Running Throughout Time

For Kathrine Switzer

"Thus, though we cannot make our sun
Stand still, yet we will make him run."

–Andrew Marvell

Roger Robinson

RUNNING
Throughout Time
THE GREATEST RUNNING STORIES EVER TOLD

Meyer & Meyer Sport

British Library of Cataloguing in Publication Data
A catalogue record for this book is available from the British Library

Running Throughout Time
Maidenhead: Meyer & Meyer Sport (UK) Ltd., 2022
ISBN: 978-1-78255-241-3

Aachen, Auckland, Beirut, Cairo, Cape Town, Dubai, Hägendorf, Hong Kong, Indianapolis, Maidenhead, Manila, New Delhi, Singapore, Sydney, Tehran, Vienna

Member of the World Sport Publishers' Association (WSPA), www.w-s-p-a.org

Printed by: by Versa Press, East Peoria, IL
Printed in the United States of America
ISBN: 978-1-78255-241-3
Email: info@m-m-sports.com
www.thesportspublisher.com

CONTENTS

ACKNOWLEDGMENTS

My love of stories about running began at age 16, when the prize for winning a schools race near London was a slightly faded copy of the *History of the International Cross-Country Union 1903-1953*. My imagination was caught by the muddy triumphs of heroes like Alf Shrubb and Alain Mimoun, and teams who were photographed standing in formal lines wearing baggy England or France tracksuits. Prominent in the book were several pages of photos of the officials who produced it. Whichever of them had the idea of awarding it as a race prize deserves my first acknowledgement.

My stories come from a lifetime of running and reading about running. The main published sources are acknowledged in the text and bibliography. But running is also a vibrant oral culture (just listen next time you are passed by two or more runners out training). I have learned much from my many friends who are runners, or writers about running, who are always generous in sharing ideas. In some personal cases, through conversation or private email correspondence, I have gained information or insight that I could not have obtained from any other source. My thanks to Professor Nicolaos Yalouris (ancient Greek athletics); Jonathan Beverly (the legend of Slievanamon, Mountain of Women); Yiannis Kouros (Greek messengers); Judge Isaac Braz (the Bible's "man of Benjamin"); Matthew W. Shores (Japanese messengers); Professor David Carnegie (seventeenth century London theater); the librarian of Shrewsbury School, and Peter Middleton (the Royal Shrewsbury School Hunt); the late Dr. David Martin (Olympic marathons and Violet Piercy); Peter Lovesey (Spyridon Louis and Violet Piercy); Mike Sandford (Windsor to Chiswick course); Alain St. Yves (Henri St. Yves); Professor Bruce Kidd (Tom Longboat); Daniel Justribo (Olympic women's 800m, 1928); the late Marty Glickman (Jesse Owens); Gary Corbitt (Ted Corbitt and Jesse Owens); Mary Lovelock and W. Robert Chapman (Jack Lovelock); Alex Khang (Sohn Kee Chung); Ian Boyd, the late Chris Chataway, and the late Chris Brasher (Roger Bannister); Peter Wood (women's cross-country); Trevor Vincent, David Mark, and Michael Peters (Adrienne Beames); Gary Cohen (Billy Mills); Barry Magee (Tokyo air pollution and 10,000m); Billy Mills and Allison Roe (their own lives); Millie Sampson (her world record marathon); Alan Stevens (the move to professionalism); and Kathrine Switzer (Jesse Owens, getting the women's marathon into the Olympics, women's running in general, and the policy of Avon Cosmetics senior management regarding Atalanta's nipples).

I have absorbed material from more articles than I could appropriately list in the bibliography from *Running Times, New Zealand Runner, Marathon & Beyond, Runner's World, Podium Runner, New York Runner, Canadian Running, Athletics Weekly,* and other magazines, newspapers, and websites. A lifetime of reading in literature and history is hard to specify as "sources," too. For biographical details, I have referred to many Wikipedia and specialist running websites and to the media guides and releases provided by World Marathon Majors and other events that I have covered as a journalist.

I have also written about runners and the history of running for many publications. The most relevant for this book are: *Running Times, Runner's World, Marathon & Beyond, New Zealand Runner, Canadian Running, VO2Max* (New Zealand), *VO2Run* (France), the *Oxford Companion to New Zealand Literature,* the *Dictionary of New Zealand Biography,* the online *Samuel Butler Project* of St. John's College, Cambridge, the *Turnbull Library Record* (Wellington), and the "Legends" section of Athletics New Zealand's website. I'm grateful for encouragement and editorial input, especially from Jonathan Beverly and Richard Benyo, and for perceptive advice (as always) from Tim Chamberlain.

My discoveries of Daniel Defoe's ground-breaking newspaper sports reports, and of the writer Samuel Butler's role in very early cross-country running, were both made during periods of literary research leave from Victoria University of Wellington, New Zealand. I remain grateful for the enlightened support of the university and many of my colleagues there.

Liz Evans (editor) and Meyer & Meyer (publisher) have been supportive and professional, and I gratefully acknowledge their contribution. The Alexander Turnbull Library (Wellington), the British Library, Cambridge University Library, Marathon Museum of Running – Berlin, the New York Public Library (especially its newspaper files), Shrewsbury School Library, and St. John's College Library (Cambridge), all held treasure. My special thanks to photographer Tony Scott (Auckland, New Zealand), artists Leon Hushcha, James Steventon, and Thomas Yeates, to Shrewsbury School (England), and Ron Carlton and Trevor Vincent (Melbourne, Australia) for permission to use images. Other credits accompany the illustrations.

Not many writers thank their reviewers, but I'm grateful to all those writers, interviewers, and podcasters, and to many regular readers, who have been so positive about *When Running Made History* and my other books.

My deepest debt is, as always, to Kathrine Switzer. Her loving support and unfailing belief in my work are essential, her productive energy is a daily example, and her inside knowledge of running in her lifetime is unmatched. I left out her own story, one of running's best, only because she has already told it so well in *Marathon Woman,* and a movie is imminent. I hope this book's dedication to her makes up a little for that omission.

Support from
World Athletics Heritage
is very much appreciated.

INTRODUCTION

Every child that learns to walk will soon begin to run. Ask any parent – that instinctive and joyous moment is important in the narrative of every life. The human species has survived and flourished only because we can run. So it's no surprise that there are so many stories about running. It's no surprise that so many people today who identify themselves in part as runners should find inspiration from learning that their own small story is part of a long tradition of great stories.

This book is a selection of the best and most important. The stories come from many different eras, from mythical ancient Greece when goddesses advised on race tactics, through centuries when running was a key mode of communication and an emergent sport, to our world of televised Olympic races and mass city marathons, a world where running is a vibrant global community, culture, and industry. Some of this book's stories are about the most iconic names in running history – Atalanta, Pheidippides, Spyridon Louis, Dorando Pietri, Tom Longboat, Jesse Owens, Roger Bannister, Billy Mills, Joan Benoit Samuelson, Allison Roe. Others are about runners and races whose stories are less well known, but need to be celebrated. If you haven't heard of the Man of Benjamin, Mawbone and Groves, Guto Nyth Brân, Samuel Butler, Johnny Hayes, Henri St. Yves, Lina Radke, Sohn Kee Chung, or Wes Santee, please read on, because in different ways they created the tradition and the choices that you enjoy as a twenty-first century runner. We run in their footsteps. Their stories matter. And they are great to read.

This book also revises some of the stories we think we know, or clears up frequently asked questions. What did happen at Marathon? Why is a marathon 26 miles 385 yards (42.2km)? Why are runners called harriers? Who was the first woman marathoner? I'm a lifetime runner, and a writer, but also a scholar, so I like to get the story right. I've made some exciting discoveries. Research is like racing – do the training, show up, and you never know what might happen.

Among many historical firsts, this book reprints after four hundred years the world's earliest newspaper report of a footrace – the very beginning of sports journalism. It reveals the moment and place of origin of cross-country racing, and publishes for the first time the earliest graphic illustrations of that sport. It gives a detailed account of the forgotten first great running boom, 1908-12, and reports the race that was effectively the first world marathon championship. It cites new source material to clarify some key moments in the politically fraught Olympics of 1936. It tells at last exactly what really happened, in the notorious women's Olympic 800m in 1928, and shows that news reports, photographs, and even film that we have relied on for decades are false or misleading. That race changed the history of women's running, and we deserve to know the truth.

I decided against attempting a full history of running. That has been done, by Edward R. Sears in *Running Through the Ages* (2001, 2015) and by Thor Gotaas in *Running: a Global History* (2012). My contribution is to tell in more depth particular stories that readers will relate to, combined with research to get the history right, and exploring the personalities, and the significance, cultural heritage, or afterlife of each story.

That's often fun. I invite my readers to join me on a run across the farmland of Shropshire, searching for an obscure wet ditch. Locating it was a highlight of my life as a researcher. I connect the Greek legends of Atalanta to her appearances in film or television adventures, a fighter now more often than a runner, and clad not in ribbons but leather crop-top and mini-skirt. I tell the story of her modern equivalent in the 1980s, who emulated her in revising the concept of femininity. I interview some eye-witness sources that Herodotos would have needed, if the story of Pheidippides really did happen as we have come (more or less) to believe. I check on the whereabouts of the British royals, and of Sir Arthur Conan Doyle, while Dorando Pietri was desperately trying to finish his legendary marathon. I add a new footnote to *The Complete Sherlock*

Holmes. I share investigations of whether Spyridon Louis cheated, who was the mystery woman runner of Athens, and who shoved whom on the last lap of the Billy Mills 10,000m.

From the modern era, I chose that race, the 1964 Olympic 10,000m, and the first Olympic women's marathon in 1984, because those two have a good claim to be called the greatest races of all time – or the most familiar and iconic, as measured by YouTube viewing figures. I end with the story of Allison Roe, partly because she is the only iconic figure from the formative era of the women's marathon not to have published her own life story.

Any selection of "the greatest" will have its own omissions. I left out some great stories because others have already told them well, like those of Walter George, Emil Zátopek, Kathrine Switzer, or Terry Fox. I left out others because I have told them myself, in *Heroes and Sparrows*, *Running in Literature,* or *When Running Made History.* Tempting as it was to revisit the era of women's smock races, or the tragic stories of Abebe Bikila or Buddy Edelen, it seemed unfair to my earlier readers.

My *When Running Made History* (2018) is a book of history based on my own eye-witness experience, from 1948 on. This time, most of the stories happened before my own lifetime. This is a book not of observed but researched history, from 1080 B.C. to the first women's Olympic marathon in 1984. It shows that running has a significant history, and a frequent place in wider history, sometimes long before it became a formal sport.

Every topic in this book is chosen for two things: a good, significant running story, and my ability to contribute something new to the telling of it. The book as a whole hopes to catch the reader's imagination, and expresses my belief that the stories of the past are a living force in the present and the future.

Chapter 1

Atalanta: The Founding Myth for Women's Running and the First Runners' Love Story

800 BC   100 AD   1719   1896   1908   1928   1936   1964   1984   2021

When Atalanta was born, her father was angry to see a baby girl. He wanted a son. He ordered the infant to be taken away and left to die on a hilltop at the edge of a forest. Wailing with cold and hunger, she was found there by a mother bear, who adopted and nourished her as one of her own cubs. Some say the loving bear was Artemis, goddess of wild nature and of virginity, and also the protectress of women in childbirth; or that the animal had been sent by the goddess to save the baby girl.

Later, hunters took over the care of the girl child, who grew up with a deep understanding of wild nature and the craft of hunting, and became so skilled with bow and arrow that none of the men could match her. She also became a supremely fast runner, and a very attractive young woman, especially beautiful when running at full speed, with her combination of grace and power. Because of this mix of male and female attributes, her guardians named her Atalanta, which means "balanced."

Strong and resourceful, she had to confront some sexual assaults, including a double attack by two centaurs (half man, half horse). She fought them off, leaving both dead. She took a leading role as an archer in a hunt in Calydonia, near her home, for a monstrous boar that was devastating life there. With her deadly accuracy with the bow, Atalanta's arrow got the first strike, hitting the boar behind the ear. After the other heroes finished off the monster, the expedition's leader, Prince Meleager, awarded her the hide as a trophy, a decision that caused fatal quarrelling among the men. Meleager was one of several men attracted to Atalanta, but she continued to maintain the chastity advocated by her patron goddess, Artemis. Her warrior skills also won her a place among the specially selected heroes who sailed with Jason on the *Argo,* and she fully earned the respect of the other heroes during that adventurous voyage.

After these travels, her father took her back, but continued to treat her in a conformist way by insisting that she needed to get married. She delayed that decision, and gave herself scope to make the choice, by taking a vow to accept only a suitor who could beat her in a footrace. That was an assignment as tough as it was tempting, for she was as fast as she was beautiful. Defeat for the challengers was fatal, since each eager suitor that she outran was put to death. But they kept hopefully trying, and dying, until one appeared who finally matched her, though not entirely by running ability.

Melanion he was called, or in many versions Hippomenes, or Milanion in Latin. At first he was understandably reluctant to risk his life by racing her on such terms. He showed up quietly to watch her in action. When he saw Atalanta running, so svelte, smooth-striding, yet powerful, her long hair streaming out behind her bare white back, and wearing little but some alluringly fluttering ribbons, he decided he had to chance it.

Melanion astutely paid a visit to Aphrodite, the goddess of love, to ask for pre-race advice. That erotic goddess was not impressed by Atalanta's insistence on chastity. She had a plan. She gave Melanion three golden apples, telling him to drop them one by one ahead of Atalanta as they raced.

The distance of the race is never specified, but seems to have been about a mile, or 2km. That's about the distance of the long race at the ancient Greek Games, the *dolichos.* Short enough to keep the crowd whooping, yet long enough for Melanion to push too hard and get into what sounds very like oxygen debt. It was a major event, with the whole court present, all the ceremonies of trumpets and heralds summoning the runners to the start, and a big eager crowd buzzing with excitement. It adds to the sporting drama when you know the race will end with either a wedding or a funeral.

The two runners crouched side-by-side, waiting for the starter's signal, aware of each other but focused on the course ahead. Atalanta was a seductive mix of strength and serenity, Melanion youthfully ardent, yet with a mature masculine sturdiness. The crowd went quiet, awaiting the moment. Then the trumpet blared, and they were away, so fast that their flying feet seemed hardly to touch the sandy ground. This was a real race.

The crowd got behind the unknown outsider. Up on their feet, they were yelling, "Now! Go! Give it all you've got! Good job, Melanion, looking good, you can do it!"

Running with silken smoothness, judging her pace, Atalanta privately felt pleased at all the support for her challenger.

She could not bear to beat him. At last, her heart told her, after so many rejected suitors, this was the man she wanted. She felt no doubt. Every time she drew level, she gazed across with yearning affection into his face, and eased back the pace again. But it was blazing fast, and the pressure was beginning to tell. Melanion was struggling, his breath heaving, his throat burning, his mouth parched. And the finish was still way off.

Melanion pulled out the first golden apple, and rolled it glittering across the course. Atalanta, astonished at its beauty, checked, stooped, and scooped it up. The crowd went crazy as Melanion hit the lead, but she powered back into her full flowing stride, and found herself edging reluctantly ahead again. She slightly eased her pace to allow Melanion to stay close.

The second apple came bouncing by. Again, she pulled up, and bent down to grab it. This time she seriously had to pick up the pace to close the gap and get back on terms.

Now they were coming off the last bend with the finish in sight. They were side by side. Melanion gasped a quick prayer to Aphrodite, and threw the last golden apple. It went spinning and bouncing across Atalanta's path and off to the side of the course. For a stride she hesitated. An impulse of love sent her after it once more. She slowed, veered away, and stooped to gather it.

Now she was clutching three apples, with no chance of being able to sprint. She kept slowly jogging. There was no finishing burst of speed. The race was over.

Melanion jubilantly passed the finish, with the crowd on their feet cheering, all delighted that the outcome this time was going to be a marriage feast, not a beheading. Atalanta crossed the line, trotted over to Melanion, slipped the three golden apples into the crook of one arm, and with the other lovingly took him by the hand.

The winner led away his prize.

Atalanta's Message

That last line, "the winner led away his prize," is straight from the Latin of the Roman poet Ovid, the main source – *duxit sua praemia victor*. It alludes to the practice in ancient Greece of sometimes awarding slave girls as race prizes, according to Homer's *Iliad*. But this is a match of consent, not mastery. Many details show Atalanta taking initiatives to show her love, and act on it, and clearly both are equally happy with the result. That's a major reason for the timeless appeal of the story, and its special appropriateness today, in an age that values gender equality.

There's a postscript to the story in Ovid's version in *Metamorphoses*. Atalanta and Melanion enjoy a happy married life, and their sexual bond is so strong that when they are traveling together to visit Melanion's family, they feel impelled to make love, and go unwisely into a sacred temple or grove. According to Ovid, it is Aphrodite who fills them with passion at this inappropriate moment, since she feels aggrieved (as Greek goddesses often did) that Melanion hasn't given her enough grateful worship for her golden apples idea.

The temple's resident god is understandably offended, and punishes the over-ardent couple by turning them into lions. *Metamorphoses* means "transformations," and every story Ovid chose to retell had to involve some change in form. The other great running story in the collection is the god Apollo's long-distance pursuit of the swift and chaste Daphne, which ends with her being saved from the god's amorous attentions by getting turned into a laurel tree. Atalanta and Melanion's transformation into lions seems more random. Perhaps we can see a lioness as the ultimate hunter, fast and lethal, but to leave them as lions is a disappointing ending for such an action-packed romance story. It's a better closure when they leave the running arena hand-in-hand, after one of the most enthralling of all races.

My narrative above of Atalanta's life draws on many classical and English versions, primarily Ovid's account of the race. There are two loosely connected Atalanta stories, perhaps originating in different regions of what we now call Greece – Atalanta the wild-bred warrior woman who fights the boar, and Atalanta the beautiful fast runner who races for a husband. Most often they are merged, and I have done the same. Since this book is the first time that the running part of the story has been told by a runner, mainly for runners, I tried to put it in language that runners in the 2020s will find accessible. At the same time, I tried to be true to Ovid's rich and unpredictable drama, vivid action, and psychological insight into Atalanta's thoughts and emotions.

Commentators like Robert Graves have suggested that the myth of the race may originally derive from ceremonial tests of manhood, or be an allegory for sexual selection. H.A. Harris, in his classic *Greek Athletes and Athletics*, mentions several such stories, including a race to win the hand of Penelope, the faithful wife of Homer's Odysseus/Ulysses.

Many cultures have stories of races to win marriage partners, some with the women as the contestants rather than as the prize, like the Irish legend when the hero Finn McCool staged a mountain race between women to choose himself a worthy wife, only to see the winner run off after the race because she fancied his younger cousin more. The mountain is still called Slievanamon, Mountain of Women. In some Scandinavian myths, young men held orienteering races through a maze to be the first to reach the female prize at the center. The Atalanta story is unique in having the sought-after bride as a contestant against her suitors in a series of head-to-head races.

The wilderness infancy and boar hunting parts of the Atalanta story connect the heroine with her immortal patron, Artemis, whose love of wild animals, hunting skills, and virginity were transferred in Roman times to the equivalent Roman goddess, Diana. Some modern versions of the golden apples story attribute the race to a young woman called Diana.

Stories abound in many cultures about apples, often golden. The divine hero Heracles (Hercules in Roman mythology) was set as his eleventh "labor" the task of stealing three golden apples from the Garden of the Hesperides, who were nymphs, or minor earth goddesses, and the apples were guarded by a giant snake. To enter the orchard of the Hesperides (in the words of the English poet Marlowe) means to achieve full sexual love, an association that is clearly present with Atalanta's golden apples that come from the goddess of love. A helpful footnote for those who know how hard it is to carry stuff when you're running is that in earlier usage "apple" could mean any fruit larger than berries, so Melanion's may have been apricot or peach size, say, not full-scale Granny Smiths.

If you're trying to find the authentic original version of stories like Atalanta's, it's important to remember that there isn't one. The Greek myths were, in simple terms, first recorded by bards (story-singers), from about 800 B.C., retelling old tales and religious ways of explaining the world. They were elaborated by poets, artists and sculptors through the era we call "classical Greece." The most familiar versions came even later, usually from the time of the Roman Empire, when Artemis became Diana, and Aphrodite was Venus. From this long process, it's not surprising that we're left with an uncertain connection between the two myths about Atalanta the virgin-huntress-warrior-runner-bride.

Whatever its beginnings, a good story doesn't die, and Atalanta's race has stayed in the shared imagination through different ages. Ovid became enormously popular in Europe during the Renaissance, and Atalanta's race emerged as one of his most influential stories. The poet Spenser is typical in alluding to the "golden apples...which Atalanta did entice." For Shakespeare, she was an emblem of speed, when the hero of *As You Like It* is complimented for his quick wit: "You have a nimble wit; I think it was made of Atalanta's heels." The story became a favorite of artists as important as Guido Reni. Google "Atalanta images" for many more. The moment of Atalanta stooping for one of the apples while Melanion/ Hippomenes races on at full speed is an irresistible visual challenge for a painter or sculptor.

In the Victorian era, poets continued to enjoy the race story. Swinburne's poem *Atalanta in Calydon* sets the time of year in one of the best-known of all lines of poetry, "When the hounds of spring are on winter's traces," and then evokes the almost divine woman athlete preparing for the race:

> *Bind on thy sandals, O thou most fleet,*
> *Over the splendour and speed of thy feet.*

The story was so well known that comic stage versions could flourish. At the Haymarket Theatre in London in 1857, the actress Ellen Ternan, future beloved of Charles Dickens, played the "breeches" role of Hippomenes, suggesting the treatment was much like a pantomime or vaudeville.

The last fifty years have seen another upsurge in interest in Ovid, and therefore awareness of Atalanta's story, with Allen Mandelbaum and Ted Hughes the best-known poets to retranslate it. The story has timeless appeal, with its elements of violence, death, gold, sex, gender rivalry, parental authority, divine intervention, sporting contest, running speed, crowd adulation, and sudden love. See Roger Robinson, *Running in Literature,* for a fuller discussion of the Atalanta literary tradition.

Many 1950s childhood radio listeners in the wider English-speaking world still remember a hugely popular American version, a loose adaptation of the story, titled "Diana and the Golden Apples," that focused on the climactic race. The narration was later used as the voice-over for a television cartoon version. It's surprising that there's no movie yet of the story, but running never films as well as fighting does. Several feature films make use of the name, for a boat in one case, but so did Handel, who lured me to an opera called *Atalanta* that, apart from the heroine's name, has no connection whatsoever with the old story.

Now Atalanta's descendants are everywhere. An outstanding comic book version, *Atalanta: The Race against Destiny* (2008), written by Justine and Ron Fontes, was illustrated by the distinguished comic book artist Thomas Yeates, who told me his rendering was inspired by the great African American sprinter of the 1960s, Wilma Rudolph.

Not all versions are so positive. As our popular culture has rejected the stereotype of the passive woman, swooning in the face of danger, always needing to be rescued, it has replaced her with the aggressive woman warrior, deadly with bow and arrow, and usually clad in skimpy leather. The fantasy idealization of the professional killer is a particular problem of modern culture, but we didn't invent the eroticized female version. Her origins go back to Hippolyta, the Amazon queen. Her recent formulations include Diana Rigg's Emma Peele in the television series *The Avengers* (1961-69), innumerable Barbarian Queens, the television series *Xena Warrior Princess* (1995-2001), the Keira Knightley warrior interpretation of Guinevere in the Hollywood movie *King Arthur* (2004), and the Marvel Comics and blockbuster movie *Wonder Woman* (2017). That heroine is again named Diana, and is supposedly the daughter of Hippolyta.

Atalanta appears as a character in the lumbering Hollywood fantasy adventure movie *Hercules* (2014), played by Ingrid Bolso Berdal in the now regulation glossy leather top and miniskirt. This warrior Atalanta also appears in video games and young adult fiction. You can buy her sandals.

Atalanta was an emigrant ship sailing between England and Australia in the 1850s, and was the model for a hood ornament on Studebaker automobiles in the 1920s. An American poet revived her in 1972, in a romantic tribute to Kathrine Switzer published in the *New York Times* (Harry Dee, "Bouquet to Kathy Miller (America's Atalanta):"

> *Patron goddess, fair Diana,*
> *On this day is proud of you,*
> *Taking part in distance running*
> *'Gainst a hardy, manly crew! (Dee, 1972)*

Atalanta also has a sporting life as name patroness of a top-flight Italian soccer team in Bergamo, Atalanta Bergamasca Calcio. She was adopted as a "sort of patron saint," in Switzer's words, by Avon Women's Running in the 1970s-80s, gracing their stationery, awards, and medals. The image on the medals, derived from a statue in the National Museum of Athens, showed Atalanta running topless in a short skirt. A male senior manager at Avon insisted that her nipples had to be sanded off. She survived all these travails to become the nearest we have to a founding myth for women's running, the best available female equivalent to Pheidippides. That's why I'm telling her story.

Her best modern embodiment was the New Zealand marathon runner Allison Roe, who won the Boston and New York City Marathons in 1981 with exactly the "balanced" combination of physical power and feminine grace that the mythic Atalanta represented. Allison's story ends this book in chapter 14.

The meaning of Atalanta as "balanced" in gender attributes is a concept that has become wholly acceptable. (Her name can also mean "unswaying" or "resilient." It has no connection with the city of Atlanta, which derives from the "Atlantic" Ocean, and so ultimately from the Titan Atlas and mythic city of Atlantis.) The image of an accomplished and independent-minded woman competing with men, and even matching them in sporting and warrior skills, appeals to our age, the first in history to have witnessed women racing every distance in the Olympic Games, and women serving in active combat in the military.

Atalanta's race may be a myth with many possible meanings, but the story has also come down to us as recognizable human reality. Her chase after the apples could seem to be merely about female susceptibility to the glister of gold, but the poets who have retold it all agree that there is another dimension. After defeating so many suitors, Atalanta for the first time feels sudden love for this challenger. When she's running at race pace alongside Melanion, suddenly she cannot bring herself to beat him. She decides to fall for the golden apples trick. It's her love, not her susceptibility to bling, that makes her stop three times, and so lose the race. Aphrodite got it right – she is, after all, the goddess of love, not gold.

So it becomes a story about a woman's independence and freedom of choice, and about feelings of attraction, romance, love, and bonding, for both women and men, and the rewards and risks those can involve. Our generation didn't invent equality in relationships. You don't have to believe in golden apples or crafty goddesses to enjoy the story's drama of credible romance.

This very old story is still true to the inclusive modern sport of running, and to the running community, where the bond between runners is stronger than any competitive rivalry. It appeals to the many modern couples who meet through running, and whose relationship (like mine) entails giving support to each other's fulfillment as runners.

That mid-race moment when Atalanta looks lovingly across at Melanion is the key. The forgotten old poet Laurence Eusden caught it perfectly when he wrote a translation in 1717:

> *When a long distance oft she could have gained,*
> *She checked her swiftness, and her feet restrained:*
> *She sighed, and dwelt, and languished on his face,*
> *Then with unwilling speed pursued the race.*

The myth of Atalanta, the supreme woman runner, is also the first runners' love story.

Chapter 2

Pheidippides and the Battle of Marathon FAQ

800 BC   100 AD   1719   1896   1908   1928   1936   1964   1984   2021

Why "marathon?" What does it mean?

Marathon is the English form of *Marathōnos*. In ancient Greek the word means "field of fennel." It is a small seaside settlement on the Plain of Marathon, where the fennel grew, a short way inland from the Bay of Marathon, in Attica, Greece. On that beach, the invading army of the Persian Empire landed in September 490 B.C., intending to attack the city-state of Athens, twenty-five miles/forty kilometers away.

What was the war about?

During the previous decade, Athens, operating independently, as Greek city-states did at that time, had supported a revolt against Persian rule by the cities of Ionia, across the Aegean, near what is now the Turkish coast. That provoked King Darius, even though it was a fleabite against his vast empire, which covered most of the modern Middle East – Iran, Iraq, Syria, Turkey and northern Greece. Darius had put down the uprising by 494 B.C., but wanted to secure his control over the Greek cities. Most paid formal tribute to him, but at Sparta, notoriously, his ambassadors had been flung down a well. He sent an invasion force to deal first with the Athenian troublemakers and set up a puppet government. The army was led by his nephew, with the fleet under the command of the experienced Datis. Marathon was not their first landing, as they captured a number of Greek cities and islands on the way, notably Eretria after only a six-day siege (that's the small Greek city north of Marathon, not the modern Eritrea in northeastern Africa). Most other Greek city-states stayed out of the conflict, presumably getting favorable treatment for being willing to accept Persian rule.

What happened in the battle?

The underdogs won. The Persians had huge numerical and technological superiority, but the small Athenian army of infantry *hoplites* (citizen-soldiers) surprised them with a fast early-morning attack.

It can't have been that simple. How did the Greek generals succeed against such odds?

Probably by attacking before the Persian cavalry was ready. The invaders had crossed the Aegean in an armada of six hundred ships, some of them specially designed to carry lots of horses, as their main strength in battle was their horseback bow-and-arrow men. Their long-range projectiles, missiles fired from powerful catapults, were also the most advanced and destructive known at that time. The Athenians astutely decided to move quickly into close combat, thus neutralizing those two assets. The historian Herodotos doesn't even mention the Persian cavalry, leaving it a mystery as to why they were not deployed. Maybe the horses were being watered, or many of them may have been re-embarked. The Persians thought the Athenians were dithering, as they often did, and knew they would prefer to delay the fight until support came from Sparta. The Persians seem to have decided to divide their force, send part of it to sail around Cape Sounion, and take Athens directly. Whatever the reason, their cavalry was not available or for some reason ineffectual. The Persians' artillery was of course useless, because the Athenians made it instantly a hand-to-hand combat, by moving so fast.

What does that mean? How did they move so fast?

The usual hoplite method was to attack in tightly packed blocks of men (a phalanx) using big shields and jabbing outward with long spears. You see similar tactics used against modern riots by closely packed police or National Guard officers, pressing and squeezing. It sounds almost mechanical, but the Athenian hoplites were also mobile when they needed to be. It's important to know that they were an unusual kind of army, a force of free citizens, supported by slaves who carried their equipment on the march but didn't fight. Young male citizens were educated at places that were a combination of liberal arts college, military training school, and high-performance sports center, called a "gymnasium." The most famous of these in Athens were the "Academia" and the "Lyceum." That's where we get our words "gym," "academy," "academic," and the German "Gymnasium" and French "lycée" for grammar school.

Unlike us, the Athenians saw intellectual education and physical education as inseparable and equal, both necessary for preparing a citizen to be capable of participating in a democracy, and protecting the community when necessary. Smart thinking. The students spent their time practicing running, jumping and wrestling, with philosophy professors hanging about in shaded corners decorated with statues and art works, ready to chat with them during rest periods. The emphasis in every way was on competition.

"Athletic activity was not just a hobby but the basis of education. Every day the Greeks engaged in exercise and competition, in the body and in the mind. The whole of Greece was like a great palaestra or gymnasium. The spirit of *agon* [sporting contest] was the basis of their civilisation," the leading scholar of ancient Greek sport Nicolaos Yalouris told me at Olympia, in 1989. Even allowing for an element of idealization there, the point is that the young male citizens were well-informed, disciplined, and in great shape, honed by education founded day-to-day on *agon,* and trained to become *agonistes*, or contenders. As part-time soldiers, they could move fast, even carrying heavy shields.

That's the key ability they used in 490 B.C. at Marathon. They moved what we would call heavily armed infantry very quickly. They seem to have covered about a mile (1.5km) down a steady slope at a fast pace, running much or all of it, and keeping in formation. Some historians (like V.D. Hanson) are skeptical about Herodotos's use of the word *dromo* (run), and claim that tests show a mile-long run in armor is impossible without the troops' formation disintegrating in exhaustion. That's an oversimplification. Trained athlete/soldiers would be well capable of a mile-long march/jog/ run that probably accelerated as they drew near the enemy, with the overall pace moderated to keep their breathing under control. They were, at any rate, able to surprise the enemy and engage them with their moving walls of shields and spears before the Persians were ready, and certainly before they could get the artillery and cavalry into action.

Now the advantage lay with the Athenians. The Persians wore little armor. They relied on sheer numbers, and on horse-borne mobility, which the Athenians continued to prevent by hemming them in. They were vulnerable to this almost machine-like block of shields and thrusting spears that was so suddenly upon them.

That wasn't the end of having to move fast. Once the fight on the beach was won, the Athenians had to get quickly back to Athens, because the bruised Persian fleet immediately sailed off to go around Cape Sounion as planned, hoping to catch the city unprotected. Part of the fleet may have sailed even before the battle (with that missing cavalry). Heading them off was urgent. Again, the in-shape Athenians made it. They must have force-marched or partly run the twenty-five miles/forty km, with shields and spears. Their full force was in position to resist any attack by the reduced and probably demoralized Persians. All that training paid off, as it usually does. The battle – and the whole campaign – to a significant extent were won by running.

How convincing was the victory at Marathon?

The Athenians divided into two phalanxes, broke both Persian flanks, and then closed in on the center with a pincer movement. They literally crushed the Persian army between their big shields, and causing a confused retreat to the ships. There is no doubt that it was a victory against heavy odds – 10,000 against 30,000 seems a likely estimate for the rival infantry numbers, and the only support Athens had was a small force of about 1,000 from Plataea. The official casualty figures probably have an element of propaganda spin, since 6,400 Persians killed, and only 192 Athenians, as documented, seems hardly credible. But battles in those days often produced extremely uneven casualties, because a lot of killing was done after the fight was decided. At Marathon, many Persians were speared trying to struggle out of the marshy ground at the edge of the battlefield, and no doubt any ships that didn't get away quickly were boarded and cleaned out.

Why is the victory regarded as so important?

Athens had a fledgling democracy, with all male citizens (not women or slaves) participating, and a developing culture that soon produced one of the greatest artistic and intellectual flowerings in human history. The first great playwright, Aeschylus, for instance, as a young man fought in the battle. If the Persians had won, they were going to install a "tyrant" (absolute ruler under the control of the Empire). They had promised the job to an Athenian traitor called Hippias, who had helped guide them to the safe landing at the beach of Marathon. He had been kicked out once from Athens, so things would have been unpleasant under his rule. The Battle of Marathon was not as climactic or decisive as it is often portrayed, with Byron calling it the day "when Marathon became a magic word" in *Childe Harold's Pilgrimage* and one of "true Glory's stainless victories." It only rebuffed the Persians for that year. But it was the first time a Greek army had defeated the Persians on land, so was important symbolically. And it did delay colonization and enable influential Greek institutions to become more firmly established. Much that our modern world values – democracy, freedom, science, the arts, history, sports – would have been at least seriously set back if the Battle of Marathon had gone the other way.

Now, what about the runner?

A running messenger (a "day-runner") named Pheidippides, or sometimes Philippides, appears in the history of the war by Herodotos, which is our only real source. Herodotos (Latin form: Herodotus) is deservedly regarded as "the father of history," although that doesn't mean every story he told is strictly accurate. Herodotos was not born at the time of Marathon, and his *Histories*, as he titled them on the outside of the roll of papyrus, were written forty years after the battle. He did his best, interviewing ex-soldiers, but not many of the commanders were still alive. And naturally Herodotos doesn't give the Persian side.

On the runner, this is what Herodotos says:

> *Before they marched out of the city [to go to Marathon] the Athenian generals dispatched a message to the city-state of Sparta. The messenger was an Athenian named Pheidippides, a professional long-distance messenger...Pheidippides reached Sparta the day after he left Athens and delivered his message to the Spartan government...The Spartans were willing to help...but said they could not take the field until the moon was full...*

Athens to Sparta is about 150 miles (240km) over the hilly tracks he would have used. From the phrase "reached Sparta the day after he left Athens," we can guess that the run took about thirty to thirty-six hours. It's a realistic estimate that a highly trained ultra-runner accustomed to lack of sleep could average about fourteen minutes per mile over that ground, which he probably knew well. The generals needed help from Sparta, and are likely to have sent the best man in the messenger corps. He had to cross some territory already under Persian control, and may have had to cope with brigands, wolves, communities that had submitted to the Persians, and other dangers. And he had to run all the way back, too. For sure, he counts as a heroic figure in history and in running history.

Is that all?

For the running, yes, that's all. He ran from Athens to Sparta, and then ran back again with the bad news that the Spartans' response was "not just yet." Officially, they said that for religious reasons they could not enter combat until after the full moon, a week away. They were playing it safe. That was the unsatisfactory message that Pheidippides had to carry back to the Athenian army, now at Marathon, and desperately outnumbered.

Herodotos added some colorful material, perhaps not strictly historical, but calculated to attract his readers' or listeners' attention. He includes one story of how the defector Hippias had a terrible nightmare the night before the battle (serves him right), and another of how the messenger Pheidippides met the god Pan on the way back from Sparta. In his whole account of the runner, that's the episode that interested Herodotos most. It gave the story religious significance. According to Herodotos, Pheidippides reported to the Greek generals that Pan, the half-goat god of nature, called him by name as he ran across the remote Mount Parthenium, above Tegea. Pan complained that the Athenians had been lax in their worship, in spite of his friendliness towards them. He gave the runner a message promising to help them again in the future, presumably including the coming battle.

What does all that mean?

The Athenians believed Pheidippides's story, says Herodotos, and once things settled down after the war they built a shrine to the god in the Acropolis, and held an annual festival in his honor, "to court his protection." If you don't believe in the gods, you might suspect the encounter was the deluded fantasy of a very tired and sleep-deprived runner; or a convenient invention by the Greek generals to lift troop morale when the bad news arrived that the Spartans were not going to show up. Most armies claim divine support on their own side. The Athenian version is that Pan rampaged supernaturally through the battlefield, causing "pandemonium" among the invaders. Herodotos tells the story of a giant bearded figure striding through the battlefield in heavy armor, striking soldiers blind who looked at him.

But there are other meanings to the story. One that is relevant in our era, when we too have neglected nature, and when running is often a leader in conservation, is that the nature god chose a runner to carry a message telling the Athenians (and all of us) to remember and respect the natural world we live in.

What did the Spartans eventually do?

They did show up after the full moon, as promised, marching 140 miles (225km) in three days in full armor. When they arrived at the battlefield, they commented somewhat redundantly "the Athenians did well," and marched home again. They became much more active against the Persians as the war progressed.

But what about the story we all know, how Pheidippides ran from the battlefield at Marathon to Athens, with the news of victory?

Someone did, for sure. But the Athenian generals are unlikely to have chosen a runner on the edge of exhaustion who had already run three hundred miles/460km almost non-stop with no sleep for four days. The message was too important, and they had a whole corps of trained messengers to choose from. They would have sent something like, "We drove them back to their ships, but now they're sailing round Cape Sounion, so prepare to meet an attack from that direction. We're getting there as fast as we can."

So, who collapsed and died?

Consider: these messengers were highly trained, and highly trained long-distance runners do not die after running twenty-five miles/forty kilometers. If they did, there would be no one left to read books like this. Nor did messengers fight in the battles. That was the job of the hoplites. Messengers had to travel light, as sometimes they had to run all day, or for almost four days in the case of Pheidippides, and you can't do that carrying a heavy shield and spear. That throws severe doubt on the later story that tells how a messenger "ran in full armor, hot from the battle, and, bursting in at the door of the leaders of the state, could only say, 'Greetings! We are victorious!' and immediately fell dead."

That's compelling stuff and would make a great movie scene. But "hot from the battle," "bursting in at the door," and "immediately fell dead" are sensational literary effects, not factual history. It all sounds like inventive fiction by someone good at creating lurid drama.

What do you mean by "the later story?"

Herodotos's story, with the run to Sparta and the meeting with Pan, is the only version that we knew of for six hundred years. The first later reference is a straightforward mention of Pheidippides running to Sparta, in Pliny the Elder's *Natural History*, in Latin, from 79 A.D., simply following Herodotos. The first time we hear of a messenger who collapsed and died is about 110 A.D., more than six hundred years after the Battle of Marathon. That's the same historical gap as if some new story about the voyage of the Mayflower or the life of Shakespeare were to appear this week for the first time. It comes in the *Moral Essays* by Plutarch, who names the exhausted hero as Eucles (pronounced "Yoo-klees") or Thersippus. Plutarch says there are different versions of the name, but the story comes from sources that had already disappeared. That leaves him free to embellish the story with full armor, bursting in at the doors, etc. Note that the name Pheidippides is not mentioned. And Plutarch tells a markedly similar story in a different book (*Life of Aristides*), with the hero this time named Euchidas, eleven years later than Marathon – see Chapter 3. So, forgive a little suspicion that the edges of history became blurred, as they often do.

So how did Pheidippides come to be the hero who collapsed and died?

A simple mix-up by a writer called Lucian. People mix things up all the time. I often get introduced as Roger Bannister. In about 180 A.D., Lucian was writing about the greeting "Rejoice!" (much like "Have a nice day") and referred to "the anecdote of the runner Pheidippides, who announced the victory at Marathon...in these words: 'Rejoice, we are victorious!' And no sooner had he uttered them than he fell down dead."

A small mistake, conflating two old stories. There are only three references to Pheidippides in the literature of antiquity, and now one of them had him collapsing and dying, an irresistible ending. That was the bit that stuck in humanity's patchy shared memory. The next we hear of the story is in the nineteenth century, after another huge time gap – nearly two thousand years. Marathon was quite often referred to as a famous victory for freedom, but no runner features until 1820. By that time, narrative poetry about historical stories was a popular form, equivalent in appeal to our television miniseries. Two highly entertaining action poems were written about Marathon, by the dynamic duo of Elizabeth Barrett Browning and Robert Browning. Both include the running messenger. Elizabeth's teenage "The Battle of Marathon" (1820) tells only the original run to Sparta and back. But after her death, her husband Robert went back to her youthful poem, and wrote his own version, focusing on the runner, and merging both stories, following Lucian's passing remark as if it were a source. The poem is called "Pheidippides" (1879).

What is different about Browning's poem?

Browning's running messenger does it all. He's the total all-round hero. He runs to Sparta, he delivers the first message, he runs all the way back again, he meets Pan in the mountains (big scene), he delivers the Spartans' message, and Pan's, he fights in the battle (very big scene), he thinks passionately about his girlfriend (the love interest that had been missing up to now), he gallantly asks for the honor of delivering the news of victory, he runs through the fennel-fields from Marathon to Athens, and he collapses and dies, uttering the last words that have deservedly become so famous, "Rejoice, we conquer!" Those words are Browning's, an inspired version of the original "Hail, we are victorious!" or "Greetings, we win!" or "Have a nice day, we trashed them." We will never know how Greek messengers communicated, but it was probably in more military terms: "Permission requested to collapse and die, sah!"

How do we get from an English poem to the first modern Olympic Games in Athens?

Via a French professor of languages, Michel Bréal. Maybe there were other versions of the double story that he knew, as well as Browning's, since Bréal was fluent in several languages, but I haven't found any yet. Browning's poem had been recently published, and is the only source we can be pretty sure Bréal would have known. Anyway, in 1894 Bréal wrote to the committee responsible for organizing the first modern Olympic Games for 1896 in Athens, and offered to donate a cup for "a race from Marathon" on the route of "the Greek warrior." He didn't give a name, but by this time the run to the death was popularly attributed to Pheidippides.

Is this real history widely known? Does it matter?

Since the runner story gained wide currency, the word "marathon" has entered the language, for any long and arduous event – marathon journeys, marathon speeches, marathon law cases. It has become merged with other words in telethons, moviethons, etc. The influence of the story also goes far beyond running. Browning's phrase "Rejoice, we conquer!" has become iconic, part of the cultural texture of the English language. We quote another line from Browning's poem when we use the phrase "on the razor's edge," his way of expressing how dangerously close the battle would be. (He was perhaps borrowing the metaphor from the ancient Hindu *Katha Upanishad*, but the English words are all Browning's.) I know men's hairdressing businesses named "The Razor's Edge," unknowingly quoting our poem. The heroic death of the exhausted messenger has such appeal that it has lodged immovably in the cultural imagination, regardless of attempts like mine to establish the real history and its literary provenance. Almost every book about marathon running opens with a sketchy and historically inaccurate version of the dropping dead story.

I'm not disapproving or purist. It's a great story. One of the most entertaining retellings, if not one of the most convincing, was in the 1959 movie *The Giant of Marathon*, starring the bare chest, pecs, and biceps of Steve Reeves. The moment when the muscular Reeves as Pheidippides rips off his jerkin and plods heavily away toward Athens is a delight for any real distance runner. Among the countless versions of the run to Athens, the message to Sparta is sometimes included, especially in memoirs by ultra-runners, like *The Road to Sparta* by Dean Karnazes, another bare-chest celebrity. Atalanta is not alone in timeless appeal.

Runners like the story because it encapsulates the challenge of the sport they have adopted, even its element of danger, or at least its demand that you push yourself beyond what you perceive as your limit. Runners also love the sense that their sport has historical significance, and that each of them personally contributes to that history. Look how they respond to anniversary events like the one hundredth Boston Marathon (1996), or the 2,500th anniversary of the battle of Marathon in 2010, when ten thousand runners went to Greece to run from the battlefield to Athens in the (supposed) footsteps of Pheidippides. The story of his heroic run is a creation myth of our sport.

Millions of marathons are completed by individual runners every year, and every one of them commemorates that famous run that Pheidippides almost certainly never did. These modern millions are inspired by the heroic early death of a runner who probably lived to a comfortable old age in the Athens Army Messengers' Retirement Village. I hope so, anyway.

****

Epilogue

As source material for the story of Pheidippides, we have only Herodotos. This is his entire narrative:

> *Before they marched out of the city, the Athenian generals dispatched a message to the city-state of Sparta, asking for the Spartans' support.*

The messenger chosen was Pheidippides, an Athenian professional long-distance courier. When he rejoined the Athenian army after competing his mission, Pheidippides told them that during his return run he had met the god Pan on Mount Panthenium, above Tegea. Pan, he said, called out to him by name, and told him to ask the Athenians why they paid so little attention to their worship of the god, despite his goodwill toward them. Pheidippides reached Sparta the day after he left Athens, and delivered his message to the Spartan government. The Spartans said they were ready to help, but could not take the field until the moon was full (Herodotos, 430BCE).

That's all. It's not much of a foundation. Herodotos drew the account partly from old soldiers decades later. We need to remember also that his narrative was designed to be read aloud to live audiences, so it includes a performance element to impress the crowd. That's partly why Pan gets a speaking role. Everything else about Pheidippides has accrued as this brief story from Herodotos was re-told and embellished over time.

We need more sources to explain some things that we have come to believe, and (to be honest) that we enjoy believing (I have "Rejoice, we conquer" engraved inside my wedding ring). So I have invented some, imagining other sources. I call the following "Interviews by Herodotos," as if he had managed to interview not only old soldiers, but villagers, senators, etc. They are my imagined eyewitness reports of the colorful story of the running messenger. I have conflated the two stories (Sparta, and the fatal run to Athens), since that's how we all want it to be, ending with the heroic death.

To repeat, full disclosure: the rest of this chapter is made up. Sometimes, even in history, we need to imagine.

1. The retired trainer, Lidiardis, former running coach of the Athenian messenger corps of day-runners, now in his late eighties:

"Marathon? Yes, yes, that was a time my men gave good service. One man, I'll think of his name in a minute. Ran three important messages - Athens to Sparta, and back again, and then Marathon to Athens. Three hundred miles, then another twenty-five miles. Took a well-trained runner to stay on his feet for that extra after the battle. Total screw-up, giving that message to a man who'd just run to Sparta and back, generals fluffing about as usual. And he paid for it, poor fellow. But it was what the gods intended. And he did it! Fit as a mountain goat! I trained them right – proper build-up, long runs, hill running, the whole corps running fast bursts in a big pack. Best day-runners in Greece, nearly all of 'em from one corner of Athens. Talent is everywhere. They could do anything, my boys, with my system. Served the city well. What? Name? Let me think. It's a long time ago. Filippides. Something like that. Yes, that was him, one of the best I trained. Reliable and smart. Not fast in the sprint sense – he'd never take the crown for the stade at the Games – but by the gods, he could run long. Low stride, flowing rhythm, controlled breathing, no matter how rough the footing, how steep the hill. I watched him leave for that mission to Sparta when the Persians were sailing toward us. He ran up a crag of rocks like they were marble steps to the temple. And down steep hills he was surefooted as a goat, and quicker. No wonder the god Pan wanted to talk to him! No, I don't know about the gods, I'm a running coach. What I do know is that he ran nearly four days and nights, like I trained them. I had them peaked and ready soon as we knew the Persians were coming. What? Yes, tough country, across the hills to Sparta. Wolves, bandits, some of the worst mountains in all Greece, risky at the best of times, and at that time parts were hostile, Persian territory. Went over to Darius soon as he shook a spear at 'em. No backbone. That Filip, Phiddip, whatever, never put a foot wrong. And ran all the way back. Dam' yellow Spartans kept him kicking his heels for hours, while their soothsayers thought up excuses. Wait for the full moon, they told him. Useless morons. How could we wait, with thirty thousand Persians gnashing their teeth on Marathon beach? Oh, they can fight when they have to, the Spartans, but no stamina. Never followed my training. It's the only system. Long runs, hill running, then – What? Oh, did I? Yes, he was a man you could trust. That last run, after the battle, he knew he had to get back to Athens on the double once the battle was over, before the enemy fleet found a wind. Watched the terrain like I taught 'em, but most have got nothing between the ears. Runners! Ever hear some of 'em whistle as they run? It's the wind, blowing in one ear and straight out the other. Got themselves caught or eaten, half of 'em. But not Pheidippides, he was my best. Well, there we were, only Miltiades and our little part-time army between Greece and destruction. It was all bad news poor Pheidippides brought back over Mount Parnes. Did he meet the god Pan up there? It was in his report. Delirium? Never. My runners didn't get delirious. Not if they'd done my training. The Lidiardis system. They ran till they dropped. And he did.

2. *High on Mount Parthenium, in a remote shack, the historian after much searching found a shepherd who would speak about that night before the battle.*

That were a dark night, your honor. Yes, I knows there's a battle comin' like, and I quarrels with my pa because I wants to go an' fight. "You'll watch our sheep," says he, and whupps me, hard. So with these very eyes I sees the runner, coming by on the high track from Sparta at first light. Up on that there ridge, see, beyond the spring. These dark nights like betwixt moons, the wolves they come creepin' up after the sheep, so I'm there with a bit of a fire and a spear. I hears a man's steps, runnin' like, for all it's a stiffish climb, runnin' firm and strong. I backs against the rock. Maybe 'tis a bandit, says I. So I sees him clear lit up as he runs by my fire. Runnin' like a young stag – neat and light and nimble, like floatin'. Never looks aside at me. Never pauses at my fire. Just runnin', like as there's nothin' in the world but runnin'. And behind him in the firelight, I sees another, with these eyes, big and black and shadowy, runnin' at his shoulder, legs all rough, half man, half goat, he was. But big! I sees the god Pan that night, your honor. Runnin' with the runner. Watchin' over him. I knows it.

3. A woman from near Marathon recalled the day in her childhood when the messenger passed through her home village.

Yes, sir, I saw him run by. It was early evening – dry, still quite hot. We were all standing by the olive grove just below the village, sir, watching the track that comes up the hill from Marathon, waiting for news. My mother and some of the other women were crying, from worry about their husbands and sons in the battle. I wanted to cry for my father. But they wept quietly, just their shoulders shaking. How could the news be good? Our small army against that huge fleet? It looked like a city when it sailed into the bay, they said. No one wanted to show fear. We children filled the time writing in the dust, scuffing the earth with our bare feet, watching the slow movement of the shadows from the olive trees, asking, "How long will it be, the news?" And watching, always watching, down the hill towards Marathon. The olive shadows grew longer. Then there was someone moving and little puffs of dust from his feet, and the people saw the messenger running steadily up the hill towards us. We all cried out. People pointed. It is a long hill up to our village, sir, and every step he took scuffed up little clouds of dust. A small, lean man in a cloth tunic, no armor, with legs like rope and dust in his beard. I remember the legs. They worked, and his body seemed to float along above them. As he came near and saw our questioning faces, he called out one word, "Victory!" But his voice was weak and croaking. Someone gave him a vase with water. He stopped to drink but kept shuffling on a few steps, drinking then shuffling, as if compelled to keep moving forward, however slowly. The people jogged and shuffled with him, stirring up dust. Some asked about their men. My mother ran with him and said my father's name, but it was barely a whisper. The runner just shook his head. He gestured up towards Athens. He would take no food. Our village was not where his run must finish. "Victory," he said again, more clearly now, as he handed back the water vase. I saw it had the figure of Athena, with her spear and shield and plumed helmet, perhaps a sign. I always remember Athena on that vase. The runner wiped his mouth. "Great victory. We pushed them back to the sea," he said. He looked for a moment back toward Marathon.

I was standing close, and young as I was, I saw horror in his eyes. And then I saw purpose, as he set himself again towards Athens. He began to run again, back into that low yet springy uphill stride. I saw the ropes in his legs pull and push, pull and push. People ran with him, still asking him to say more, offering him food. Men, women, and children, all ran, raising more dust, so that the setting sun was turned to grey-brown. Soon only the bigger boys ran with him, falling behind one-by-one as they realized that his pace was faster than it looked. Then he passed over the crest of the hill towards Athens, and he was gone.

4. *One of the former archons (senators) of Athens, in his great old age, one moon before his death, gave this account of the Senate House on the day of the battle.*

The place was a hubbub as we waited for the news. There were speeches - what to do if we have won, if we have lost... No one listened. It was useless before we had news. The archon President dithered and fussed. The sun had set and it was the first part of the night before we heard the call outside, "The runner comes!" No one thought of telling the attendants to open the doors. Suddenly they were pushed open. All of us – statesmen, governors, greybeards – all jumped like frightened children, startled as if it was the Persian army flinging open the doors, bringing flame and swords to destroy our city. But it was one man, Athenian, thank the gods. A day-runner, in his short tunic. Small, lean, sweating, dirty. He stood gasping. There was dust on his face and his legs. He stumbled towards the President's chair, still running, though weary and limping, as if his whole being was a compulsion to keep running forward. He stopped before the President, swaying. He seemed to force his chest to stop heaving. As he panted, we were all holding our breath. What was his news? Then he gathered all his breath, and he cried out: "Nennikkamen! Rejoice, we conquer!" We rose from our marble seats, looked at each other, beginning to shout with inarticulate joy. But before we could react the runner stumbled again, ran a few shuffling steps, then bent forward as runners do after a race, both hands on his knees, face to the ground, his body heaving. Then, he fell. Not heavily, but just as if sliding from life into death. He fell. Some ran to him, lifted his head, splashed water on his dusty face. But we knew. Athens was saved. The Persians were back in their ships. But it cost us our best runner. "Rejoice, we conquer!" he said. And then he died.

Your command I obeyed,
Ran and raced: like stubble, some field which a fire runs through,
Was the space between city and city: two days, two nights did I burn
Over the hills, under the dales, down pits and up peaks...

He [the god] was gone. If I ran hitherto –
Be sure that, the rest of my journey, I ran no longer, but flew.
Parnes to Athens – earth no more, the air was my road:
Here I am back. Praise Pan, we stand no more on the razor's edge!...

He flung down his shield,
Ran like fire once more: and the space 'twixt the Fennel-field
And Athens was stubble again, a field which a fire runs through,
Till in he broke: "Rejoice, we conquer!" Like wine through clay,
Joy in his blood bursting his heart, he died – the bliss!

—From Robert Browning, "Pheidippides" in Dramatic Idyls, 1879

Chapter 3

The Messengers

The world's first great long-distance runners were not the graceful nude racers idealized on ancient Greek vases, and commemorated in elaborate award-winning odes, but generations of down and, no doubt, often dirty mailmen, whose modestly paid day-job was to run many miles a day, all day if necessary, carrying messages, or goods. Their names are rarely recorded, but their endurance was vital to human communication in every era before we had cell phones, radio, or even the pony express. Running messengers made up one of the world's oldest, most global, and most important professions.

Pheidippides was a *hemerodromoi*, a military day-runner, working for the army, while the *dromokirikes* were the civic letter carriers of ancient Greece. Pheidippides was not quite the first running messenger to achieve some lasting fame, however fictionalized. The first Book of Samuel in the Old Testament of the Bible tells how six hundred years before the Battle of Marathon, a similar messenger ran with similar news, of the defeat of the Israelis at the Battle of Even Ha'ezer, in 1080 B.C.:

"That same day a Benjaminite ran from the battle line and went to Shiloh with his clothes torn and dust on his head." (1 Sm 4:12).

The messenger is identified only by his tribe – "a Benjaminite," or, in the Authorized Version, "a man of Benjamin." The distance from that battlefield to the city is about the same as from Marathon to Athens, a coincidence that inspired Judge Isaac Braz to create a "Modern Benjaminite Race" under marathon rules, first run on April 14, 1968.

The Biblical story, again like Pheidippides, has a tragic ending, although this time it is not the messenger who dies. Eli, the ninety-eight-year-old High Priest and judge, is so shocked by the news that his sons have been killed and the Ark of the Covenant lost to the enemy that he falls from his seat and his neck is broken.

Every army depended on its running messengers, and so did every society. Faster over long distances than horses, more flexible than messages sent by river or coastal boat, running messengers were almost unconstrained by terrain or weather, and were capable of initiative and decision making. Tireless and often intrepid, for thousands of years they conveyed royal commands, military orders, legal documents, summonses, trading deals, news of the day, love letters, begging letters, business letters, "Dear John" letters, pleas for payment, notices of births, deaths, and marriages, advertising, shipping notices, offers of employment, market prices, publishers' rejection notes, and every other kind of text message, email, or tweet. Our very word "courier" means "runner," from the Latin word *currere* (to run), which also gives us words like "current" (the latest news), "course" (something you run along), "cursor" (something that runs around your screen), and "precursor" (someone who ran before us).

They deserve more honor than they have received in the history of running. The class-conscious "amateur" code that dominated the sport and wrote its history until the 1980s preferred to take track athletes from antiquity as its originating role models, since they were untainted by being paid, and were lauded in poetry. Humble messengers who were employed to run were disregarded until the world found inspiration in the almost certainly fictitious exploit of Pheidippides.

Yet their role was so important that the ancient Greeks worshipped a messenger god, the winged-footed Hermes, whose name became Mercury for the Romans, acting as messenger among the gods and intermediary between them and us mortals. Native Americans of the southwest explained the very creation of the world by myths of runners and running. Peter Nabokov, in his seminal *Indian Running*, explains the belief that the Sacramento River is the wake of a running messenger racing inland, and the Milky Way is dust raised by a race between the coyote and the wildcat as the earth was being formed.

All cultures respect messengers as entitled to protection, no matter how unwelcome the message they bring. When Shakespeare's Cleopatra has a messenger whipped, it is the most inexcusable of all her offences. We still give way to the mailman's truck or bicycle, as if it were an ambulance. Some regarded the messenger as sacred. In Christian cultures, messages were quite often carried by friars, who were nomadic, unlike monks. Friar John fatally fails to deliver an important message in *Romeo and Juliet* when he gets quarantined because of an epidemic. In Japan, John Stevens has told us of Tendai Buddhist monks whose tradition is to conduct a "moving meditation," of *kaih gy,* running more than fifty miles a day in a seven-year, one thousand-day "mountain marathon," no doubt related to an understanding of the endorphin effect of long running. In Tibet, the *lung-gum-pa* messenger-monks ran effortlessly (it seems) all day, in a trance that modern marathoners may aspire to.

The sacred dimension explains why one early messenger's name is still remembered: Euchidas of Plataea. In 479 B.C., eleven years after the Battle of Marathon, combined Greek armies won an even more important victory against the Persians, outside the walls of Plataea. Despite driving out the invaders, they felt their land and its temples had been desecrated, and Euchidas, their star running messenger was sent to the shrine of Delphi, to bring back holy fire from the altar of Apollo, and regenerate their sacred flames. He did the round trip of 113 miles/182km in twenty-four hours (this chapter will be full of such dubious stats), saluted his fellow citizens, delivered the flame, and (in a now familiar ending) collapsed and died. He was buried in the temple of Artemis Eucleia, with the inscription "Euchidas ran to Delphi and back in one day." His name survives because his feat is recorded by Plutarch in his *Life of Aristides* (the general who led the Athenian forces), written soon after 100 A.D. – five hundred years later. Not an immediate source, but the best we have.

One sure way for a runner to be turned into legend is to drop dead at the finish line. Another who famously did that was the legendary Welsh shepherd, Griffith Morgan, or Guto (pronounced "Gitto") Nyth Brân, taking that version of his name from the farm (Crow's Nest Farm) where he grew up, in the Cynon Valley in mid-Glamorgan. Born in 1700, Guto was the swiftest of many fleet-footed shepherds on that hilly terrain, and began life single-handedly rounding up his father's sheep and bringing them into the fold for the night. The first story about him as a child is the time he was home late from herding the sheep and told his father "I had trouble with the small brown one tonight." When his father went to investigate, he found a hare panting with exhaustion among the sheep in the pen, a Welsh running equivalent to Davy Crockett shooting his childhood bear.

A fast runner will always be given messages to carry and errands to run. Dorando Pietri began his running career that way – see Chapter 7. As a boy, Guto was once sent to Pontypridd to collect something for his mother, and ran the seven-mile/twelve-kilometer return journey (so the story goes) before her kettle had boiled. Once he chased and caught a bird, snatching it in flight from the air. But he found his vocation only after he was romantically smitten by Jane of the Shop (Siân o'r Slop), who became his manager and muse as well as fiancée. Jane arranged races for Guto at high stakes, starting with a bet of five hundred (or four hundred) pounds on a three (or four) mile race over Hirwaun Common, against an army captain stationed at the camp there. The details vary, but Guto won easily, and was launched on the career of a part-time professional "pedestrian."

For more than ten years, he ran many daily miles on the hills, he slept in a midden before races so that the warmth of the manure would make his legs supple (I might propose that idea in *Runner's World*), he beat all comers at all distances, on cross-country, along the dirt roads, or in some cases up steep hill sprints, and Jane reputedly grew rich on the proceeds. But it is his last race that stirs the imagination of runners three hundred years later. Guto was 37, and few challengers had been found in recent years. Then a young upstart calling himself "Prince" laid down a challenge, for the huge sum of a thousand guineas, over a twelve-mile course from St. Woolos Church, Newport, to St. Barrwg's Church, Bedwas, near Caerphilly. Many reputedly wagered their life savings, including Jane (though that sounds unlikely for a lady so canny).

The equally canny Guto allowed Prince to take a big lead, but, alert to the advantage of running negative splits, caught the over-confident younger man at ten miles, and accelerated on the final uphill to win convincingly, racing between the fervently cheering crowds who lined the finish. They were wildly jubilant, none more so than Jane, who rushed over to embrace Guto, crying "Bravo, Guto bach, bravo!" and passionately slapped him on the back. Guto fell dead on the spot. Whether from exhaustion, or from the vigor of Jane's back-slaps, which reputedly "displaced his heart," or from the stress of having officially run twelve miles in 53 minutes, Guto died, his last race a triumph that became a tragedy.

He was carried in solemn procession to St. Gwynno's Churchyard, and there he rested in peace for more than two centuries, until an enterprising local runner, running historian, teacher, and promotional genius, Bernard Baldwin, found and retold the old story, and had the idea in 1958 of staging a New Year's Eve race to commemorate Guto Nyth Brân. He named it Nos Galan, after a Welsh mid-winter carol. It has grown into a major running festival, mainly because of Baldwin's inspired idea of inviting an annual "mystery runner" celebrity, whose identity is kept strictly secret, and who embodies Guto, a lone runner emerging out of the darkness with a lighted torch, which he or she carries to Guto's graveside in St. Gwynno's Churchyard, and then on down the mountainside to the town of Mountain Ash, to be the starter of the road race. The first mystery runner was 1948 Olympic Marathon silver medalist (and Welshman) Tom Richards, and since then many luminaries of British sports have run out of the shadows to represent the humble running-messenger shepherd.

Baldwin's main sources were William Thomas Glanffryd, *Plwy Llanwynno (Parish of Llanwynno)*, 1888, and the poem "Guto Nyth Brân" by Isaac Daniel Hooson, published after Hooson's death in 1948. Guto's large imposing gravestone, erected in 1866, more than a hundred years after his death, suggests that his story was very much alive locally, despite a lack of written evidence. It took Baldwin to link it to modern road running and fire one of the first shots in the running boom.

Baldwin, who died at 91 in 2017, should be remembered. He created a race in his little home town that was ahead of the forefront of running as it evolved from a small eccentric sport into an inspirational mass movement. Nos Galan is a road race that is also a celebration, with the appeal of a significant story, some magical mystery, mildly religious ritual, the appeal of a folk hero, and surefire media impact. It is an open-to-all fun run, a street party, and a tourist destination event. All those things came into mainstream running well after the imaginative Baldwin envisaged them for Nos Galan in 1958. The format and timing have changed over the years, and traffic concerns forced the event to be canceled for some years, but it is now back again as the culminating highlight of a program of family entertainment that brings ten thousand people into the town, including eight hundred runners. Guto Nyth Brân has his own statue; Baldwin received an honor from the Queen; and the Freedom of the Borough – Rhondda Cynon Taf; and his race was declared the "Best Fun Run in Great Britain." There's lot to be said for dropping dead at the finish.

A more triumphal modern celebration is run on Ninety Mile Beach in the far north of New Zealand (Te Oneroa-a-Tōhē/the long beach of Tōhē). The firm sand of that seemingly limitless surf-loud thrust of land between the South Pacific and the Tasman is an irresistible location for an epic running legend. Te Houtaewa was a young *rangitira* (Māori chief) of Te Aupōuri, a warrior, and a famed runner. When his mother (or perhaps grandmother) lamented that she didn't have enough *kumara* (sweet potato) to feed her family, he set out to run the entire length of the beach, trespassing into the territory of the rival Te Rarawa people, at the southern end of the long beach, to forage from their unguarded stores. No doubt there was an element of youthful provocation about it, not unknown among feisty young warriors, or runners. Of course, they caught him in the act. Surrounded by indignant enemies, and with no weapon, Te Houtaewa defied, dodged, and eluded them, running up the hill of Whangatuatia, and as they gasped after him, suddenly racing down and breaking through their line.

Running home at full speed, Te Houtaewa's pace left their best runners struggling behind him on the long return journey. He arrived home laden with vegetables for his mother's earth oven, and with the stuff of oral legend for future generations. The historical background is the pre-European tradition of warfare between Te Aupōuri and Te Rawara, with frequent raids, and (according to the Māori guide when I visited in 2021), the wounding of Te Houtaewa in a battle at Mount Camel when only Te Rawara had obtained European muskets.

His legendary feat is now commemorated every March by the Te Houtaewa Challenge/Te Wero o te Houtaewa, which offers the world's only full marathon run entirely on a surface of firm beach sand. Other events include a 60km ultra run, and other running, walking, and Māori canoeing events, with a Māori arts festival, the same mix of sports and ethnic culture that works on the other side of the world in the Nos Galan.

Euchidas, Guto Nyth Brân, and Te Houtaewa are commemorated by name, but thousands of runners whose names are forgotten sustained the communication networks that enabled human society to develop, literally from China to Peru. The Inca *chasqui* and Aztec *titlantil* systems were fully established in South America before the arrival of the Spanish, couriers covering the empire at a rate of 240km/150 miles a day, with well-developed routes, a relay system, and rest houses, often portering fresh fish, game, and fruit from coastal regions to the mountain capital. They also carried numerical or financial information encoded on a set of knotted strings (see picture).

When the Spanish landed at Chianiztlan in May 1519, they were surprised to find that detailed reports of their ships and forces had reached Montezuma, 260 miles/420km away, within twenty-four hours. A similar communication network enabled the Native Americans of the widespread Southwest Pueblos to rise successfully against the Spanish and take Santa Fe in August 1660. Indigenous runners in Bengal in 1857 used a "chain-letter" system of divided chapatti to summon the scattered villages to join the uprising again British rule known as the Indian Mutiny. On these occasions, these humble running messengers contributed to making history in radical ways.

Another early documented account dates from 1333, when a Moroccan traveler to India, Ibn Battuta, admiringly described the sophisticated relay network of runners created by the Sultan Muhammad Tughluq from 1324 to 1351, based in his capital in Delhi. Foot couriers were stationed in pavilions, "girded up ready to move off," and alerted by the sounds of bells carried by the letter-carrier at the top of a brass rod, so that the next runner moved off with no delay, jingling his bells in turn to warn the next. As well as mail, Battuta reports that they carried fruit, water, and sometimes condemned criminals (lashed to stretchers on the runners' heads), and were faster than any mounted post.

It could be a dangerous profession. A history of the Indian postal services records one mail runner being eaten by a tiger, and that his family was refused compensation on the grounds that "the man was only carrying out his ordinary duty." Runners anxious about tigers will be relieved to know that this unkind decision was overruled on appeal, and the audit officer reprimanded. The foothills of the Himalayas were particularly notorious for the threat of beasts and brigands for the *hikaras*, or mail runners, who among other routes covered the mountain terrain between Kalka and Shimla, now one of the world's most spectacular rail journeys.

Japan maintained an equally efficient system of running couriers, the *hikyaku*, which means literally "fleet feet." They kept the country organized and coherent at a time when Japan had almost no contact with the outside world. Matthew W. Shores (scholar of Japanese literature and a marathoner) has provided the following outline of their work and history.

The shogunal structure meant the government needed to send official documents throughout the country, with five national corridor trails leading to and from the capital, Edo (Tokyo). As in India, *tsugi-hikyaku* (a relay system) ensured express delivery, and it seems that they operated in pairs to guard against attack or injury. Different groups divided the route into different distances, as names have survived for *shichiri no mono* (seventeen milers) and *ichiri tsugi* (2.4-mile relayers). Each major city had its own *hikyaku* who were adept at finding their way through the convoluted maze of backstreets that characterizes Japan's urban areas. Other specialties developed, like the *hikyaku* sprinters who brought instant information on market prices to a riverside salt broker in the 1600s. Soon there were runners bringing the latest prices in rice, silk, the money market, and more. Running messengers were crucial to the development of modern commerce.

The first Western observers in Japan were impressed by the couriers' speed, Sir Rutherford Alcock (1809-97) giving an account that they could cover 850 miles/13,700km in nine days. But even more astonishing to Westerners was the traditional near-nudity of the runners. Rudolf Lindau (1829-1910) recorded them in summer and winter as wearing only a thin white loincloth, with straw sandals, and carrying a bamboo pole, with a box of letters at one end and the name of their employing provincial lord at the other. Japanese woodcut prints by Hokusai and others confirm this dress code.

Like the runners in India, the *hikyaku* also carried a bell, rung to demand safe passage and to alert the next relay runner. This seems to have been an almost global convention. The Grand Turk's corps of eighty to a hundred runners in the fifteenth through eighteenth centuries, routinely travelling 386km/240 miles between Constantinople and Adrianople, wore belts and garters covered with little bells, and a high bonnet topped with a plume of ostrich feathers, a uniform that announced their approach, and provided some protection against marauders. The running footmen of England carried a staff and were decorated with bells. The equivalent in ancient Peru was to signal their approach by blowing on a conch shell, like the later European posthorn. It's fascinating that the conventions are so closely similar, even in parts of the earth that supposedly had no contact with each other. Running messengers, as we might suspect, seem to have got around.

In Tudor England, the couriers' traditional dress was simpler, a sort of kilt or long linen shirt coming down to the knees but, like the Japanese loincloths, leaving ample freedom for running. "Our village maids delight," wrote a mid-1500s chronicler, "to see the Running Footman fly bare-arsed over the dusty road."

The Grand Turk's runners were usually native Persians/Iranians from mountain areas, an early indication of the benefits of altitude for endurance running. For the same reason, in France and Spain, the couriers were traditionally Basques, giving rise to a French proverbial expression, "run like a Basque." References go back to Rabelais in the 1540s, and in 1566, the Basque servant of a French aristocrat was recorded as running from Le Puy to Paris (543km/337 miles) and back, in seven and a half days. The reputation of the Basques was such that another sixteenth century writer, Henri Estienne, urges anyone wanting to send important correspondence to use "your Basque, who runs like the wind." Because of this tradition, the Basques developed Europe's earliest structure of competitive long-distance races, the *korrikalaris*, which began in the eighteenth century, possibly as wagers among retired running footmen. These precursive races have been chronicled by Andy Millroy, in "The Great Running Traditions of the Basques." The Basque tradition has been sustained in modern times by such stellar runners as Mariano Haro, Francisco Aritmendi, Martin Fiz, and among the women, Carmen Valero.

And so around the world. In Hawai'i the messengers were *Ka'ili* (recorded in the Bishop Museum). In Ethiopia they were *malacténia*, mostly coming (no surprise) from Bekoji. Noel Tamini cites a source from the early twentieth century that a porter/messenger named Yayi carried a sum of money over very rugged terrain to Addis Ababa, 65-70km away, arriving in ten hours, and returning the next morning with the receipt.

In North America, "Indian runners" were the communication network before the pony express, and always in forest country where horses could not easily penetrate. They make key appearances in J. Fenimore Cooper's novels. Magua, the enigmatic and dangerous Huron chief, first enters *The Last of the Mohicans* as "the still, upright, and rigid form of the 'Indian runner,' who had borne to the camp the unwelcome tidings of the previous evening." Hollywood likes dramatically galloping horse-borne news, but in reality the running messengers were more efficient.

Developing communities regularly employed "footposts" as they were called in England, like Bartholomew Moore, who travelled on foot from Leicester to London and back once a week in the 1600s (320km/200 miles round trip). His name suggests he was Irish, which fits with many of the early running footmen. In New Zealand's South Island in the 1850s, "Black Andy," an Australian aboriginal, worked as a mail carrier between the sheep stations of South Canterbury and the city of Christchurch, covering the 160km/100 miles in each direction, with several dangerous river crossings, between sunrise and sundown, "at a quick trot all the way." Knowing his own weakness for brandy, Andy used to check himself into the Christchurch police cells for the night, recalls Ellen Tripp in *My Early Days*. Farther north at the same date, a Māori called Nga Mapu carried mail twice a week between Auckland and the "fencible" (defended) early settlement of Howick, running the 12 miles/21km each way, and living in a raupō thatched cottage that can still be visited, among the wooden buildings of the settlers in a "historic village."

Probably the most famous runner who also worked as a messenger was Tom Longboat, who will be one of the key figures in Chapters 7 and 8. He volunteered for the Canadian army in World War I in 1916. He won regimental races, and then did duty so dangerous as a messenger-runner in the trenches that he was twice reported dead. The main figures in Jack Bennett's novel *Gallipoli* (1981), later a successful film are, like the real Longboat – military runners in the lethal trenches.

For centuries, all around the world, these usually nameless messengers were the true precursors of our modern running. Their heroic individual stories add up to one big and overlooked story that has had a profound effect on the progress of human society. They included, no doubt, some very great runners, who in a different context would have been elite marathoners and ultra-runners. Only now do we understand how they could sustain such distances day after day. It took us (the competitive sport) until the late twentieth century to learn that the human body's powers of adaptation include the ability to acquire an almost unlimited increase in endurance. Those who risked running training mileages ahead of their time, like Tom Longboat, Clarence DeMar, Paavo Nurmi, Jim Peters, or Doris Brown Heritage, reaped the benefits in the races they won. Scientist/runner Bruce Tulloh, in his eloquent account of breaking the record for running coast-to-coast across America, affirmed that "I was fitter as a running machine at the end of the 65 days than I was when I started." Tulloh's daily mileage rose as the run progressed (Tulloh, 2019).

But the messengers were only doing their job. The messages they carried were more important than they were as individuals, just as with modern mailmen or couriers. Their achievements were not documented, and they received few literary tributes. So, in their honor, here are three.

Willa Cather gives a glimpse of runners in the American Southwest in her novel *Death Comes for the Archbishop*. She perfectly evinces the Native Americans' empathy with the land, their ability to "pass through a country without disturbing anything...like fish through the water, or birds through the air." In one of the most exquisite images ever created for runners, Cather beautifully describes how two messengers run across the land in this natural harmony with the environment:

> *North of Laguna two Zuni runners sped by them,*
> *going somewhere east on 'Indian business'...*
> *They coursed over the sand with the fleetness*
> *of young antelopes, their bodies disappearing*
> *and reappearing among the sand dunes, like the*
> *shadows that eagles cast in their strong unhurried*
> *flight (Cather, 1926).*

There's a glimpse of mail runners in British Ceylon in Katherine Mansfield's story *The Daughters of the Late Colonel*, when the two spinster sisters in London think back to their girlhood days in Ceylon, before their young mother died from a snake bite, and both recall mental images of the courier:

> *Both paused to watch a black man in white linen drawers running through pale fields for dear life, with a large brown-paper parcel in his hands. Josephine's black man was tiny; he scurried along glistening like an ant. But there was something blind and tireless about Constantia's tall, thin fellow...*

To end this story of history's running messengers, here is a wonderfully witty poem about them (1886) by Rudyard Kipling, perfectly poised between admiration and humor. A eulogistic encomium for the faithful mail runners (in British India this time), with their bags and their bells, it pays sincere respect to their intrepidity, the fearsome terrain they had to traverse, and their importance to settler society, while enjoying some tongue in cheek comedy at the expense of the "exiles," the ruling British. For those homesick ex-pats, the tiger, the tempest, the brigand, and the hot Indian sun itself are concerns much less important than the arrival of mail from "home."

The Overland Mail
(foot-service to the hills)
> *In the name of the Empress of India, make way,*
> *O lords of the Jungle, wherever you roam,*
> *The woods are astir at the close of the day –*
> *We exiles are waiting for letters from Home.*
> *Let the robber retreat – let the tiger turn tail –*
> *In the Name of the Empress, the overland Mail!*

With a jingle of bells as the dusk gathers in,
He turns to the footpath that heads up the hill –
The bags on his back and a cloth round his chin,
And, tucked in his waistbelt, the Post Office bill:-
"Despatched on this date, as received by the rail,
Per runner, two bags of the Overland Mail!"

Is the torrent in spate? He must ford it or swim.
Has the rain wrecked the road? He must climb by the cliff.
Does the tempest cry halt? What are tempests to him?
The service admits not a "but" or an "if".
While the breath's in his mouth, he must bear without fail,
In the Name of the Empress, the Overland Mail.

From aloe to rose-oak, from rose-oak to fir,
From level to upland, from upland to crest,
From rice-field to rock-ridge, from rock-ridge to spur,
Fly the soft-sandalled feet, strains the brawny, brown chest.
From rail to ravine – to the peak from the vale -
Up, up through the night goes the Overland Mail.

There's a speck on the hillside, a dot on the road –
A jingle of bells on the footpath below -
There's a scuffle above in the monkey's abode -
The world is awake and the clouds are aglow.
For the great Sun himself must attend to the hail:-
"In the Name of the Empress, the Overland Mail!"

Chapter 4

Hell and Fury Sykes

800 BC   100 AD   1719   1896   1908   1928   1936   1964   1984   2021

Journalism, Theater, Nudity, and Crime: The Era of the Running Footmen

Newmarket Heath, on the Suffolk/Cambridgeshire boundary line in Eastern England has been famed for four hundred years as the center of horse racing in England. The first recorded horse race on the expanse of rough chalky grassland was in 1622, and in 1671 King Charles II became the first and only monarch to ride a winner. Races in the spring and fall were on the "Rowley Mile," named after Old Rowley, the favorite horse of Charles II, and summer races were on the "July Course." In the winter, Newmarket became a favorite venue for another sport – foot racing.

February 1719: The lean racehorses are in the stables, warm under their blankets, pressing their proud hoofs on the trampled straw. The wintry heath outside is dank and misty, too cold for thoroughbred horses. Today a different kind of race has brought crowds, color, excitement, and money to Newmarket. Two "running footmen" are ready for a match foot race, over two miles, on two laps of the thick grass of the Rowley Mile course. It's not an easy course, with an uphill slope that drains the energy on this footing. "Match" means just the two of them, head to head, like a boxing championship. There is rich prize money, which will go to the winning employer, not the footmen, just as in a horse race the prize money goes to the owner, not the horse or the jockey. The runners are domestic servants, their status barely equivalent to a good horse, employed for little more than their keep, and a small allowance "to washhe his hose" (stockings), as one letter of appointment said. In a report of this race, they are identified only as "the Duke of Wharton's Running Footman, and the Lord Castlemain's."

In fact, they are William Mawbone and Thomas Groves (or Grove – the spelling varies), racing the second of a series of four match races over different distances – one, two, three, and four miles, held at one-month intervals, always on the tenth of the month, January to April. *The Original Weekly Journal* gives us that information. The races attracted great public interest and betting. When the series was announced, each race was said to be worth one hundred pounds in prize money. By the second race, the purse is already "several hundred Guineas," and much more would be staked in bets. The betting is the aristocrats' main interest in setting up this amusing diversion for the winter months, when their horses have to keep to their stables.

The sums gambled during that era were mind-boggling. In 1720, the newspaper reported that the same Duke of Wharton, Mawbone's boss, "has lost near 6000 pounds by Horse-Racing, etc.," several millions in modern terms. With such money at stake, no doubt the runners got a good bonus, as well as whatever they made (or lost) on their own bets.

The two footmen prance in their rival liveries of colored jackets, breeches tucked into high white socks, leather shoes, and a cap, much like the apparel of a modern jockey. Their breath shows white in the chill damp air of the low-lying ground of East Anglia, only a few miles from the watery Fens. Their aristocratic patrons in long ornate coats and elaborate curling white-powdered wigs cluster expectantly near gilt coaches at the finish, surrounded by their guests and followers. Pastel-colored cloaks and long wide skirts that sweep and swish on the grass mark the few women. Grooms stand quietly by the coach horses, and servants move about to bring refreshments and carry bets. The bookmakers prowl the fringes of the scattered crowd. Some eager boys wanting a better view climb up on one of the dome-shaped Bronze Age burial mounds that still dot the edge of the racecourse.

The race begins. They go out fast. With big partisan crowds, the high stakes, just two competitors inexperienced at pace control under pressure in racing, we can imagine how fervently they would begin.

"Both of 'em Ran with such Fury and Violence" went the newspaper report. Oxygen debt inevitably strikes by halfway, and brings on the searing lungs and aching enfeebled legs suffered by all runners who start too fast. Over coarse grass and uneven footing, with a long uphill drag in each lap, inevitably the pace slows, to not much more than a gasping shuffle in the second mile. Then, with the finish in sight, the two stir themselves to a desperate scramble. Neither gives up, though their legs are buckling. Almost side by side, with a flailing gasping sprint, they lunge across the line, and collapse exhausted. "They both drop'd down for Dead when they came in" concluded the report.

That race on Tuesday, February 10, 1719, is important as a historical milestone. It wasn't the first race between footmen, not by more than a hundred years, but it was the first to be reported in a newspaper. The report that I've quoted from was the first time ever that a running race was recorded in a factual, eye-witness account in a print newspaper for public sale. It is the earliest extant piece of running journalism.

It appeared in *The Original Weekly Journal*. Here is the paragraph in full, a concise yet vivid piece of writing:

> *Last Tuesday the second match between the Duke of Wharton's Running Footman, and the Lord Castlemain's, was Run at New-Market, for several hundred Guineas, and the Duke's Man won. Both of 'em Ran with such Fury and Violence, that, tho' it was but a two-Mile Course, they drop'd down for Dead when they came in.*
> *(The Original Weekly Journal, February 14, 1719)*

Factual reporting of running for a public readership was unprecedented. There are exciting, dramatic, even fatal foot races in imaginative literature, from Homer's *Iliad* onward, with the gods often affecting the result. From the late 1500s through the 1600s there was a flourishing real-life competitive scene of races between footmen. Those provided colorful material for some stage plays, and there are accounts of races in private correspondence and diaries. Samuel Pepys recorded footmen races. His diary is the most famous of all, but it was of course private (extremely so in places) and was not published until 1825, more than a hundred years later. Some of Pepys's references are important historically, as I'll show. But none has the detail, the objectivity, and the immediacy of reporting journalism, which in 1719 was in the very early stages of its development.

Newspapers at that date had existed for barely thirty years. They began to appear in the late 1600s. They could not exist until printing became widespread and cheap, and literate urban populations were big enough to supply an adequate reader market. And the earliest newspapers (as we now call them) did not immediately take on the function of reporting news. They were established as calendars of coming events, *diurnals*, that is "of the day"; in the French version of the Latin, *diurnal* was pronounced "journal." They were more concerned with providing "notices" than reporting news in the sense we understand it. Even today, many print and online publications still retain this "coming events" or "what's on this week" preview function.

It was only when a leisured gentlemen's coffee house social life developed in the late 1710s that the "journals" began to add such matters as social gossip, and occasional items about leisure activities like horse racing. Even then, these are the merest scraps, still notices of coming events more often than reports of events after they have happened.

Many of the innovations were made by that extraordinary genius of journalism, Daniel Defoe, in his three-times-weekly *The Review* (1704-13) and other ventures. Even his famous novel, *Robinson Crusoe*, is a first-person semi-invented remake of the news story of the real-life castaway Alexander Selkirk.

The Original Weekly Journal, where the "Fury and Violence" race was reported, was indeed the world's inaugural, or original, weekly. Again, much of it (exactly how much is a matter of speculation) was the work of the workaholic Defoe. He wrote for it under the pen name Applebee. Soon the name changed to *Applebee's Original Weekly Journal*, which may mean it was mostly a one-man publication, like *The Review*. Mostly "notices" of coming events, *Applebee's* began to include concise paragraphs of what we would call breaking news, enlivened with snippets of vivid and dramatic writing. The footman race provides one of the best examples: "Both of 'em ran with such Fury and Violence that... they drop'd down for Dead when they came in." I think that's Defoe, writing with the same vivid observation as in *Robinson Crusoe* or *Moll Flanders*. It's for sure a writer who knows his business, how to capture the reader's attention, how to get the intensity of sporting contest into a few words, with the powerful hyperbole of "Fury and Violence," and the timeless appeal of dropping down dead at the finish, even if on a more careful reading it says only that they "drop'd down for Dead," or "as if they were dead." In fact, they raced each other again a month later.

Reported information relating to an actual event, brought to narrative life, and heightened by colorful and emotive language – this is sports journalism at the moment of its birth.

In early January, the paper announced the scheduled four races, and the time and terms of the first in the series, to be held on January 10 – "a Mile on the Flat at New-Market for 100 pounds." But the result of that first race was never published, nor any report, to my historian's frustration. It is the first known one-mile race in history. This notice tells when it happened, and I have deduced below who won; but there is no published record after the event.

Mawbone won the second race, the "Fury and Violence" two miles at Newmarket on February 10 – "and the Duke's Man won." For the third, announced beforehand as three miles on March 10, there is again no report, no result. (In the stillness of the British Library Reading Room, I emitted an inward howl of disappointment.)

Happily, there was a report of the fourth race. It went decisively to Groves.

> *Last Friday 7. night [i.e., Friday last week, April 10, 1719], the Foot Race, spoken of in our last, was Ran at New-Market, between Mawbone, the Duke of Wharton's Running Footman, and Groves, the Lord Castlemain's, and the former was beat above two Miles. (The Original Weekly Journal, Saturday, April 18, 1719)*

Reconstructing these sparse bones of information from a runner's or running journalist's perspective, my deduction is that Mawbone was the middle-distance man, the 800/miler, as almost certainly he won the first race, which was a mile. Then his miler's finishing speed, and the endurance training from his daily work, was enough to take the second race, over two miles, after a desperate sprint that left both men "drop't down for Dead." That is still the distance, two miles/3,000m, where middle-distance and long-distance specialists are most closely matched, usually to the advantage of the former. Groves would be the distance man, probably smaller and lighter, who took the final four-mile race decisively, dropping Mawbone at halfway ("the former was beat above two Miles"). It's a safe deduction that Mawbone won the one-mile first race, and Groves won the unreported three-miles third encounter, since the stakes for the fourth race were high, meaning that the overall series was still open.

The Running Footmen

I wish I could recapture the personalities of these early runners, the Western world's first competitive long-distance runners. They have been too long forgotten. That is mainly because history was for a century idealistically confined to the amateur sport, and the footmen were professionals in the sense that running was one requirement of their employment, and they ran to win prize money for their employers. But even at the time, the newspapers were more interested in celebrity trivia than actual performances (nothing changes), and gave far more space to the Dukes than their mere footmen. *Applebee's* in various issues, for instance, tells us about the Duke of Wharton's comings and goings from his Westminster residence, about his generosity at Christmas to his country tenants in Buckinghamshire, of his horse-racing exploits (he often rode himself), of his musicians, his "set of the finest Harriers, or Hare-Hunters" (Beagles), and the birth of a son, "to the great joy of that noble Family." The runners are little more than names, most times not even that.

Footmen's duties could include waiting at table, but their main roles were to carry messages and to provide an escort on foot to their employer, who rode on horseback or in a carriage. In large aristocratic households, the running footmen were an on-call communication service, running from house to house in London, and when necessary from town to town. If the Duke of Wharton decided to move from his town house in Westminster to his country property near Buckingham, it was Mawbone or a footman colleague who ran the fifty miles/eighty km to tell the household to prepare. In the city, they ran ahead of the carriage to check oncoming traffic in the narrow streets, and on the roads outside the city they paid tolls when the new turnpike roads came in, and set up proper reception and change of horses at the next inn. They could run all day if they had to, like Pheidippides, and the other early messengers of chapter 3. Like them, they were the running equivalent of the cell phone, email, and courier service, with a touch of public relations frontman or herald thrown in. They wore livery, and they traditionally flourished a long cane of office, to clear inferior persons out of the way, with a hollow silver ball at the top where they carried sustenance ("a little white wine" or "hard-boiled egg").

The cane or staff, sometimes a long horn, recurs in later accounts of the footmen in their ceremonial role. Sir Walter Scott's *The Bride of Lammermoor* (1819), set in Scotland in the early 1700s, describes "running footmen, dressed in white, with black jockey caps, and long staffs in their hands," and adds a footnote citing contemporary sources. One old play, Scott says, sums up a footman as "linen stocking, and three score [60] miles a day." William Thackeray's scene of running footmen in his historical *The Four Georges* (1860) seems at least idealized: "a pair or a half-dozen of running footmen scudding along by the side of the vehicle, with conical caps, long silver-headed maces, which they poised as they ran, and splendid jackets laced all over with silver and gold."

I'm not convinced that a runner can "scud along" while carrying a long mace and wearing a high conical cap. I recall the great Greek ultra-runner, Yiannis Kouros, dressed for the part of Pheidippides for a television documentary that I had scripted (see images in chapter 2), throwing away his short sword in disgust after a few strides. "No runner could run all day with that thing banging against his leg," Yiannis said.

I decided to check. I did a scientific experiment into whether it is possible to run with a "long silver-headed mace," or even a light five-foot cane. What does Thackeray's "poised as they ran" mean? The ways to carry a mace or pole while running are in one hand, as strong people sometimes now carry flags while running marathons; or in the curious two-handed grip shown in one old footman illustration; or on the shoulder, as shown in another illustration, with the employer on horseback and escorts on foot, carrying canes like rifles. I conducted my research experiments in New York's Central Park, because that's the one place on earth where no one would think it strange to see a skinny bald person in shorts running at a six-minute-mile pace carrying a five-foot-long tree branch.

It can be done, I concluded. But I wouldn't like to do it all day. There are easier ways of getting access to white wine or an egg. I decided against experimenting, even in Central Park, with running in a high conical cap.

If there are runners, there will be rivalries between them. The earliest modern-era reference to racing seems to be in Coverdale's first English translation of the Bible in 1535, when he rendered what in the Hebrew is probably a reference to foot-soldiers (*ragli*), in terms that sound as if he has competitive runners in mind: "Seinge thou art weery in runnynge with the fote men, how wilt thou then runne wt horses?" The *New Revised Standard Version* (1989) keeps the allusion to competitive racing: "If you have raced with foot-runners and they have wearied you, how will you compete with horses?" (Jeremiah, 12:5)

The young Shakespeare probably saw some long races, too, since in his early *Henry VI, Part 3* (ca. 1589), he has the battle-weary Earl of Warwick say, "Forspent with toil, as runners with a race, / I lay me down a little while to breathe" (3.2.1-2).

Andy Milroy collected references that show that prize-money racing between footmen was underway by the 1580s. When in 1587 or 1588 a footman called Brown raced an unnamed opponent, on a course from St. John Street to Highgate and back, the fifteen pound prize became a matter of dispute, which went to court, and hence produced a written record. In April 1618, King James I and his court watched "the unusually notorious race," as one correspondent called it, between a royal footman and an Irish runner, from St. Alban's to Clerkenwell, about twenty miles/35km. "The betting on the race was great," but the Irish favorite lost, and the "lord of Buckingham went away with 3000 pounds." In the same year, the chaplain to the Venetian ambassador in London wrote, "It is a custom of this kingdom to make the footmen run races of fifteen or twenty miles," saying that one "famous" winner was presented with "a life rent of 80 crowns" as well as being taken into the King's service (Milroy).

This custom of racing footmen was familiar enough in London to feature quite often in the theater of the time, the early 1600s. Theater scholar David Carnegie's essay "Theatrical Running" is a suitably lively account of references to running and running footmen in the plays of that era, which he wrote for *Running Writing Robinson* (2011). Carnegie cites one scene, for instance, where a gentleman invites the ladies to "make a fling to London," to visit the resorts of pleasure, including "Hyde Park to see the races, horse and foot."

The appeal was never purely sporting. In private correspondence and in drama the emphasis is always on the prize money and the betting. In one play, a master trying to choose between hiring a butler, a cook, and others, says to the prospective footman, "you can win me wagers, / Footman, in running races," to which the footman confidently replies, "I dare boast it, sir."

But there was obviously an eager following. The playwright John Webster was a fan. He includes a fascinating glimpse of pre-race preparation in his little-known Roman play *Appius and Virginia* (ca. 1620). In a discussion of political ambition, Appius says that those who aspire to high office should "load themselves with excuse and faint denial," so they can leap to power all the faster, just as

> *I have heard of cunning footmen that have worn*
> *Shoes made of lead some ten days 'fore a race*
> *To give them nimble and more active feet.*
> *(1.1.55-58; I have modernized the spellings.)*

And in his comedy *A Cure for a Cuckold* (printed in 1661), Webster uses a competitive footman as a simile for how fast your money goes once you hire a lawyer: "Your purse must run by like a footman then." This prompts a response that implies that a litigant's purse is like a gasping runner, on the edge of exhaustion: "My purse shall run open-mouth'd at thee" (Carnegie, 2011). Quite likely some big race had just been run in London that the actors could ham up as they spoke the lines.

Webster also wrote "A Footman," a comic-satirical "character," or pen portrait, which is full of complex puns, and therefore hard to decipher now. Among the footman's defining characteristics, according to Webster, are his restless compulsion to keep moving, his attractiveness to women, and (not unrelated) the skimpy tattered condition of his clothing. Carnegie daringly suggests that, on occasion, racers stripped totally. One play offers the opportunity to "see the Adamites run naked afore the ladies." Adamites were a religious nudist sect. In another play, the independent-minded Lady Carol demands to "see / Plays when I have a mind to't, and the races, / Though men should run Adamites before me." When her friend comments that the race was "a most immodest sight...It would fright the women," Lady Carol responds, "Some are of opinion it brings us hither!" (Carnegie, 2011)

Carnegie also shows that many of the on-stage footmen are presented as Irish, which seems historically accurate as well as a source of comedy, with jokes about the unkempt wildness of appearance, the broad Irish accent, and the tendency to crude oaths that were supposed to define them.

Only one play actually shows a race on stage – James Shirley's social comedy, *Hyde Park*, performed in 1632. The race is between an Irish footman, Teague, and an English one, who dash twice across the stage, accompanied by cries of "A Teague!" and "Well run, Irish!" and followed by panting gentry anxious about their wagers. The stage direction is explicit: "The two runners cross the stage, followed by Lord Bonvile, Venture, and others." Carnegie discusses how the running might have been done, whether in stylized slow motion or by looping around the stage, but it's important that this is the first instance in history of a foot race on stage.

Without doubt, the audience is assumed to be conversant with foot races and how to wager money on them. There's a similar level of expected recognition in all the various comic running-and-gasping gags, and references to footmen's races, that Carnegie shows were common in these plays. The well-read Walter Scott, who did good research for his historical novels, made the same observation in *The Bride of Lammermoor*: "Such running footmen are often alluded to in old plays...and perhaps may still be remembered by some old persons in Scotland." It's an unusual example of a popular sporting entertainment being incorporated into the theatrical entertainment of the time.

The story goes quiet after the 1630s, a period of civil war followed by the Puritan Commonwealth's suppression of all sports and entertainments.

But no sooner was King Charles II back in town than Samuel Pepys was in Hyde Park with his friends Moore and Creed (both Irish, probably), and as he wrote in his diary (August 10, 1660), "saw a fine foot-race, three times round the park, between an Irishman and Crow, that was once my Lord Claypooles footman. Crow beat the other by above two miles." By 1663, a big race could again bring out royalty, as Pepys wrote on July 30 of that year: "The town talke this day is of nothing but the great foot race run this day on Banstead Downes, between Lee, the Duke of Richmonds footman, and a Tyler, a famous runner. And Lee hath beat him – though the King and Duke of Yorke, and all men almost, did bet three or four to one upon the Tyler's head."

Those Pepys entries are known by running historians, but perhaps the most historically significant foot race entry in his diary has been missed, the first race when actual women are identified by name as racing – Barker and Jane – even though the event was highly informal. It was a Sunday, and Pepys was in holiday humor, possibly because his day began with an illicit visit to the bed of his girlfriend, Mrs. Martin, followed by a quarrel, which I will tactfully omit.

> ...by and by away home, and there took out my wife and the two Mercers and two of our maids, Barker and Jane, and over the water to the Jamaica house, where I never was before; and there the girls did run for wagers over the bowling green. And there with much pleasure, spent little, and so home (The Diary of Samuel Pepys, April 14, 1667).

Another first came in May 1719, the first race in the modern sense. All the contests I have mentioned so far were match races, head-to-head between two runners like two rival boxers, or two racehorses entered by the "owners." In September 1718, *The Original Weekly Journal* announced a different kind of event, a race open to all footmen, to be run the following May, a month after the completion of the four-race

"Fury and Violence" series at Newmarket. Records are so patchy up to this time that we can only say it was probably the first open-entry race. But for sure it was the first when a call for entries was published by a newspaper.

> *A Twenty Pound Plate is to be given to all Footmen that will run for it at Woodstock next May [date illegible]. Those that are desirous to try their Agility that way, if they please to enquire of Mr. Edward Jones at the Crown in Pallmall near the Gloucester Tavern (The Original Weekly Journal, September 13, 1718).*

Sadly, no result was published. We can only hope it took place. If it did, open to all footmen "desirous to try," it was a significant step toward making the sport of running open to all comers as we know it.

Another notable event at Woodstock, on the grounds of Blenheim Palace, was an echo of Greek athletics, or perhaps the soft porn side of fashionable Hellenism (the craze for things Greek). Green's history of Blenheim Palace, quoting Thomas Hearne, says it was a four-mile race in 1720 with "the contestants running quite naked, without even shoes or pumps. Such a display of nudity was 'looked upon deservedly as the Height of Impudence, and the greatest Affront to Ladies, of which there was a great number.'" Lady Carol was not alone in liking to watch men race naked, it seems.

An unobtrusive detail in a piece of *The Original Weekly Journal* news for February 24, 1720, is of even greater significance for the beginnings of running history. The article reports a kind of equestrian/human double-header, two gentlemen betting on a race between their horse-drawn chaises, followed by a foot race, three times round St. James's Park, between two servants. As usual, to the gambling-mad upper classes, their runners were much like their horses. But this is worth reading for another reason.

On Monday last 'Squire Cunningham's Chaise with six horses ran against Captain Lister's Chaise and two Horses on the Long Course at Epsom, for 140 Guineas, and the former won; and 'Squire Cunningham having matched a Boy belonging to Williams's Coffee-House in St. James's Street, against Captain Luter's Negro Boy, to run three times round St. James's Park, for 100 l [pounds]. They ran on Wednesday Morning, and the Coffee Boy beat (The Original Weekly Journal, February 24, 1720).

"Luter's" is almost certainly a typo for "Lister's" (since the double bet was between the same two gentlemen). The notable item is Lister's "Negro Boy." Black servants were beginning to appear in London – Pepys had a "blackmore" cook, and Hogarth's paintings and engravings feature a number of Black servants, like the boy pointing to the cuckold horns in *Marriage à la Mode: the Countess's Levee*. This "Negro Boy" is important because he is the first recorded African competitive runner.

When St. James's Park was used as the venue for the 2020 elites-only London Marathon, the world watched on television as the greatest African runners – men and women – chased world records and took almost all the top places. No one knew, but they were running in the footsteps of that pioneering young African in 1720, racing that same course around St. James's Park, exactly three hundred years before. Given the looseness of the term "Negro" at the time, he may have been from almost anywhere in Africa, or the African Caribbean. Most likely, for a distance runner at a date when Kenya and Ethiopia were almost unknown, he was Moroccan, like Shakespeare's Othello and Aaron.

The Hell and Fury Chairman

It is time for the villain to enter. James Sykes was for a while a running footman for the Duke of Wharton, probably sharing duties with William

Mawbone of "Fury and Violence" fame. But Sykes seems to have been of restless temperament, and he had already left the Duke when he achieved his most famous running feat:

> *Last Monday, one Sykes, late a Running Footman*
> *to the Duke of Wharton, beat all the Post Horses*
> *between the White Hart Inn, Southwark, and Dover.*
> *(The Original Weekly Journal, May 14, 1719)*

That feat is not unlikely for a well-trained ultra-runner on seventy miles/112km of roads that in 1719 were still so rutted and muddy that heavy goods were carried by pack-horse rather than wagon. But it gave Sykes a reputation.

He won many match races, coinciding with the emergence of newspapers in 1719 to 1722, and feeding their hunger for sensation. He was the first runner to have a nickname, "Hell and Fury Sykes," or later, when he was employed carrying sedan chairs, "the Hell and Fury Chairman." The name was probably appropriated from the report of Mawbone's "Fury and Violence" race, either by careless journalists or by Sykes himself. Confusion between Sykes and Mawbone is understandable, as both had been employed by the Duke of Wharton. But Sykes did his best to live up to the name and made it into a successful piece of branding.

Sykes was still racing, and still getting the *Original Weekly Journal's* media attention, in 1722. "Lovet and the famous James Sykes, the 'Hell and Fury Chairman,' are to run for 100 Guineas…" Sykes was no longer in service as a footman, and no patrons are named, so he may have been running for the prize money and the betting. It that sense, running for the proceeds of the race rather than as part of his regular employment, it is possible to describe him as the first professional competitive runner.

But he wanted an easier source of income, or a more adventurous one. By 1723, he is mentioned as a footpad, or city-street mugger, a member of the most notorious criminal gang in London. The city was a cesspool of crime in those years, with primitive policing still based on an outmoded structure of parish constables. That was replaced in the 1750s by a mobile force of "thief-takers" under the Bow Street magistrate. The Bow Street Runners were not a London running club, but the city's first effective police force. They had their hands full. *The Original Weekly Journal* from 1719-20 carries reports of weavers' riots in which women had calico dresses ripped off them in the street, and one week in which "all the Stage Coaches coming from Surrey to London were robb'd by Highwaymen," and an incident in which a footman who protested about unfair dismissal was "oaked heartily" by thugs hired by his former employer.

Sykes thrived in this dark world. A year later, he earned an even less enviable fame by turning traitor and luring the famed super-crook Jack Sheppard into the arms of the constables in an ale house. Sheppard was a folk hero, beloved for his ingenious jail-breaks, and this time it took him only a few hours to break out through the roof of St. Giles's Roundhouse. He left his escape later on another occasion, when Defoe was obliged to hastily revise the book-length "gallows confession" he had written for Sheppard, ready to be released immediately after the hanging. There couldn't be a confession because there was no criminal to die – the night before execution Sheppard escaped again.

So, another hundred years on, when Sykes appeared as the informer in Harrison Ainsworth's historical crime novel, *Jack Sheppard* (1839-40), he was the despised villain, and was hissed off the stage in every melodrama theater version. Charles Dickens also borrowed his name for his burglar and murderer Bill Sikes in *Oliver Twist* (1836-38). That was published just ahead of *Jack Sheppard,* and the two novelists became rivalrous about their low-life sources. For a runner, James Sykes had an unusually active afterlife.

Running footmen apparently did quite often become footpads. It must be the outdoor life. Jonathan Swift, in his satirical *Directions to Servants* (written in 1731), offered footmen the advice that they should never grow old in the job, and if they cannot find comfort by "running away with your Master's Niece or Daughter, I directly advise you to go upon the

Road...There you will find many of your old Comrades." "Go upon the road" means "become a highwayman."

One much-retold story is about the Duke of Queensbury, who liked to test potential appointees as running footmen by giving them a trial run, dressed in full livery, while he watched from his balcony. One candidate finished his run and stood before the balcony, waiting for the Duke's judgment. "You'll do very well for me," drawled the Duke. "And your livery will do very well for me," replied the man, and ran off with the full outfit. It sounds like Hell and Fury Sykes again; but runners are often opportunists.

In the twenty-first century, the running footmen have been noticed as a possible art form. British artist James Steventon offers what he describes as "running based performance," delivering messages for special occasions like weddings, in costume researched from old etchings and created by the costume-maker Amy Cunningham. Seeking the mental state of operation defined by Csikszentmihalyi as "flow," Steventon achieves it by both endurance running and endurance drawing, not unlike the Tendai monks of Chapter 3.

Another living link to the old footmen is the London pub that until recently bore the historic and curiously assertive name, "I Am the Only Running Footman." It's on the corner of Charles Street and Hay's Mews, near Berkeley Square in Mayfair, one of the world's most affluent neighborhoods. In Mayfair's aristocratic prime, thousands of domestic servants were employed to manage its many opulent mansions. The name "I Am the Only Running Footman" was inscribed in gold letters above the bow window of the little tavern, which had small leaded panes in thick Queen Anne glass. It's perhaps testimony to the independent temperament of runners that the footmen, alone among the various branches of domestic servants, contrived to have their own resort. Or at least to have one named for them, since it was described in the Victorian period as "much frequented by the servants of the neighboring gentry."

The footmen were socializing there as early as 1720, when the hostelry was called "The Running Horse." The name was changed to "I

Am the Only Running Footman" sometime before 1800. No explanation is known, but perhaps (like the boxer who called himself "The Real McCoy") there was a rival Running Footman bidding for business. Martha Grimes took the name as the title of one of her mystery novels, and the signboard is featured on posters and postcards of notable London public houses. A succession of artistic images of running footmen has swung above the door for at least two hundred years. Until recently, the cramped and characterful lounge bar boasted a ceiling painting, depicting a liveried footman running ahead of the carriage, and announcing its approach with his horn. It was painted about 1910, I'd guess.

That period art piece was lost, along with the pub's unique full title, when its trendy current owners carved away three hundred years of history by "renovating" the interior and reducing the name to merely "The Footman." Shame on them, and all like them, eager to make a profit on the prestige of history at the same time as they obliterate it. As E.M. Forster said of an earlier phase of commercial destruction in London, they "spilt the precious distillation of the years."

Before those obtuse obliterations, a runner tourist could sip a pint of English beer in the bar of the "I Am the Only Running Footman," and enjoy the redolence of so much unpretentious running history. Here, Mawbone, Groves, and Sykes, fit, lean, mileage-hardened men, used to share a drink and a joke. Here, no doubt they talked, as runners always do, of last week's race, and next week's, and whether the course was short, complained about the hills, or their running shoes, and gossiped about who is in shape, and who has the best kick. Maybe they had a laugh about that novelty phenomenon, the weekly newspaper. Maybe one of them read aloud the lurid claim in this week's issue that in the latest footmen race, they ran "with such Fury and Violence that both of 'em drop'd down for Dead when they came in." That is, if any of them could read.

Chapter 5

Sam Runs With the Hounds and Three Great Sports Begin: An Experiment in Biography

800 BC   100 AD   1719   1896   1908   1928   1936   1964   1984   2021

Sam Butler had an unhappy childhood. The comfortable house in rural England, with its elegant Georgian windows, mansard roof, and portico over the front door, looks the embodiment of the Victorian ideal of ordered family bliss. But for little Samuel the big comfy furniture and empty religious rituals embodied repression and cruelty. His clever but ill-tempered clergyman father was home all week, a darkening presence, especially severe on Sundays, banning the children from any games or toys, and on that night often so tired and grumpy that he was capable of vicious punishment for any lapse. Samuel Butler's novel, *The Way of All Flesh* (written between 1872 and 1884 and published in 1903), has a harrowing scene when the father thrashes his four-year-old son for not being able to pronounce his c's (he says "tum" for "come"), and the chapter ends, "'and now, Christina, I think we will have the servants in to prayers,' and he rang the bell for them, red-handed as he was."

The fluttery, pious, manipulative mother (named Christina in the novel) supported her husband, and was given to trapping the boy on the sofa, and softening him with frilly charm until he confessed to any crimes. His three siblings seem not to have been much company. The midlands village of Langar, Nottinghamshire, was scattered and remote (it still is). In the novel he named it Battersby, or "batters-boy." His father took charge of his education, and battered into him knowledge of Latin and Greek grammars and the Bible before he was ten. Rarely allowed out, the child Sam found the place a prison, and longed to wander. He suffered from what later, in his revenge-raid of a novel, he bitterly called "home-sickness...The children were white and puny...they were starving, through being over-crammed with the wrong things." His only emotional outlet was his love of the cats.

At almost thirteen, in 1848, after two years of yet more Greek and Latin at a small private school, Sam was sent to be a nervous boarder at the prestigious Shrewsbury School. There, he had big shoes to fill. His famous grandfather, Dr. (later Bishop) Samuel Butler, had been an innovative and all-powerful headmaster, and his father Thomas an almost star pupil. (The "almost" explains a lot.) The Principal when Sam was enrolled in 1848 was another great classical scholar, Dr. Benjamin Kennedy, whose *Elementary Latin Primer* (1843) has enlightened or tortured generations of school and college students from then till now (the "tortured" include me). It is probably the most long-lived of all school textbooks, and Dr. Kennedy, who later became Regius Professor at Cambridge, is still admired as a scholar, and for his advocacy for women's higher education. But for the teenage Sam, Dr. Kennedy was too much like another version of his father – clever, devoted to the classics and the Church of England, but vain, despotic, and utterly lacking in compassion for a boy's anxieties. Small in physique, low in confidence, only a bit above average at academics, and no good at the School's early version of soccer, Sam could have drifted through adolescence as just another unnoticed teen who never came to anything.

But he discovered running.

In *The Way of All Flesh*, Butler wrote an episode where Ernest, the fictional version of himself as a boy, impulsively runs several miles across the fields to give a parting present to a servant, Ellen, who has been unkindly dismissed by his father.

One of the most popular amusements at Roughborough [the novel's name for Shrewsbury] was an institution called 'the hounds'...Ernest's want of muscular strength did not tell against him here...if it came to mere endurance he was as good as anyone else...[and so] a run of six or seven miles [10-12km] across country was not more than he was used to. (Samuel Butler, The Way of All Flesh, Chapter 39)

The Hounds Club, or more formally the Royal Shrewsbury School Hunt, was well established by the time Sam arrived at the school in 1848. It was, in fact, the first running club in the world, with its origins in 1820 or before. The sport of cross-country began here, at Shrewsbury, not at Rugby School as is still widely believed. That error came about because of the huge popularity of the novel *Tom Brown's Schooldays*, by Thomas Hughes (1857), set in Hughes's own time at Rugby School, from 1834 to 1842, with a vivid, action-packed chapter where Tom Brown runs in Rugby's Hare and Hounds. That account became the inspiration for the world's first adult running club, Thames Hare and Hounds, near London, founded in 1868. Rugby School did indeed have the sport very early and its "Crick Run" is deservedly famous. Hughes's novel also has a fascinating scene where two Rugby runners run a mile time-trial against the arriving stagecoach, with the coach guard timing them at 4:56 between two milestones.

But Shrewsbury thought of it first. About ten years before Rugby, they were already calling their boy paper-chasers "fox and hounds," or "the Hunt." It's all documented in old hand-written notebooks that I found more exciting than the fictional *Tom Brown's Schooldays*. Known as the "Hound Books," they are a week-by-week record of the sport from its beginning. Finding them in the Shrewsbury School Library was a magic moment for a historian.

Crackly old exercise books, such as you'd find forgotten in any dusty attic, their pages are hand-written in scratchy black ink. The writing changes year by year, with each new schoolboy secretary of the club. The oldest surviving one is dated 1831. A separate letter indicates that the sport was established no later than October 1820. Twice a week in the winter term, the Hound Books record a narrative of every run. Officially, I was there to track down references to the schoolboy Samuel Butler, for my research into his development into a major Victorian writer. But as I read in that quiet library, I realized that in my hands I was holding absolutely authentic evidence from before the reign of Queen Victoria of the very beginnings of the whole vast modern sport of organized running.

Of course, people have always raced, from Mycenaean funeral games recorded in Homer's *Iliad* to the village sports of nineteenth-century Europe. And boys have always chased. A game called "Hunt the Fox" or "Hunt the Hare" was played in England's schools during the reign of Queen Elizabeth I, so Strutt's *Sports and Pastimes of the People of England* tells us. The boy William Shakespeare probably played it. When Hamlet is eluding the Elsinore security guards, he teasingly calls out "Hide, fox, and all after."

At first, the Shrewsbury runs or "hunts" were organized by dormitories, or "houses." A precursor of the main series of Hound Books is called "The Journal of the Hunts of Mr. Iliff's Fox-Hounds." The runs were structured to imitate the fox-and-hounds hunting that was the vigorous amusement of many of the boys' fathers. (Not Sam's father, whose hobby was botany.) There is often a touch of self-mockery in the young runners' reports, acknowledging that it's all a game. The earliest record, October 16, 1831, is signed tongue-in-cheek by "J. Sayle, dog-feeder and Veterinary Surgeon also Horse-Butcher to the Establishment."

Yet they also took the running seriously. Every outing finished with a competitive race or "run-in," and there are records of rivalries between House clubs with names like Iliff's, Gee's, Jollyboys, and Butler's Hounds – Dr. Butler, the earlier headmaster, our Sam's grandfather. Evidently, he actively encouraged the sport, earlier than Dr. Thomas Arnold, Headmaster of Rugby, who usually gets the credit.

By 1839, there was the single Royal Shrewsbury School Hunt, open to every boy in the school. When Sam arrived in 1848, a small, shy, and – in his own words – "puny" boy three months short of his thirteenth birthday, almost straight from the cruel prison of his childhood, he found himself living in a crowded, rat-infested dormitory on the school's cramped and unhygienic old town site, studying in gloomy, rigidly disciplined academic classrooms, and as a pastime forced into rowdy shoving soccer games that he hated. The Hounds must have been in every way a breath of fresh air.

Fitness, fun, friendship, running over miles of different farmland and woodland areas twice a week – it's a powerful combination for a repressed and lonely child who has longed for thirteen years for some freedom of movement. Shared adventure outdoors in an energetic, co-operative pack was the opposite in every way of any experience he knew. The club captain, known as the "huntsman," wearing a red jacket and carrying an old hunting horn, explained things to the new recruits.

(This is slightly dramatized from notes on the club's rituals and rules in the Hound Books, and the list of mock-hunting vernacular terms in Peter Middleton's seminal history, 2011.)

Foxes, Are you ready? – Go! And away they run! Give them a cheer – hip-hip- hooray! Now, welcome, all new hounds. There go the two foxes, off and away, carrying scent bags. Once out of sight, they'll drop a trail of shredded paper. That represents the fox's scent. You're the hounds, and you have each been allocated a hound name. We give the foxes a good lead – that's called 'law.' Then, at my signal, we run off in that direction. I will say 'Gently forward!' Make it gentle, as first, we have to find the trail, and then we follow the scent, working together as a pack. And you have a long way to run – about ten miles today. We know the general direction for each run – today the course is "The Drayton," passing near Drayton village. But the foxes set the course, and if they're good, it will test you. Hounds – your task is to scurry about to find the trail, eyes peeled, noses down, like good hounds, and the Gentlemen of the Runs follow and help to organise you. The foxes will lay false trails – they're cunning – and there may be 'checks,' that's when the trail is lost. The scent may go across water or marshland. There will be fences and hedges – learn how to cross them. Sometimes I'll blow my horn and call an 'all-up,' which means we rest a little and regroup. When we finally sight the foxes, listen for the 'view halloa!' That means it's the 'run-in,' when we all chase as hard as we can, and the first gentleman or hound to touch the fox gets the kill, and will be awarded the brush. Now, do the foxes have enough law? Hounds, get ready! Start when I blow this horn. Wait for it! All hounds who wish to run, run hard and run well, and may the devil take the hindmost!

How did Sam do on that first run? We'll never know, as juniors were identified only by their Hound names, like Challenger, Trojan, Traveller, Driver, or Merlin. So there is no way we can find Sam's "results" in those first two years. For a fearful boy like him, with a sense of inadequacy thrashed into him, and now at a highly competitive academic school, his anonymity as a mere Hound must have conferred some welcome escape. It's also worth noticing that even on the competitive "run-in" at the end of each hunt, only the first three were ever recorded in the Hound Books. So despite the huntsman's "devil take the hindmost" incantation (a ritual that dates from the club's earliest years), no one came last. They were a pack, and could all be proud of how well they worked and ran together.

They created a culture of non-judgmental collaboration that you still see, in a different form, when runners help each other through difficulties in modern marathons. They got a lot of things right, those imaginative teenage boys in the early 1800s.

They gave us a sport, and some of its words. Taking the word from fox-hunting hounds, they hunted in a "pack," the word we still use for a group of runners. They gave us "leader" for the front-of-pack runner. We still run on a "course," a word they took from horse racing and the running footmen. Sometimes we still say "run-in" for the approach to the finish. The paper trail scent was laid by "foxes" at Shrewsbury, and by "hares" in most other places, probably because hare hunting is done on foot, not on horseback. And that's how we get the word "harriers" (hare hunters) to describe cross-country runners. Hare-hunting hounds are beagles, a smaller version of foxhounds, and bassetts, the short-legged big-eared guys with scent skills second only to bloodhounds. They are the original harriers. Hawk species also have that name for their hare-hunting ability.

These paperchase pack runs were twice weekly in the winter term before Christmas. After the Christmas break, the focus became the annual "Royal Salopian Steeplechase." That was a foot-racing version of the adult sport of racing on horseback across country from village to village – chasing from one church steeple to another – leaping every stream and hedge along the way. On horseback or on foot, it was a sport of daring and danger, challenge, unpredictability, and inventiveness. Our modern 3,000m steeplechase, not even two miles, confined to laps around an artificial track, with formal, measured hurdles and a water-jump trimmed into a token imitation of a brush hedge, is a feeble conformist descendant, not meriting the old name.

The Shrewsbury Steeplechase was a much more worthy foot race version of the original equestrian sport. It was what we would call the school's cross-country championship, and again, it was the first, and is now the oldest annual foot race in existence, dating from 1834. (Rugby's Crick Run began about 1837.) The runners pitted their pace, strength, and nimbleness against the challenge of true cross-country, wet and hilly farmland, with glutinous fields of raw plough or lumpy stubble, woodland where the surface was woven with treacherous roots, river crossings of unknown depths, gullies, waterlogged natural bowls, gates, and high thorn hedges, which had to be traversed by an agile technique, disturbingly called "belly-hedging" in the Hound Books.

Visiting Shrewsbury for Butler research in my fifties, still capable of running well on hills or rough footing, I found and ran most of their courses, "The Drayton," "The Bog," "The Tucks," and "The Long." I must confess that I omitted the "belly-hedging," and the "good leaps and stiff fences" that the Hound Books enthused about. There are limits to what I will suffer for historical research.

The boys invented all this, adapting their fathers' sports. The Hounds were organized wholly by the boys themselves. No teaching staff, no coach, no letters, no official awards, no sports scholarships, no redshirting. Every year, the boys themselves elected their own "huntsman" (captain), a secretary, and "whips" (club officers), they allocated the Hound names, they appointed the roster of "foxes," they planned every run, and arranged the timing to fit in with the school's timetable, and each year's secretary recorded it all with some sense of history and more than a little wit in the Hound Books. It was still much like that when I ran in my school cross-country club in England in 1954.

In the early years, the Hounds were encouraged by Dr. Butler, who in some way sponsored or hosted one of the packs. But his more narrowly academic successor, Dr. Kennedy, detested them. He resented their independence. By Sam's time, it was close to open war. The Hound Books show why. The reports of the runs make wonderfully wicked reading. They are detailed, spirited, full of energy and mischief, and sometimes very funny. The Hounds were, like most true runners in my experience, adventuresome, a little maverick, and they enjoyed a vigorous social life. They often took a break during the run, to imbibe some energy.

"At the Fox Hotel Atherton kept by Mr. Brown...the gentlemen refreshed themselves with a hearty glass of ale," reports the Hound Book.

Another time, they paused to "imbibe punch at the farm of N. Lloyd Esq...They "washed the hounds mouths out with some beer" ("hounds" means the younger boys, aged 13-15) and they "regaled our pack with punch & c." During the run called "The Long," all 14 miles/22.5km of it, they drank beer and sherry at the inn at Atcham. On special occasions, they took full meals ("were regaled with a substantial repast"), often at "Mother Wade's," and then ran on.

They vaulted fences, they went "belly-hedging" over high thorn hedges, they waded streams and canals, they dodged dogs, relished trespassing, and had confrontations with angry farmers, one wielding "an immense cudgel." And with special teenage glee they ran wide-eyed along the secluded byway named in the official school history as "Lovers' Lane," but in the Hound Books more explicitly as "fornicators' lane."

Dr. Kennedy was not amused. Receiving complaints from farmers about trespassing, the fussy despot tried to make rules about where the boys were allowed to run. The Hound Book irrepressibly comments, "as stolen fruit is always the sweetest, we determined to...revive the good old custom of running out of bounds."

Dr. Kennedy tried making them wear mortarboards (academic caps) as they ran. He locked their dormitories so that he could catch them coming in. He once stood out in the cold to take the names of those breaking bounds. They whooped by in defiance on the other side of the hedge. His most lethal strike, they indignantly reported, was when "Ben nabbed the scent bag." The scent bag was their holy grail. Used to carry the shredded paper that marked the trail, its theft had to be avenged.

With an eloquent gesture of reprisal, they ripped up copies of the Latin textbook the hostile headmaster had recently published – Dr.Kennedy's *Elementary Latin Primer* - and dropped the shredded pages as paper trail around the Shropshire countryside. Fragments of the book that would be Dr. Kennedy's greatest legacy for almost two hundred years were left rotting in wet grass and trampled by farm horses in fields of sodden plough. Remembering my own schoolboy sufferings from Dr. Kennedy's *Primer*, my heart leapt up in support of their rebellion.

"Frantic but fruitless" was how the Hound Book described the Head's efforts to control the running dissidents.

That's when Sam Butler joined the Hounds. And that is where the reality that I discovered in the Hound Books simply does not fit with Butler's own published versions of his schooldays. In *The Way of All Flesh*, Dr. Kennedy is the fearsome Dr. Skinner, who intimidates Ernest by being "much too like his father," and terrifies him by his bad temper, and his habit of suddenly rushing at Ernest like a ferocious lion, or falling on him "like a landslip." Dr. Kennedy/Dr. Skinner is devastatingly portrayed in the novel as a pompous, posturing, superficially learned "passionate half-turkey-cock half-gander of a man whose sallow, bilious face and hobble-gobble voice could scare the timid."

The novelist Samuel Butler portrayed Ernest, his teenage self, as timid and submissive, a less-than-popular outsider among the boys, "listless," "feeble," "a young muff, a mollycoddle," and "no greater lover of his school work than of the games." There may have been some selective truth in that self-portrait. Yet in real life he was also a faithful and respected member of the Hounds. Not only a member, but evidently a good runner, soon regularly appointed as a "fox," and finally elected as the "huntsman." So he was chosen by his peers to lead the club, at a time when it was in more or less open warfare with Dr. Kennedy, who in the Hound Books is never called anything more fearsome than "Ben" or "K." The episode when Dr. Kennedy stole the scent bag and the Hounds shredded his Latin primer was in 1849, Sam's second season. He was too young to have initiated that defiance, but he must have been part of its enactment. In 1853, when Sam was the "huntsman" (though away on a family tour of Italy for some of his tenure), the war continued. The Hound Book reports, "we met on Thursday instead of Saturday in consequence of K. keeping a sharp look out for us on Saturday."

So Sam was in the thick of it throughout his five years in the Hunt. From his third year, after graduating to be a "gentleman," he was identified in the Hound Books by surname, and through two winter seasons, twice a week, in all weathers, the records show that he never missed a run. Soon, when he was sixteen and seventeen, he became a frequent choice as "fox."

That's a surprise, if you have believed in the muff and mollycoddle version. The "foxes" were chosen by the "huntsman" and "whips," based on popular approval, and they would have been selected for being both reliable and inventive. The success of every run depended on them. They had to plan and pioneer a challenging and innovative route, while keeping to the main outline of the day's traditional course. They needed to work well together, lay false trails, stay ahead of the eager pack until they all had a good run, and finally provide a good clear "run-in" at the end, all the time carrying a heavy scent bag and dropping the right amount of paper. They had to get it right. The secretary writing one day's Hound Book report is critical of the "foxes" (not Butler that day) who led a run that didn't have enough "leaps." Being a "fox" was a skilled job, liable to be critically assessed.

A young Sam who was so capable, so resourceful, and so often appointed to the role by peer esteem, does not fit with the unpopular nerdy mollycoddle of his own versions, "a mere bag of bones with...no strength or stamina whatever." Every Butler biographer (about twenty in all) has accepted that version without question. The Hound Books showed me a different Sam. Take November 3, 1852.

One month before Sam's seventeenth birthday, he was one of the two "foxes" appointed for a run that followed days of heavy rain. On the way to the village of Hencott, they reached a low-lying field that was covered by shallow water. Sam and his fellow "fox" craftily laid the paper trail so that it seemed to go directly across the field, straight toward the hill on other side. In fact, across the middle of the field, concealed under the sheet of flood water, lay what the Hound Book calls "a treacherous drain," a ditch about one meter (three to four feet) deep. It was invisible beneath what looked to be a simple shallow flood only inches deep. Seeing the paper "scent" go on up the opposite hillside, the runners splashed forward through the innocently shallow water, until they reached the unseen deeper ditch. And they all fell in.

The Hound Book reports with some relish, "both hounds and gentlemen, some head first, some tail were one after the other seen to disappear in the water; this however only cooled our legs without cooling our ardour, and we went along at a brisk pace up the fields towards Hencott."

Was Sam concealed on the hillside with his fellow "fox," chortling at the comedy they had created? Probably not, with several miles still to run, carrying half-full scent bags, before they showed themselves to prompt the view halloa and the final run-in. But he must have enjoyed the Hound Book report. It's a moment that reveals a mischievous and self-confident Sam, accepted as a leader (or misleader) among his peer group, roguishly inventive, perpetrating a hilarious practical joke. That's credible for the Samuel Butler who would go on to be an intrepid mountain explorer in New Zealand's Southern Alps, write long letters to the newspaper on both sides of the Darwin debate, publish a tongue-in-cheek hostile review of his own first book, and write the wickedly ingenious ironic masterpiece of *Erewhon*. The listless and neurotic young Butler of his own fictional creation, which he ensured was perpetuated by his first biographer, is hard to reconcile with those things.

That created, or highly selective, version of his schooldays in *The Way of All Flesh* continues the story of his childhood misery. It works well for fictional consistency, and for Butler's interpretation of his own life as one of recovery from a damaged beginning. It takes its place with *David Copperfield* and *Jane Eyre* as a vivid nineteenth-century narrative of schooldays suffering. But unlike other Butler scholars, I am disinclined to take that version as biographical truth. The rebellious hand-written Hound Books are not conventional scholarly sources, but they are absolutely authentic and contemporary, and give priceless access to how young Sam was seen by the teenagers he mixed with.

I had my own hunting adventures when I decided to try to search for the ditch in the low-lying field where Sam lured the pack into deep water. That September week, every late afternoon, after reading the Hound Books and other documents all day in the Shrewsbury School Library,

I went exploring the Hounds' traditional runs, so far as I could locate them among urban sprawl, screaming highways, and ever-burgeoning Sainsbury's supermarkets. I managed to run past landmarks familiar from the Hound Books (and from Ellis Peters's *Brother Cadfael* novels) – the mighty Severn River and little grass-clogged Berwick Brook, Coton Hill and Sundorne Farm (still there, squeezed next to a giant retail park), Battlefield (where King Henry IV retained his title in 1403) and the tiny communities of Hencott and Atcham. In a car, you would call this country rolling, but for a runner it is hard hilly going. I scratched my shins on stubble and plodded across what the Hound Books often call "heavy ploughed land." I couldn't "run in" on the narrow lanes as freely as they did, since I got pressed against the hedgerow every few seconds by the whang of some frenzied car.

North of the town, trying to run "The Bog" or "The Drayton," I looked out for the field with the treacherous ditch. I searched through faceless 1950s housing developments to find the route the Hounds took that day after their soaking, when they "went along at a brisk pace up the fields towards Hencott." No trace. Most likely it was all buried under the suburbs and supermarkets. It hardly mattered. After all, I was only looking for a wet field.

On my last day, I made one last attempt, looking once more for a footpath I'd found marked on an old map. After more "checks" (as the Hounds would have said), I found a promising narrow lane between Coton Hill and the railroad. That rail line, I'd established, was built later than 1852, so the barrier it presented to me would not have existed when Butler ran. I jogged up the lane hopefully, but it led only to an opulent white house. The scent had died. But as I ran regretfully back, I suddenly saw a tiny foot track I'd missed on the way up, twisting steeply down through long grass. It was almost overgrown. Pushing through weeds and undergrowth, I scrambled down.

And there, at the bottom of the hill, I found it: a low-lying field between two hills, clumped with marsh grass, with the remnants of a dark green ditch running straight across it. Soggy now in September, it would be flooded after the November rains. Secluded, too wet for cultivation, with only two straggly struggling trees, it had a sort of sadness about it, or the sense of a spot that time had passed by. Its moment in history was modest enough, a practical joke among schoolboys. Real biographers would sneer at all the trouble I'd taken to find such an obscure and boggy bit of England, but I felt as if I'd made contact with the living young Sam Butler, and was confirming a side of him that had eluded other researchers. Also, beneath my feet I felt the textures of the same piece of earth where lively lads had run soon after the very beginning of the sport I loved. I was literally in contact with the grass roots. I even took some incompetent photos.

There is still more to this curious story, a literary life intersecting with the early history of modern running. As he became senior, and especially in his last year, when he was the "huntsman," Sam had responsibilities for organizing the two major running events of the year, the cross-country Steeplechase, which was held in March, and the "Second Spring Meeting," which was the school sports or track-and-field championships, held in May. Like the Steeplechase, the Second Spring Meeting was set up to imitate horse racing.

The runners in both events were entered as if they were jockeys, supposedly riding horses, which were given names like "Vesuvius" or "Family Herald." I choose those names as examples because they were given to young Sam Butler on two occasions when he raced. It occurred to me that intelligent and mischievous schoolboys might put special meaning into the names they invented for their friends. "Vesuvius" I suspect referred to Sam's early smoking habit, which he maintained until he died, probably of lung cancer, at age 66. "Family Herald" surely satirized a tendency to boast about his ancestry, especially his famous grandfather, another surprise in assessing his youthful character. On another occasion he ran under the name "Backbiter," suggesting that his later tendency to be over-sensitive about himself and sharply critical of others began early.

Other "horse" names given to various boy runners make me suspect that teenage humor and teenage testosterone were about as active in the early years of Queen Victoria as at any other date. I found "Adonis," "Heart-breaker," "The Perfumer," "The Beaver Hunter," and others even less politely suggestive, which I'll pass over.

Each horse was entered by an "owner," a senior student or supportive staff member, who probably put up a small stake. The Second Spring Meeting was modeled on racecourse horse racing, with Stewards and Clerks of the Course, and included, taking the 1854 race card as an example, the Derby Stakes (about one mile), the Hurdle Race, the Trial Stakes (for horses under 5ft. 4in.), and the Two-Year-Old Stakes (for juniors). There were also "throwing the cricket ball," "high leap," "distance leap," "sack race," and "match," which seems to have been a two-man head-to-head sprint. It thus amounted to what we would call a track-and-field athletics meeting. Well established by 1850, on this evidence it is the world's oldest still-existing track-and-field athletics meeting, though it has never received that recognition, probably because of its title. In 1856 it became the "May Races" or "Athletics," and moved away from the Royal Shrewsbury School Hunt (the Hounds) as its organizers.

The meeting usually credited as the oldest is the sports of Exeter College, Oxford, dating from 1850. That too was originally based on horse racing, the runners even carrying weight handicaps. Later in the 1800s, that horse-racing form of athletics merged with the old rural village sports, bringing in events like the shotput, hammer throw, and pole vault. Then at the end of the century there came another merger, with the trendy, more upper-crust Hellenist and Olympic revival, which added Greek events like the discus and javelin.

Those three converging streams made track-and-field athletics the weird mixture it is, with human creatures as different as hammer throwers and 10,000 meter runners on the same team. A glimpse of this strange tripartite history helps to understand how it happened. That diverse mix is also the sport's unique strength, giving opportunity to such contrasting physical disciplines, all together in one arena. Universities considering cutting their track-and-field programs should weigh very carefully the fact that no other sport provides gender-equal competition for every physical type, and brings them together in one team.

Sam's part was played in the early years of the horse-race version. He returned from the family tour of Italy in time to fulfill his duties as "one of the stewards" (he wrote to his parents), or in effect co-race director, for the Steeplechase in March 1854, and then steward/meeting manager again for the Second Spring Meeting in May. He didn't run in the Steeplechase, he wrote to his mother, "not being at all in condition." For the athletics, his duties as "huntsman" stopped him running. "[T]he stewards are not expected to run as they have the pacing of the ground and the height of the hurdles," he wrote to his sister Harriet (Butler/ Silver, 1962).

So Samuel Butler ended his career in the foundation era of running as race director of an early version of the world's first modern cross-country race, and as meeting manager of the earliest still-existing athletics meeting. And he made one more, totally unique contribution, this time to the pre-history of the sport of cross-country running. He drew its earliest ever images.

A genial mathematics teacher at Shrewsbury, A.T. Paget, used to invite older boys to his room for tea, and with their help compiled a scrapbook that is now a treasure house of information about school life in his years, 1840 to 1855. Paget stuck into his scrapbook all kinds of miscellaneous bits and pieces – lists of marks, newspaper clippings, autographs, notes from the headmaster (including one reprimanding the amused Paget for being late with his marks), tickets, jokes, sketches, what librarians call ephemera. Among them are several "race cards" for the annual Steeplechase and Second Spring Meeting, the entry lists of owners, horses, and jockeys that have enabled me to piece together how those events were conducted. One of those, the card for the Steeplechase in March 1853, is decorated almost like a medieval illuminated manuscript by a vivid pen-and-ink sketch of runners wading through a quite deep stream and scrambling up the bank. The sketch was done by the seventeen-year-old Sam Butler.

That is beyond question, as the style is exactly like other Butler sketches attributed to him by name in Paget's Scrapbook. At school Sam also produced very competent watercolors; in New Zealand in the 1860s he drew important sketches of his remote mountain property (now featured in "Lord of the Rings" tours); and later he painted oils good enough to be selected for exhibition by the Royal Academy.

Another sketch by Sam in Paget's Scrapbook shows a run that seemingly involved a runaway pig, or someone represented as a pig, followed across rough ground by three runners. The names attached to the runners – "Warren" etc. – are all to be found in the race cards for that year's Steeplechase and Second Spring Meeting. The runners' mixed apparel is interesting, but so is the fact that clearly they are running long-distance, with low arm carriage and stride. Sam knew what he was about as well as the artists who painted runners on Greek vases.

My biographical hunt on the scent of young Sam Butler had led me over some fascinating and unexpected ground. I'd found a teenage life that he chose to suppress in his later writings, and in the version he gave to Henry Festing Jones, his friend and biddable chosen biographer. The Sam I followed was a strong runner, and a lively and mischievous young man, respected by his peers. They gently mocked him for his boastfulness about his family, and made him pay for his sharp tongue, but they also saw him as capable of taking the responsibility of organizing important and complex events. They recognized that he had the inventiveness and practical sense to lay their trails, and the initiative and resilience to be their leader at a time when they were challenging authority. He was "fox," race director, meeting manager, and unofficial artist, drawing pictorial images of cross-country racing that are the earliest known, and until now have never been reproduced.

It may be an oversimplification to see Samuel Butler as someone whose life was rescued or transformed by running, but it's not something to dismiss out of hand. In our own era, it is a commonplace that thousands of lives have benefitted from just such a transformation, including the lives of many who will be reading this book. I have been on teams with men who could have become criminals but for their running ability. There can be no doubt that the strength, endurance, and resourcefulness that Sam developed as a runner served him well in his five years as a pioneering explorer and settler in New Zealand.

It's also certain that the habit of long-distance endurance exercise stayed with him for life. He made annual summer excursions among the European mountains, and when he was home in London he walked vigorously two afternoons a week in the countryside around the city, scrupulously marking his routes on maps – the same habit he had acquired as a Hound at Shrewsbury. His long European walks gave him material for books on the Swiss Alps, Italian popular religious art, and Homer's *Odyssey,* as well as scenes and subjects for some impressive oil paintings and innovative photography.

Sam also laid a paper trail that unexpectedly led me back to the very beginnings of much modern running. In his footsteps, I discovered the earliest records of pack runs, paperchasing (still practiced worldwide by the Hash House Harriers, though they use chalk now instead of paper), club running, cross-country races, the steeplechase, and even modern track-and-field athletics. I also discovered the first visual images of cross-country racing. Sam made me hunt for days to find a soggy ditch, but on the other side lay one of the best stories in the age-old history of running.

Chapter 6

Spyridon Louis and the Art of Pace Judgment – Athens 1896

800 BC   100 AD   1719   1896   1908   1928   1936   1964   1984   2021

If Pheidippides really ran from Marathon to Athens (but see Chapter 2), he would have passed close to Amaroússion (or Maroússi) near the fatal end of his journey. About eight miles (13km) northeast of the city, today it's an Athens suburb and home of a major sports complex. In the ancient Greek era, it would have been a tiny settlement. In the 1890s, it was a peasant community surviving mainly because of its fresh-water spring. At that date, the Louis family were small-scale farmers in Amaroússion, with a business transporting barrels of water from their spring into Athens every day, using mules. Spyridon Louis (Spyros for short), a son of the family, spent much of his youth walking or jogging alongside the mules, eight miles each way, every day, year round. Probably the return journey was faster, with the barrels empty, and the mules eager for home. We can only guess. The certain fact is that Spyridon Louis covered the distance very often.

Louis had no coach, no specialized training, no managed diet, almost no race experience, little education. Only those low-level miles on his feet every day made him the first great marathon winner. Although some coaches speak contemptuously of "junk miles," truly there is no such thing.

Greece was excited by the revived Olympic Games in 1896, especially by the idea of a race to commemorate the patriotic legend of Pheidippides.

A poor but proud people struggling to emerge from many centuries of oppression, with few organized sports, the Greeks could not hope to compete with affluent college-trained athletes from America and Europe in most Olympic events. But the "marathon race" would demand simple endurance and courage, for which their history had prepared them. True, the idea of the race came from a Frenchman, a professor of languages named Michel Bréal, and, true, he was drawing on a skimpy legend revived mainly by an English poem, Robert Browning's *Pheidippides*. And true again, there was no precedent for such a long foot race in the Games of ancient Greece, whose longest race, the *dolichos*, was about two miles (3km). But Bréal was an inventive antiquarian, and the Greeks were eager to believe any good story about their past heroic greatness.

Bréal had the anachronistic idea that, "If we knew the time the Greek warrior took, we could establish the record." (Letter to Pierre de Coubertin, Sept 15, 1884: *Si nous savions le temps qu'a mis le guerrier grec, nous pourrions établir le record.*) It was shaky history, to impose a modern notion of timed "records" on a fictional ancient story that came from long before the invention of clocks or watches, and that was not even clear about what route the warrior was supposed to have taken, or how far he ran. But the Greeks saw their opportunity. In hope of inspiring a local winner, the businessman Georgios Averoff, who supported (an understatement) the Games financially, added an antique vase to the silver marathon cup donated by Bréal as incentive for the winner. There are stories that Averoff offered his daughter in marriage with a large cash dowry to any Greek winner. But there are many stories about this first and most romantic of marathons.

Another enthusiast for the revived Games was Colonel Papadiamontopoulos, an aide to the king of Greece, who would be the race director and starter for the marathon. (He may have been only Major at the time but I'll stay with Colonel.) The Colonel was eager to get Greek representation in the experimental new event, so tracked down some men who had shown promise as runners when they did military training under his command in the Athenian division of the battalion of honor guards. One was Spyridon Louis, now twenty-four years old, still jogging from home to the city and back with the family water barrels. One story is that the Colonel had been a customer for Amaroússion spring water when Louis was a boy. It seems sure that it was the Colonel who persuaded him to try out for the marathon.

Trivia question: what was the first marathon in history? The obvious and wrong answer is the 1896 Olympic race. In fact, the Greeks held two pre-Olympic races over the Marathon-to-Athens course, which served as selection trials. These runners were the true progenitors of the marathon foot race. The start was the same as for the Olympics – by the bridge in Marathon, alongside some modest buildings with kids clambering on the roof for a good view. They ran over the same unpaved roads that the Olympic race would use, along the flatter coastal road first, then at the port of Rafina turning into the Pendeli hills, though the village of Pikermi, up again into the Hymettus hills, skirting Amaroússion, and at last downhill through the suburbs of Athens to finish in Averoff's superbly restored marble Panathenaikon Stadium at the edge of the city itself. The distance was about 25 miles/40km, but that was not the point. No one measured it. It was the heroic, historic, life-threatening, long-distance challenge that mattered.

Outside the two trials, some hopeful aspirants, or exploitative attention-seekers, staged informal runs from Marathon to Athens, solo runs or two-man races, claiming decent times, and getting some publicity; but we have no way of knowing the source or reliability of the reports.

The first real race, on March 10, 1896, with twelve starters, was run as part of the Pan-Hellenic Sports Celebration designed to develop Greek talent for the coming Games. Kharilaos Vasilakos was the winner, running it in 3:18:00, and thus becoming the first person in the world ever to finish a marathon foot race. In the Olympic marathon a month later, Vasilakos, a customs officer, improved by twelve minutes to come second. He is "one of the most important but least-known marathoners in history," write the historians of the Olympic marathon (Martin and Gynn, 2000).

The second trial, on March 24, 1896, was faster, despite a cold, rainy day and a sodden dirt course. Ionnis Lavrentis won, finishing in 3:11:27. (Remember these times are for 25 miles/40km, approximately, not a modern marathon.) Seven minutes behind him, in fifth place out of 38 starters, was Spyridon Louis, the young water carrier. Familiar with moving over these unpaved roads in all types of weather, Louis was not surprised to find the surface churned at times into mud. Baron de Coubertin described the course in drier weather as "rough and stony." In his first race other than during his army training, Louis repaid the Colonel's confidence, with a time (3:18:27) that would have come close to winning the first trial. He was a contender.

Those two selection races are also an overlooked factor in assessing the rumor that a Greek woman made a last-minute attempt to enter the Olympic race, and was refused (see Chapter 13).

Thirteen Greeks were selected from the two trials as the Olympic team. Limitations on the size of national teams did not begin until after World War I and became three per nation in 1932.The thirteen were transported out to Marathon the day before the race, probably feeling like most of us do on the bus to Hopkinton or Staten Island, appalled by how far it is. On the starting line in Marathon, that famous April 10, 1896, they were joined by four overseas runners, three of them boosted by having taken the top places in the Olympic 1,500m two days earlier. The young (22) London-based Australian accountant Edwin "Teddy" Flack had in fact completed the double by winning the 800m only two hours before they departed for Marathon. He also played in the Olympic tennis tournament that same busy day.

Only the Hungarian Gyula Kellner had long-distance experience. Flack was probably the favorite, already a double Olympic champion, and a good cross-country runner, a member of the prestigious Thames Hare and Hounds club near London. He had prepared in the lightly-trained manner of the time. Cross-country courses were often nine or ten miles at that time, but Flack had no idea of what lay ahead in twenty-five miles of racing.

It was cool with clear skies. The Greek team took the sacrament from local priests. Minutes before 2 p.m., the seventeen runners gathered at the bridge in Marathon, standing in four short rows. They wore shirts, drawers, caps, some in national colors, most not. Flack wore his old Melbourne Grammar School cap and shirt, dark blue with an emblazoned Church of England miter. The Frenchman Albin Lermusiaux was dapper, in a dark shirt, probably French blue, with gleaming white gloves. Louis was in an all-white shirt and long shorts. Their bicycle or horse-borne attendants also waited, each ready to pedal or trot behind his runner and provide refreshments and encouragement. Flack's very English attendant, a member of the British Embassy staff who had Australian connections, wore a bowler hat. Behind them, Greek officials and soldiers on horseback completed what one observer called "an odd caravan of attendants."

Colonel Papadiamontopoulos urged his horse forward. Still mounted, as quoted in Morites's biography of Louis, he gave a short, stirringly patriotic speech, in Greek:

> *Men, think of your country; think of your flag on*
> *the pole inside the stadium; that flag wants you to*
> *do honor for her. Hooray for your country, Hooray*
> *for the Olympic Games!*

One of the Greek runners, Sokratis Lagoudakis, a medical student, added a friendly comment in French for the four visiting runners: "If you win, we will still think of you as brothers" (Morites, 1997).

It was now 2 p.m., April 10, 1896. Colonel Papadiamontopoulos fired his starting pistol. The first Olympic marathon began.

The course was relatively flat as they left the village and followed the seacoast road to Rafina. Thanks to recent rain, there was little dust. Predictably, the visiting track runners went out fast, led by Lermusiaux, his white gloves twinkling. The Frenchman had placed third in the 1,500m, and won his heat in the 800m, but did not start in the final, perhaps saving himself for the marathon next day. The tall Flack followed, prancing along in his tasseled cap, with the American runner-up in the 1,500m, Arthur Blake, close behind. The rest of the field, all Greek plus the experienced Kellner of Hungary, straggled behind.

Lermusiaux raced away with Gallic verve, and by nine miles/15km had a lead said to be almost two miles/3km (though these estimated times and distances are highly unreliable). The Greeks, who had experience of the distance from their trials, chose their pace more carefully. Lavrentis, winner of the second trial, was closest to the confident foreigners at first, but faded and dropped out, to be replaced by Vasilakos, the first trial winner, and Louis. They knew the real race had not yet begun.

From the seaport of Rafina, at about ten miles/16km, the course turned inland and headed into the hills. At a *taverna* in Pikermi, about halfway, Louis is reported to have accepted a glass of wine, and cheerfully announced that he would win the race. It's a good story and could perhaps be true. He was tall and thin, with an impressive stride at this easy early pace. Yet even the eagerly patriotic crowd outside the *taverna* must have thought his prediction of victory (if he truly made it) was wildly optimistic. Lermusiaux was well on the way to Athens, and Flack and Blake also were out of sight and moving well. But soon after, things changed.

At 15 miles, Blake was blistered and struggling. He fell, and could barely climb into the hospital wagon that collected exhausted runners. Several Greeks were already aboard. By 16 miles, Lermusiaux was fading. His huge lead was vanishing, as leads do in marathons. At the next cluster of houses, Pallini, the villagers had erected a triumphal arch with a crown of leaves for the race leader, a tribute that Lermusiaux enjoyed briefly, before he reached another uphill. There, the dark monster of the marathon seized him. He repulsed Flack's first move to pass him, but it couldn't last. The Australian skipped into the lead. The Frenchman began to weave, even (it was reported) colliding with his bicycle attendant. He stumbled a little further, staggered to a stop, and lay down for a rub with alcohol by his attendant. Fatal. When he tried to resume, his race was over.

Now Flack, the debonair Australian, was sensing a third victor's wreath. With his English cross-country background, he was better prepared than a pure middle-distance track man like Blake or Lermusiaux. The news that Flack was winning was carried ahead by a frantic bicyclist, and produced a mass groan of disappointment from the packed crowds in the Panathenaikon Stadium. They had been watching yet more American victories on the track. They were pining for one by a Greek.

If there had been a giant screen to show the race in progress, they might have had more hope. According to the official report, Vasilakos and Louis were within reach of the foreigner, and running strongly. Louis had a lot more miles in his legs than even Flack the ten-mile cross-country man. He was also well used to pacing himself. He did it every day. Even when Vasilakos slowed on the last major uphill, at 20 miles/32km, Louis waited. Then, at 21 miles/33km, passing near to Amaroússion, he moved quickly away from his teammate, surprised Flack, and at 34km was in the lead.

There are stories, stories. Louis was so confident that after passing other runners, he pretended to slow down, and then surged again. Louis had prayed on his knees for two days before the race. Louis had fasted for twenty-four hours. Louis had eaten a whole chicken the day before the race. Louis cut distance off the course by running through a forest. Louis covered some miles leaning on the stirrup of a supporter's horse.

All colorful, all appealing to those who prefer belief to fact. (It was a Greek, Plato, who first drew that distinction.) But in reality this marathon, even this one, so romantic in so many ways, was in essence prosaic. Louis controlled his pace. That is the whole story. He knew precisely how far it was to the finish, how much weary running that distance would take. He alone knew that 30km does not mean you're nearly there. Flack, whose advocates even now seem to believe that delusion, struggled briefly, but his race was over. Louis was away, his strength saved, his stride strong, his mind focused on the reality of what still lay ahead. Yet romance did await him. At 23 miles/37km, still close to Amaroússion, Louis's girlfriend Eleni was waiting with orange segments, and no doubt words of love and encouragement. Every report includes that detail. I hope it's true.

Now at last the course was downhill, Louis picked up the pace, and behind him Flack reeled, fell, and (more stories) was reportedly delirious when they put him with Lermusiaux in the horse-drawn sag-wagon. Louis ran on.

And the excitement grew. At the city boundary, a cannon was fired to give notice of the leader's approach. A cyclist pedaled ahead, crying "Ellene! Ellene!" ("Greek! Greek!"). Hordes of small boys began to romp alongside, and girls are said to have thrown flower petals under Louis's feet. Colonel Papadiamontopoulos, the starter, who had ridden the entire course on horseback, saw his dream coming true, and galloped to the stadium to inform King Georgios that a Greek was near to victory. The word spread around the packed crowd, variously estimated as 60,000 up to 125,000. The atmosphere became fervent. The pole vault was halted. (A vaulter from Boston was winning.)

"A man wearing white, sunburnt, and covered in perspiration, is seen to enter," wrote the official Olympic reporter. The whole crowd were on their feet, wildly cheering. "Enthusiasm swelled like an unstoppable wave," wrote Pierre de Coubertin, the founder of the modern Olympics, and advocate for their nationalism. Every woman waved a handkerchief or fan. Every man waved his hat. The king reputedly "nearly ripped off the visor of his naval uniform cap in waving it wildly." His sons, the two adult royal princes, got closer, flourishing their hats as they ran alongside Louis for most of the length of the stadium.

The crowd "went mad for joy" as Louis broke the string across the track at the top of the tightly curved bend (2:58:50 for about 25 miles/40km). He stopped at last, bowed to the king, and stood as the band played the Greek national anthem. After that pause, the crowd's jubilation was even more passionate. "It was a moment I could never have imagined. The crowds were calling my name. Flowers and bouquets were raining down on me, and hats were flying in the air," Louis was quoted as saying by the French sports newspaper *L'Equipe*. (It's a good description but sounds a little too polished to be credible as spontaneous post-race comment.)

The wave of enthusiasm surged again when Vasilakos arrived at the stadium, a second Greek, seven minutes behind Louis, in 3:06:03. The customs agent (who won the first-ever marathon, the first Greek trial, remember) had his moment of glory, and presumably so did Spyridon Belokas when he stole the crowd's acclamation in third place, seeming to complete the Greeks' day of bliss. That was short-lived, as there was an immediate outraged protest from the Hungarian Gyula Kellner, on the grounds that Belokas had ridden most of the later miles in a carriage, jumping out in time to run fresh and strong into the stadium and revel in the cheers to the finish. He was disqualified, the first known cheater in the history of the marathon. Kellner deservedly took third.

But nothing detracted from the triumph of Spyros Louis. He became an instant Greek myth. He was the focus of national ecstasy. Eye-witness reports colorfully describe ladies tossing flowers and jewels to him across the track, and it is certain that in the days after the event he was showered with gifts that included meals, haircuts, watches, jewelry, a sewing machine, and, from the king himself, a new horse and cart for the water carrying business. That was kind, although I worry about what became of the faithful mules, who had played their part in one of running's great stories.

The awards ceremony for all Olympic events came on the concluding day of the Games, five days after the marathon, in the Panathenaikon Stadium. The king presented Louis with a silver medal (the convention of gold/silver/bronze did not begin until 1904), a diploma, a branch of wild olive, the ancient Greek vase decorated with *dolichos* runners donated by Averoff, and the silver cup donated by Bréal that had started the whole story.

The effects of Louis's victory were long-lasting and profoundly important. "Without Louis, the Athens Games would have had no epic hero, no master symbol...Indeed, it may fairly be said of Louis that, more than any man but Coubertin, he created the modern Olympic Games,"

John MacAloon has argued. Louis's triumph transformed two unlikely experiments – the revived Olympic Games, and the marathon foot race – into successes that would in time grow into two of the most remarkable and most positive social phenomena of our modern world. It's perfectly possible to imagine an 1896 marathon won competently by Kellner, say, worthy though he was, that would have fallen well short of the zealous hysteria that Louis inspired, and that would have left the Olympic Games marathon as a short-lived local re-enactment.

The Hellenic zeal that Louis inspired was also proof to the instigators of the new Olympics that international sports competition would foster national pride, exactly as Colonel Papadiamontopoulos exhorted the runners in his speech at the start. National pride was a big issue in 1896. Europe was trying to regroup after Prussia's victory over France in the war of 1870 and the subsequent unification of the separate German states into the modern German nation. Italy had been one nation for only thirty-five years. British imperialism was at its height, and America was beginning to flex its empire-seeking muscles. Nationalistic aspirations were surging across Central and Southeast Europe, but were stifled under the Austro-Hungarian Empire. Greece was anxious to reaffirm its historic national identity after centuries under a series of occupying powers.

All that adds up to a big burden for a humble water carrier to bear. Nationalism in international sport is almost always positive, and great fun, a game of flags and chants and young women with painted faces, yet sometimes a darker underside is exposed. The flag worship that Papadiamontopoulos asserted in his speech was among the causes of the First World War. The one occasion when Louis was honored at a later Olympics was in 1936, in Berlin, at the most abhorrently nationalistic of all Games. In photographs, wearing the soft hat, puff-sleeved white shirt, and short white skirt of Greek national costume, the poor old man looks pathetically out of place among the grandiose militarism of the Nazi uniforms, like an aging rabbit among wolves.

That public moment in Berlin was an exception in his quiet post-Olympic life. As soon as he politely could, Louis retired from the limelight, put his Greek national costume away, married Eleni in 1897, and settled to obscure privacy in Amaroússion, where his ancestors had lived, conceivably since 490 B.C., when they might have seen Pheidippides run by. Spyridon Louis was buried in the Amaroússion cemetery in March 1940. I hope it didn't occur to him that he had innocently contributed to the world-destroying nationalism of that terrible year.

Aftermath

Louis struck the spark, and everyone in Athens that day was warmed by the flame. Those from overseas carried it home with them. The imitators came fast. The first "marathon race" outside Greece was only four months later, on July 19, 1896, a prize-money event near Paris. On September 20 came the first amateur open "marathon," when thirty men ran, walked, and floundered through twenty-five miles of muddy roads from Stamford, Connecticut, to Columbia Oval in New York City. Similar races recreating the point-to-point "hero's journey" into the heart of a city were run in Hungary, Sweden, and Norway in the later months of 1896. Most significant in the long term, on April 19, 1897, just over a year after the Athens Olympic race, fifteen runners lined up at Ashland, Massachusetts, under the auspices of the Boston Athletic Association (B.A.A.), to run twenty-five miles into Boston.

The B.A.A. had raised money and sent its own representatives to Athens, who joined with Princeton athletes to make up most of the USA "team." William Milligan Sloane, Professor of French History at Princeton, was an ally of de Coubertin, and cobbled together that part of the American squad, while coach John Graham led seven B.A.A. athletes. The four in track-and-field took home three firsts, and one second, Arthur Blake in the 1500m. With Blake well placed in the early stages of the marathon, and B.A.A. pole vaulter Ellery Clark having to delay his winning vaults while marathon ecstasy obsessed the crowd, almost certainly the Boston men were all in the stadium at the unforgettable moment of Louis's victory. They carried the image and its crowd reception home, and within weeks, coach Graham was working with other B.A.A. officials on establishing a "marathon race" for Boston. As an equivalent to the Battle of Marathon victory over the colonizing Persians, they planned it for Patriots' Day, commemorating what America sees as its own fight for liberty, the Battle of Lexington on April 19, 1775. As equivalent to the "Greek warrior" Pheidippides, they found an American messenger hero in Paul Revere, even though for reasons of distance and logistics they chose a different route into Boston.

Boston, the world's first annual marathon, was only one of many, as the new races inspired by Louis began to merge with existing long races in Europe and Canada. Hamilton, Ontario, for instance, founded its annual Around the Bay 30K in 1894. It is therefore unique in today's long-distance running calendar in needing to pay no tribute to Spyros Louis.

Interpretations: Did Louis Cheat?

Some friends of Teddy Flack (though not Flack himself) were so astonished and outraged at how quickly Louis closed the big gap at about 20 miles/32km that they later led some writers, mostly British, to speculate about cheating. Journalist/historian John Bryant offered two different versions in two books, one that Louis hitched a ride on the stirrup of one of the Greek cavalry soldiers accompanying the race, the other that Louis had taken unfair advantage of his local knowledge: "familiar with the local landscape, [he] had taken a short cut through the forest" (Bryant, 2004, 2008).

One problem with both theories is that Louis was frequently observed and reported as running confidently alongside Vasilakos at the time he was supposed to be either hanging on a horse or dodging alone through a forest, well off the course. The two Greeks were officially reported as closing in together on Flack. Another problem is that although that forest was long ago turned into paved suburbs, it's hard from contemporary maps to see where it could have provided a short-cut worth several minutes, especially as forests rarely offer clear trails or good footing, and tend to be more severely hilly than the road. Anyway, why should Louis be "familiar" with obscure forest tracks five miles/8km or more distant from his daily return route into Athens? He had to work the family farm as well as maintain the water-carrying business. He is unlikely to have spent his free time on Sundays, if he had any, plotting routes through forests more than an hour's walk away.

If you're going to accuse a runner of cutting the course, at least produce a map to show where it happened. That forest story originated years after the event with the Greek poet, George Katsimbalis. His credibility is undercut by the complete lack of geographical information about the mysterious shortcut, and by the over-colorful detail that as Louis sneaked through the forest, "he was followed by six of the Greek runners." At that point (somewhere before 30km) Louis was not running alone, but was closely following or running alongside Vasilakos. All the other Greek runners were so far behind those two that there is no way they could have "followed." I have experience of poets, and do not regard them as factually reliable.

The whole question of Louis's integrity has been researched by one of the sport's most distinguished historians, Peter Lovesey, who is kind to the doubters, and in his (to be published) account reaches the conclusion that "it must remain an open question whether Louis broke the rules." If he did, Papadiamontopoulos must have been complicit, Lovesey says. So must Vasilakos, I would add, a respected public servant. So must officials and spectators at the points where Louis is accused of leaving and rejoining the route. And so it grows into a conspiracy theory.

It's true that the Greeks were desperate for a winner, but my view is that none of the speculative accusations stand up against the known facts. Louis was observed often on the course, mostly with Vasilakos; he passed several overseas athletes, none of whom reported anything amiss like stirrup-hanging; most important, he was a twice-daily jogger, and on the day he judged his pace astutely. I'm not willing to take seriously stories that surfaced more than sixty years after the event, that consist largely of second-hand reporting or rumor, and that seem to have been motivated in part by attention seeking. One doubter cited by Lovesey called it "the greatest sports scoop ever," the worst possible starting-point for seeking the truth.

The main instigator, though he didn't raise any doubts until as late as 1964, was Sir George Robertson, who was a British competitor at the Games as a young man, and roommate with Flack, making him less than objective. The main reason he and Bryant offer for any doubt about Louis is simply that at 30km Flack was running strongly and no other runner was in sight, so his victory looked assured. That argument is pure marathon ignorance.

Sorry – try going out too fast before you claim that someone running well with a big lead at 30km is a certain winner. Try watching past marathons, as runners as great and experienced as Charles Hefferon, Etienne Gailly, Jim Peters, Juma Ikaanga, or Mary Keitany lose leads that looked unassailable at 30km. Where Flack floundered and Louis came past, 34km, is exactly where we all know now that an 880/mile specialist with some cross-country experience who had never run beyond ten miles will "hit the wall," marathon slang for reaching the point where your glycogen is expended and the body has to make the switch to burning stored fat. We have seen it over and over. Most marathon runners on some unhappy day have experienced the sudden loss of power it inflicts. The only unusual thing about 1896 is that this was the first time it ever happened.

Flack never complained. Ian Jobling has given us access to Flack's own description, in a letter home to his father dated eight days after the race. It is absolutely consistent with the version that sees him as predictably and suddenly running out of glycogen while Louis benefitted from his years of slow miles, and his even or negative splits on the day. Flack wrote:

> *About the 30 kilo post I caught the Frenchman and passed him…I then began to feel rather done myself and I had the feeling that I should not be able to finish. I felt fairly well except for my legs which I feared would fail to carry me through.*

However, I kept going because a friend who was riding near me on a bicycle [almost certainly Robertson] said that I must win if I could only keep going as there was no one in sight. I managed to struggle on to the 34 kilo post when I felt that I should not be able to go another kilo as I had no feeling in my legs whatever at this time.

Just as I was on the point of giving in a Greek came past me looking very fresh and running well. I staggered for another 100 yards rolling about from one side of the road to another, then stopped as I should have fallen if I had gone any further. I got into the carriage and was driven to the stadium… All along the roads there were crowds of people…
(Jobling, 2018)

If you're less than fully trained for a marathon, the wall of sudden glycogen depletion awaits you. Thus big leads disappear. There's no need for lurid inventions about cheating. British doubters like Robertson and Bryant seem to feel entitlement for their man Flack to win. With Bryant, full disclosure, it's partly club loyalty, as at the time he wrote his books, he also was president of the London club that Flack had joined, Thames Hare and Hounds. I'm also proudly a member of Thames, but I don't believe that membership confers special rights to win Olympic marathons. It must also be stated that there is an element of British jingoism, or class snobbery, in the campaign against Louis. Robertson and Bryant describe Louis so recurrently as a "peasant" that I can't help being reminded of all those who refuse to believe that a mere provincial Stratford glover's son could have written the plays of Shakespeare.

The Vase

To end on a more positive note, the antique Greek vase donated to the winner by the beneficent Averoff recently returned to its proper home, Greece. It was appropriated by the occupying Nazis during World War II, presumably from Louis's family in Amaroússion. It was rediscovered and presented back to Greece in 2019 by its then owner, the University of Münster, Germany, to their great credit. Now safely in the Museum of Olympic History, it is a wine-drinking vessel with an image representing two *dolichos* runners in the ancient Games, under the watchful eye of judges. Most runner images on vases represent sprinters, but these can be identified as longer distance runners from their low arm carriage and knee lift. Probably that's much how Spyridon Louis ran on April 10, 1896.

Footnote

In 1989, I was in Greece as writer for a TV documentary about the history of marathon. A bonus of the job was the long, late dinners with the crew in local *tavernas*. One night in Rafina, near the 1896 Olympic course, a very small boy was romping around the tables, as happens in Greece late at night. A local man called out (in Greek), "Run! Be like Louis!" Our interpreter confirmed it. "Run like Louis!" is a common proverb in modern Greece, meaning "Move quickly, and succeed!" Spyridon Louis has become part of the language.

Chapter 7

The Fascinating Struggle: Near-Death Drama at the Great White City – London 1908

800 BC   100 AD   1719   1896   1908   1928   1936   1964   1984   2021

He has gone to the extreme of human endurance... It is horrible, and yet fascinating, this struggle between a set purpose and an utterly exhausted frame.

–Arthur Conan Doyle on Dorando Pietri

The crowd was fervid with anticipation. A hundred thousand people watched for one man to appear. Who would he be? Their only information had come from a big leaderboard that was paraded around the field for people to read the top positions. A sudden gunshot hushed the crowd, then a shouted announcement through a long megaphone: "The runners are in sight!" That call was repeated from left to right, to each side of the giant stadium. No names were given. The crowd buzzed with speculation. They watched the top of the ramp where the first runner would appear. They felt certain it would be the South African Hefferon. He had been four minutes ahead the last they knew from the leaderboard.

When you're waiting for the marathon leader, nothing is certain, especially on a hot and humid day. There was a scurry of action at the top of the sloping ramp. Officials and police moved about, some shouting or pointing. Among them, the crowd could glimpse a small dark man with a white kerchief knotted on his head, in a sodden white shirt and baggy red shorts, stumbling down the ramp. He seemed unsure of where he was and where to go. As he came out on to the cinder track, he moved like a marionette, unevenly, as if not in control, as if at any moment the strings would break, and he would collapse.

The entry of a marathon leader into the stadium is like no other moment in sport. There are great touchdowns, and goals, and home runs, and sprint finishes, but with each of these, the spectators have been witnesses to the whole developing drama. At the finish of a marathon, the stadium crowd sees only the final minute or so of more than two hours of action. The leader's entry to the stadium is almost the end of the story, yet not quite. We greet the arriving hero, almost finished, almost triumphant, yet visibly vulnerable. Even as we shout in praise, we're looking for the next runner, who might change everything.

And for the runner, after twenty-six miles of inward effort, suddenly this acclaim from the encompassing walls of people. The journey is almost done, but the distance still to run can be cruel. There have been many dramatic marathon entrances in running history, some of them narrated in this book – Spyridon Louis, Sohn Kee Chung, Joan Benoit. The tradition started with the legend of Pheidippides. The most dramatic of them all was this one, the Olympic marathon finish in London on July 24, 1908. The small dark man stumbling down the ramp was Dorando Pietri of Italy. What happened to him in the next few minutes has become inseparable from the story of the marathon and of the Olympic Games. The photo images have become iconic, instantly familiar, arousing universal sympathy, distress, and admiration.

Witnesses said it "would never be forgotten," and they were right. There have been countless retellings, but all the details in the narrative that follows, like those words, are taken from reliable eye-witness reports, most often those in the *New York Times*, and the report by Arthur Conan Doyle, originally for the *Daily Mail*, revised for his autobiography, *Memoirs and Adventures*. The visual evidence is also important. To get the story right (as it deserves), I'll try to pick my way through many old beliefs that don't hold up. (How did it get to be 26 miles 385 yards/42.2km? Where were the royal children? What was Arthur Conan Doyle doing there?)

The crowd hoped to see Charles Hefferon arrive first. A South African winner who had been born in Berkshire was almost as good as a Briton, only six years after a bruising war had given imperial Britain that last major colony. Better the British-born South African than the young Canadian Indian Tom Longboat, who was the pre-race betting favorite after his record-breaking win in the Boston marathon in 1907, but who was suspected of having taken money for running. Far better any winner, most of the crowd thought, than one of the twelve Americans, whose track and field team had won so many events and so few friends in those conflict-ridden Games. That partisan context would have an effect on how some key people acted in the next minutes.

The crowd who actually saw Dorando Pietri were moved by something that lies deeper than partisanship. The human frailty and courage embodied in the struggle of the little Italian to move himself around the track stirred them to profound sympathy mixed with horrified fascination. He could barely walk, swerving haplessly from side to side, dazed and bewildered, unsure which direction to go, tilting at first to his right, staggering forward. The crowd's roar faded to an anxious murmur. Primitive early film footage lets us see and study the moment. Pietri stutters slowly out onto the cinder track, tries to turn the wrong way, blunders among a cluster of officials and police who shout and gesticulate at him. He hesitates and wavers about in confusion. Looking groggy and semi-conscious, he turns (or to be accurate he is turned) the right way. He shuffles forward rather than runs.

Different reporters tried that day to find the right word for his unstable motion: "tottered," "staggered," "floundered," "reeled," "a strange automatic amble," "like a man in a dream." Weaving and stumbling, looking likely to fall at any moment, he covered about twenty yards, and then his legs crumpled, and he fell. He was directly in front of a tightly packed stand, and the people gasped. Some thought he had died.

We are familiar now with this sight from film of later occasions – Jim Peters in 1954, Gabriela Andersen-Schiess in 1984 – and it is still heart-wrenching. These people were seeing it for the first time. They had no understanding of the medical implications. Potential tragedy was being enacted right in front of them.

We might think that the noise and heat of the stadium, those sudden towering tiers of watchers, overcame Pietri, but it is a little-known detail that he had already collapsed on the way into the arena. The marathon medical officer, Dr. Michael Bulger, stated in the official report, "I was first called to Dorando in the passage leading to the stadium. He was in a state of absolute collapse and quite pulseless. In a short time he recovered sufficiently to enter the stadium" (Cook, 1909). That's why Bulger and race director Jack Andrew are always prominent among the officials helping to steer Pietri in the film footage of his entrance to the stadium and in the photographs.

It was the second time he collapsed, therefore, when he first fell in full view of the crowd. He looked to be down and out. Officials including Bulger surrounded him and tried to help him. Later, Pietri lamented that his official attendant was not there to assist, but the film and photographic evidence shows it could not have made any difference, as he was too far gone. The rules were anyway specific that "No attendant will be allowed on the track" (Rule 8).

"There were wild gesticulations. Men stooped and rose again," wrote Conan Doyle (Doyle, 1924). All was confusion. Even eyewitness reports vary wildly. "He had to do one round of the arena [in fact it was half a lap] where unfortunately he was helped up, and so disqualified." (Lady Metcalfe, letter to the *Daily Telegraph*, September 1965). "My recollection is that Dorando, on arriving at the track, was followed by a few enthusiasts...who patted him on the back. This no doubt caused his collapse." (G. Chapman, letter to the *Daily Telegraph*, August 1965). Think how hard it is to get agreement on exactly what happened in the Budd/Decker incident in 1984, and that was televised live and recorded on video.

The official Olympic report seems to provide a clear account. "As it was impossible to leave him there, for it looked as if he might die in the very presence of the Queen and that enormous crowd, the doctors and attendants rushed to his assistance. When he was slightly resuscitated the excitement of his compatriots was so intense that the officials did not put him on an ambulance and send him out, as they no would doubt have done under less agitating circumstances" (Cook, 1909). Even that official and supposedly objective summary puts blame on the excitable Italians ("his compatriots") and glaringly omits the crucial vexed issue of the assistance Pietri was given, both when he was down and when he was upright and moving toward the tape.

Pietri was helped to his feet, and tottered along the rest of the long straight, "the little red legs going incoherently," Doyle wrote, and astutely, "driven by a supreme will within." He reached the curve, his legs sagging, and then the crowd groaned in pity and terror as he fell again. They shouted for him to be helped, to be saved. Again, they thought he was dying. But again he was up, and again they cheered, in relief and admiration. Poor Pietri covered only a few yards before crumpling helplessly yet again at the top of the bend. This time there is a photograph, showing him lying on his back, supported in the arms of Dr. Bulger, with another man touching, perhaps massaging, his leg. Pietri looks inert, totally out of it – eyes shut, limbs soggy, face shattered. He seems to have passed out.

But not quite. An unnoticed detail is that throughout the whole drama of repeated crumpling collapse, he somehow kept hold of his handkerchief, which flutters from his right hand in the finish-line photo, and at least one "grip" or "cork," which is visible clutched within his fist. This was a short lightweight hollow tube of wood, usually bamboo cane, or a round piece of cork. Pietri's looks like cane. He may have one in his left hand, too – you can't see, but his hand is in a clutching position. Runners a hundred years ago carried such a grip in one or both hands in the belief that it helped style and concentration to have something to hold. Alf Shrubb, the great English multiple world record holder of the same era, habitually ran with "corks," and in various photos I have spotted them also in the fist of Tom Longboat and others. Later, runners wrapped a handkerchief round one hand; see Sohn and Harper in the photograph of the 1936 Olympic marathon. I remember older runners gripping a handkerchief at the beginning of my own running career in the 1950s.

So Pietri was never totally unconscious, although he looked bad enough for many to think he was dying. How he got to his feet again after this fifth collapse is hard to imagine, but he did, almost certainly with plenty of help. (The film coverage is patchy.) Briefly, he seemed capable of finishing, still teetering yet also somehow pushing forward. He got around the bend, and then, horrifically, collapsed once more. This time "kind hands" (said Doyle) were alongside to help, and he was saved from a heavy fall. Again, the crowd gasped. Only about sixty yards remained to the white tape stretched across the track in the middle of the straight. But Pietri was down.

"Surely he is done now. He cannot rise again," writes Doyle, with the dramatic present-tense immediacy of a commentator on live radio or TV.

And now things became really exciting. The next runner appeared, with the striped shield of the USA on his white shirt. It was Johnny Hayes, a New Yorker of Irish parentage. And he was charging, with a sure stride. The crowd had no idea of how he got there, but it is a crucial part of the story of this extraordinary day. Hayes had run a perfectly judged race when everyone else was going bananas. The first Brits ran the first mile in 5:01, sheer folly. 1908 training and 1908 road surfaces and 1908 shoe leather simply did not give you a 2:11 marathon. Perhaps they were carried away by the presence at the start of Mary, Princess of Wales, who signalled Lord Desborough to fire the gun. With that royal inspiration, Tom Jack reached four miles in a suicidal 27:01, and after Jack drifted, two other Brits, Jack Price and Fred Lord, passed ten miles in a still fatal 56:53 (2:29:00 marathon pace). Hefferon and Pietri were on 57:12, not far behind, also much too fast, on that training, on a hot day, on a course that was mostly dirt and stone, and crossed cow paddocks at 25 miles.

Everything favored careful pace judgment, we now understand. Hayes was the one who was careful.

Far ahead of Hayes's steady progress, a war of folly was being waged. Approaching 14 miles, Hefferon and Pietri had enough in reserve to sweep up the Brits, Price and Lord. It was too soon. Then Hefferon moved powerfully away – too powerfully. During the fifteenth mile, he went ahead by two minutes. Then Tom Longboat came up fast – too fast. At 16 miles, he was in second. At 17 he was walking. He soon gave up. ("A Special Car will follow to carry competitors who abandon the race," promised the official instructions.) Longboat's bicycle assistant was plying him with champagne to quench his thirst and stimulate him, which probably did not help.

The whole race was a litany of self-destruction. None showed pace planning or control, except for Johnny Hayes. He alone among the potential winners seemed to understand that a marathon is longer than eighteen miles. He ran the first few miles well back in the field of fifty-six. Some say dead last, but his teammate Joseph Forshaw of Missouri, who also ran a sensible race and came through to third (fourth, counting Pietri), told the *New York Times* that Hayes was always ahead of him. Anyway, Hayes went out slow. At 17 miles, probably running with two teammates, he was still six minutes behind Hefferon, the leader. Six minutes is almost a mile, eternity when you're waiting for the next runner. It looked decisive, and no doubt Hefferon thought it was decisive, but in fact it meant that Hayes was running perfectly, with nine miles still to run. One photo taken at 23 miles shows Hayes, now alone, looking composed and resolute, with a firm stride. Pietri in a photo and in film footage at the same point looks wobbly – his head on one side, down on his hips.

Pietri was still moving, however. At 25 miles he had caught the much taller Hefferon, and they were side by side, battling for the lead. It must have been a battle in slow motion. By contrast, ominously, though they didn't know it, Hayes was coming on strong, relentlessly closing. When Hefferon dropped behind Pietri, he must have almost stopped, as Hayes quickly scooped him up, and was in second. While Pietri was a crumpled heap inside the stadium, Hayes was powering over the cow tracks that crossed the open space of Wormwood Scrubs toward the ramp into the arena, running close to six-minute miles. Spectators who perched in their dozens in the overhanging trees saw the action, but inside the stadium the crowd and waiting cameras missed it. The drama outside was as great as the one inside. And then the two converged.

Hayes appeared. The crowd roared again – not entirely in acclamation. He ran down the ramp "gallantly" (in Doyle's word), on to the track, and began the final pursuit.

How did Pietri ever reach the finish? With plenty of help, for sure, even to be on his feet. He got there as Hayes was on the final bend, a mere 150 yards behind. The famous finish-line photo shows Pietri with liquid legs and glazed expression. Chief Clerk of the Course (Race Director in our terms) Jack Andrew is helping him through the tape, with a good grip on Pietri's right upper arm, holding a huge megaphone in the other hand. Andrew claimed later that he "only caught Dorando as he was falling at the tape," and Dr. Bulger, who is alongside, wrote as his official report, "I exercised my right in having precautions taken that he should not fall again. Hence the slight assistance rendered by Mr. J.M. Andrew just before the goal was reached."

The photo does not bear out either of those explanations. Andrew is supporting and steering the sagging Italian, and film footage shows he had that grip on the arm for some time. Given Doyle's phrase, "kindly hands saving him from a heavy fall," and their appearance in every photograph, Andrew, Bulger, and others were close alongside him all the way from the second time he fell (within the stadium). They were indisputably giving him more than "slight assistance." Reports talk of the officials dragging him along, clearly reluctant to see him lose. If that seems a little exaggerated, one reminiscence long after turns the scene into pure Charlie Chaplin: "They picked him up and threw him over the tape" (Major N. Leith-Hay-Clark, letter to the *Sunday Times*, 1964).

To say that Andrew gave what has to be interpreted as "assistance" is not to overly criticize. The instinct to help a courageous and dangerously exhausted man is a decent one. Dr. Bulger had been close to Pietri since the very first collapse on the ramp into the stadium and seems properly to have taken responsibility on medical grounds. The huge crowd was noisily pleading for Pietri to be helped. His "compatriots" (probably his assistant and some Italian officials in the arena) were "excited." Pietri was showing extraordinary willpower and resilience at the very edge of unconsciousness. Hayes was coming on fast. The only communication by the Race Director was by bellowing into a giant megaphone. Decisions had to be made on impulse. The place must have been bedlam. Now we all know that if you give assistance by supporting or steering, the runner has to be disqualified. But we only know that because of what happened in London that day.

While all eyes were (and still are) on Pietri's painful progress, Hayes was still running his own well-judged and well-completed race, moving strongly around the track. He finished thirty-two seconds behind, 2:55:18.4 to Pietri's 2:54:46.4. That gave Andrew time to run back, and attempt to steer Hayes by the arm as he had with Pietri. Defending the help he gave to Pietri, he said "I assisted Hayes in the same way."

Again, that's a little flexible as truth. Photographic evidence shows that he only stretched out an arm toward Hayes, who does not look as if he needs or would welcome any assistance. His stride still looks smooth and has some lift. He is disregarding Andrew's outstretched arm. It's an important question whether he was charging after Pietri or struggling along in a similar state of near-collapse. One American spectator said that Hayes "trotted into the stadium as fresh as a daisy," but other accounts say things like he "struggled in second, apparently befuddled by strychnine." What shape was he in? The first-hand evidence shows him far from befuddled and in no need of help.

An Italian observer's sketch (Martin and Gynn, 1979) shows the points where Pietri collapsed, and marks with an X Hayes's position on the last bend as Pietri reached the tape. Assuming it is accurate (and it fits with Doyle's account, which is otherwise reliable), this puts Hayes 150 yards behind as Pietri reaches the tape. The gap was officially timed as 32 seconds. 150 yards in 32 seconds is 93-second 440 speed, or 6:12 per mile pace. That's good running, at the end of a 2:55 marathon, average pace 6:41. "Fresh as a daisy" might be wishful thinking, but those stats suggest that Doyle's description of Hayes as "well within his strength" is credible. Hayes finished fast, by almost any standard. To imagine him at six-minute mile speed in pursuit of the tottering Pietri, who might fall and pass out again at any moment, is to understand the full frantic drama of that scene. No wonder the crowd was in frenzy. No wonder the officials who so much wanted Pietri to win were in a state of near panic.

Andrew's motives in seeking to give Hayes the same "assistance" as he gave Pietri may not have been as pure as he would like us to think. Even from the photo, it looks to me (I regret to say) like quick thinking to make it look equivalent to the assistance Pietri received. In fact, if there was any contact at all with Hayes, it was trivial, by comparison with all the manifest catching and cradling and lifting and steering and supporting that Pietri was given every time he fell, every time he got up, and all the way in between. Andrew clearly wanted Pietri to complete the course, and equally clearly didn't want Hayes to be the winner. You don't need assisting if you're running at six-minute mile pace. If (and it's a real if) Hayes "collapsed" or fell down after the line, as some reports say, well, so do plenty of us after a hot day marathon, and it doesn't mean we were not running strong to the line.

Andrew promptly declared Pietri the winner, presumably announcing it through his megaphone. The poor little Italian was the briefest champion in Olympic marathon history. The American team immediately lodged a protest, which properly and inevitably was upheld.

Pietri's collapse looked serious and was considered to be life-threatening. He was carried off on a stretcher. But he did not die. He was taken to a hospital where the official report said he "lay between life and death for two hours and a half." He was "almost too weak to answer questions." The "almost" is suggestive. He was voluble enough to complain that his assistant had not been allowed on to the track.

The awards ceremony was not until the next day, when the mood was very different. Queen Alexandra had announced that she would present a specially engraved gold cup to Pietri, who was given a hero's welcome. He looks quite perky in the picture where he is receiving the cup from the Queen. The *New York Times* said he "walked briskly around the track and up the steps," which is more than I could ever do the day after a marathon. He received a great ovation, with people rising and cheering him, some say for fifteen minutes. Americans in the crowd were generously exuberant in support.

The engraving of Pietri's consolation cup (to "Pietri Dorando" – see below) was completed quickly, by royal command. Hayes was awarded the gold medal, and a statue of a dying Greek warrior, presumably Pheidippides. He now received the unqualified acclaim that he had missed on his half lap of the track. With the trophy at his feet, and smiling modestly, he was carried off the track on a table held by six American teammates. At the front left corner, by the way, is Louis (sometimes spelled Lewis) Tewanima, one of the first great Native American marathon runners, who the previous day had placed ninth (fourth American), and who will appear again in this book.

Hayes was a guest of Britain's Parliament after the ceremony, but it was Pietri who was the celebrity hero of the hour. The British public took the plucky Italian to their hearts. Those words come from the poster that advertised his nightly appearances at the Hammersmith Palace theater: "The Plucky Italian Runner Signior Dorando (first past the post in the Great Marathon Race) will appear here every evening." He became a symbol of gallantry, and of noble breeding. Doyle pronounced portentously, "No Roman of the prime ever bore himself better than Dorando...The great breed is not yet extinct." If it seems a bit of a stretch to dress up the small-town cake-maker in a toga as one of the noblest Romans of them all, well, the British in 1908 believed in "great breeds," especially their own, and saw themselves as inheritors of Rome's imperial destiny. Some of this spin campaign to apotheosize Pietri as the true ("first past the post") winner was calculated to take the smile off the Americans' faces. They, after all, had chosen to split off from the great breed. The Irish were seeking to do the same.

There is no question that Pietri was heroically courageous and determined. He misjudged by probably only five minutes and kept running amazingly well after that foolhardy 57:12 at ten miles. He was desperately unlucky that the course was extended beyond the usual, beyond what had been promised, by more than a mile. His heroism after he lapsed into exhaustion fully earned his iconic place as a symbol of the enduring human spirit. To get to your feet once after collapsing with heat exhaustion near the end of a marathon is tough. To do it six times, even with help, is astonishing.

But for my money, as a runner, it takes just as much courage to let the entire field in a major race run away from you at the start, sit sedately back while British spectators jeer from the sidewalks, allow the leaders to go away by nearly ten minutes, and wait till after fifteen miles before you even begin to make any significant ground on them. That's really gutsy. And really smart. The marathon is a sporting event that tests judgment and self-knowledge, as well as stamina and resolve. By that full test, Johnny Hayes was emphatically the winner.

He may have run negative splits. No halfway times were taken, but if he really was six minutes behind Hefferon at seventeen miles, a negative split at halfway seems possible. Before the Olympics, in 1906, 1907, and 1908, Hayes had placed fifth, third, and second at Boston, and won the Mercury A.C. (later Yonkers) Marathon in 1907, so he was experienced at running well over difficult marathon courses. We know that at least in the 1908 Boston, he had tested the tactic of sitting well back off the pace, since he was recorded in thirty-second place at South Framingham, about four miles, and finished second. He knew what he was doing, at a time when very few marathon runners had any clue. The final judgment is that on that hot day, on that long course, Hayes was the one who got it exactly right, and that's ultimately what matters.

That 1908 Olympic marathon is a wonderful story, an essence of the human drama of long-distance running, enacted by memorable personalities confronting an extreme challenge, some emerging as truly heroic, others more fallible, with a darker undercurrent, too, of international hostility, and partisan officials subverting the rules they are appointed to uphold. Historically, the race is a key reference point in the development of the marathon and the Olympic Games. It's worth getting the story right, as nearly as we can, and correcting some long-cherished errors. Even some eye-witness reports, as I have shown, are inventive rather than factual, and original sources are hard to find.

What really did happen? and why? What follows is an investigation as close as is possible, more than a century after the fact. Much of my evidence is new. A lot of old beliefs simply don't hold up.

The Distance

There was no precise set distance for a "marathon race" at that time, and many so-called marathons were prize-money events, so not subject anyway to amateur rules. The International Amateur Athletic Federation was not even founded until 1912. Any long race could call itself a "marathon." That title was good for publicity, as it still is today, when "half-marathons" and "marathon relays" have become prominent purely on the allure of the word "marathon." When Johnny Hayes won the Mercury A.C. race in 1907, the big silver cup (now displayed by the Shore Athletic Club in New Jersey) is inscribed "25 Mile Marathon Run." Because several runners collapsed that year in the last five miles, the race officials planned to reduce the distance in 1908 to twenty miles, still calling it a "marathon run." The official Olympic rules in 1908 said only that the event would be a "marathon race of about 40 kilometres marked out on public roads." That meant a road race of more or less the same distance as at Athens (1896), Paris (1900) and St Louis (1904), with no expectation that the distance had to be exact.

The decision to make the London course two kilometers longer was not last-minute, but made at least three months beforehand, when a

British trial was held. As with Athens in 1896 (see Chapters 6 and 13), the story takes on new light when we know that a trial race was held. On April 25, 1908, it was run on the Olympic course, except that the start was on the Long Walk, south of Windsor Castle, not within the Castle grounds. Race director Jack Andrew, who would be the key man in the whole Pietri controversy, had measured it. At the time of the Olympics, the distance was stated in the competitors' Race Instructions, which were also publicised in the London *Times* for July 22, two days before the race. The measurement is given as: "26 = 41.84 Entrance of Stadium," along with "26 miles 385 yards = 42.263 kilometres. Full distance." (I can't explain why the conversion here is 42.263 rather than 42.195.) The official report published after the Games gives "42 kilometres." For interpreting Pietri's pace judgment, a lot depends on whether he or his managers ever read that small print about the extra two kilometers. If he went into the race expecting the distance to be "about 40 kilometres," his two extra kilometers of despair are only too understandable.

Since we all now have to run every precisely measured yard and meter of the supposed "London distance" of 26 miles 385 yards, or 26.219 miles/42.195 km, it's worth pausing to know exactly how that came about.

The traditional, almost universally accepted version is that the start of the race was outside the Royal Family's nursery at Windsor Castle, so that the grandchildren could watch from the windows or balcony. (A variant that I discovered only recently is that the start was placed there for the benefit of a member of the Royal Family who was unwell.) It's also usually said that the finish was extended to place the tape directly beneath the Royal Stand in the Great White City.

Both are wrong. Let's walk through what really happened.

The support of the Royal Family was indeed important for the Games to be a popular success. King Edward VII, whose sporting interests were shooting, yachting, horse racing, and adultery, showed little interest, performing the opening ceremony but nothing else; his son, the Prince of Wales (the future King George V), was on a state visit to Québec. So the work was done by Queen Alexandra and her daughter-in-law, Mary, Princess of Wales.

It was agreed that the marathon would start on the grounds of Windsor Castle, to highlight the royal endorsement. But it was well away from the nursery, on a broad gravel path across a lawn beyond the East Terrace. A film clip exists, and a photograph in the official Olympic report. Both show most of the royal grandchildren among a cluster of high-ranking spectators out on the lawn, spiffily dressed in boaters and little sailor suits and the like, standing close to runners who are apparently very soon going to start, as all are walking purposefully in the same direction downhill, with the children watching, a kind of informal pre-race parade. The official report provides the caption, "H.R.H. The Princess of Wales at the start at Windsor." In the photo, she is the tall figure on the left, wearing an appropriately regal hat.

The report text says the Princess of Wales "was present with her children" (Cook, 1909). Four are visible, probably Prince Albert (later King George VI) age 12, Mary, 11, Henry, 8, and George, 5. The oldest and the youngest of the six children, Edward (later briefly King Edward VIII), 14, and John, 3, are not evident. So there were no little noses pressed to the windows of the nursery, because they were outside, on a different lawn, getting a privileged close-up view of the runners a few minutes before the action.

Being within the private grounds of the castle, the start was not open to public spectators. The exact location needed to be 700 yards from the statue of Queen Victoria in the town of Windsor, to pick up Andrew's course measurement from that point on public roads. At the statue, the Olympic course joined the Long Walk route that had been used for the trial on April 25. Mike Sandford, Measurement Secretary for the South of England Athletic Association, established in 2008 (partly by trigonometric readings from photographs) that "the actual start line... was on a path that leads just South of East away from the SE corner of the Castle...about 150 yards distant from the East Terrace," on what is marked on a contemporary map as the "South Slopes."

The field lined up in four rows, drawn by lot. At a signal by Princess Mary, Lord Desborough fired the gun. The official report is specific.

Sandford also found a separate report by Andrew on the course and its measurement in the program for the trial race on April 25, which expressed the "hope" that royal permission would be given for the Olympic start to be "from the terrace of Windsor Castle, in which event the distance will be about 26 miles to the edge of the stadium track."

So the distance from the lawn at Windsor to the edge of the track at the Great White City stadium at Shepherd's Bush in Chiswick (pronounced "Chissick") was always going to be "*about* 26 miles" (my italics). We can't know why that was rendered in the official instructions as "about 40 kilometres." Perhaps it was to conceal the change that had been made. For the precise actual distance, that word "about" is troubling. "About" has since been interpreted as meaning "exactly." The official Olympic report then states, "385 yards were run on the cinder track to the finish, below the Royal Box" (Cook, 1908). And thus the weird distance we all know.

It took another sixteen years to become official, ending an era of rivalry. The British didn't much like the European dominance of the Olympic movement. When Britain became stand-in hosts for 1908 after the disastrous eruption of Mount Vesuvius in 1906 forced Italy to withdraw Rome as the venue, the British insisted on making the London Games as "imperial" (non-metric) as possible. The program included, for the only time, a 5-mile race, a 10-mile track walk, and a 3-mile team race, as well as Jack Andrew's marathon length of 26 miles and 385 yards, with all intermediate times recorded in miles. The only other non-metric event in Olympic history was an exhibition 4-mile team race in St. Louis in 1904. After 1908, the contest between Britain and France to own the "marathon" distance raged until 1921 when the International Olympic Committee adopted the "London distance" for the 1924 Olympic marathon in Paris. The Olympic marathon in Stockholm in 1912 had been 40.2km, and in Antwerp in 1920 42.75km. In Paris in 1924, it was 42.195km, the supposed 1908 distance, which then became standard, not only for the Olympics. Boston, the oldest annual marathon, also toed the 26 mile and 385 yards line for the first time in 1924.

The 385 yards on the track seems likely to be accurate, but it's misleading to say the race was extended to that distance for royal pleasure. All races on the track finished at the same line, directly under the Royal Stand, whether or not the Queen was in attendance. Sandford cites the trial program to show that the original intention was to finish with one complete lap of the track, one third of a mile (see below). It's not known why that changed; perhaps it was a matter of where access to the track for the marathon runners occurred, which became clear only after construction of the stadium was completed. The outcome anyway was a little more than half a lap of the track to reach the regular Games finish line, measured as 385 yards.

The Great White City

A key factor in understanding the drama that happened on the track is the stadium itself. Many writers construct their Pietri narrative on the assumption that by running 385 yards inside the stadium, the runners were covering almost a whole lap, as if that were the now familiar 400m/440yd. But although the 1908 events were mostly metric, the British had built the track at White City as 1,760 feet, or 536.45 meters, three laps to the mile, as British tracks quite often were at that time. Perhaps it was a "Britocentric" snub against metric measurements, but the big lap was common at that time. The whole sport was new. As late as Colombes Stadium for the Paris Olympics in 1924, the track was 500 meters, meaning that Paavo Nurmi won the 1,500m over a tidy three laps, and throwing interesting light on Eric Liddell's famous 400m win – running less than one lap with only one bend made it less of a disadvantage for Liddell to draw the outside lane. The Merseyside track used as the setting in *Chariots of Fire* did not measure up.

So the Great White City was a huge arena, well capable of holding 100,000 spectators. The marathon runners entered from a ramp alongside a large covered stand, and rounded just one big bend, to reach the finish under the royal seats in the middle of the stand on the opposite straight. The direction became a problem for poor Pietri. The marathoners had to turn to their left, and run around the bend clockwise, with the curb on their right. That oddity may partly explain Pietri's confused wandering as he entered and tried to turn right. The Olympic track races were in the standard counter-clockwise direction, and he had run in the 3-mile team race ten days before the marathon (he did not finish, withdrawing once Italy had no chance of qualifying for the final). He was not to blame if he was confused. The official instructions for athletics that were issued to all competitors end with the rules for the marathon, and immediately following those comes a "Note" that first states that the track is measured "12 inches from the inside edge" and then "The direction of running will be left hand inside." That's all – it's intended to apply to all track events, but it comes immediately after the instructions for the marathon, and makes no exception for that event, where the direction of running for the half lap of the track was, on the contrary, to be "right hand inside." If Pietri had that instruction translated for him, no wonder he wavered about when officials swarmed "expostulating" around him. Look at the film footage and imagine.

British/American Rivalry

The 1908 Games were fraught with contention between the hosts and their most successful guests. When the Americans protested against the announcement of Pietri as the winner, it was their fifth formal protest in as many days. The controversy started when the American flag was missing from the display above the stadium during the Games' opening. The position allocated to the Americans during the formal entry of the teams, immediately ahead of "British colonies," was interpreted as a further insult. The U.S. flag bearer therefore declined to dip the American flag to King Edward.

Well, the controversy really started in 1776. British Imperialism was at its height in 1908, and America represented its one great failure.

That historic resentment was exacerbated by the fact that most of the American team were of Irish ethnicity or birth, members of the Irish American Athletic Club, and in 1908, Ireland and Irish Americans were bitter that the move toward Ireland's independence had stalled. Athletes from Ireland were indignant at having to represent Great Britain, and at the 1906 "intercalated" Games in Athens, one gold medal winner had rushed the flagpole after his ceremony, hauled down the Union Jack, and replaced it with a green Irish flag.

And Johnny Hayes was as Irish as he was American. He was probably born in New York, but his parents had very recently emigrated from Nenagh, Tipperary, and he belonged to the Irish American A.C. The *New York Sun* (July 25, 1908) enthused (or perhaps gloated, given the rivalries I have described), "Jack Hayes is as Irish as you find them, with black hair, blue eyes, a good humored and freckled face and a ton of confidence in himself."

The 400m was the high point of the 1908 Games conflict between Britain and the U.S. The American winner was disqualified for supposedly cutting across in front of the British runner, and the race was declared void. A re-run was ordered, but all four Americans withdrew in protest, leaving the single Brit to circle the track alone in that strange second final. Newspapers in the two countries published accounts of the various incidents that were so colorfully biased as to be almost unrecognizable as describing the same event. This tradition of contrasting perceptions continues in recent historical work: e.g., the British John Bryant in *The Marathon Makers* (2008) and Roger McGrath writing in *Irish America* ("Running Rings Round the Empire," August-September 2012).

An attempt to defuse the controversy was made by the American Bishop of Pennsylvania when he was invited to deliver the Sunday sermon at St. Paul's Cathedral in London in the middle of the Games, and charitably coined the phrase "the important thing in the Olympic Games is not so much winning as taking part." Baron Pierre de Coubertin at the post-Games government banquet, only a few hours after the Hayes/Pietri drama, quoted that line (translating it into French) and it has become enshrined almost as a mantra in the Olympic creed. What Hayes and Pietri thought about it is not recorded.

To put it bluntly, the British officials wanted Pietri to win, not Hayes. Clearly there was an undercurrent of anti-American resentment in the British officials' efforts to ensure Pietri's victory. America had the last word, however, taking first, third, fourth, ninth, and fourteenth in the marathon, by far the best national performance. By unofficial team scoring (3 to score) Britain didn't even get second, as Canada headed them. Americans could now be gracious in victory, cheering Pietri the longest when he received his gold cup. Resentments were "forgotten," wrote the *New York Times* next day.

A good note to end on, though "temporarily suppressed" would be more accurate.

Dorando Pietri

One persistent error about Pietri is his name. The official entry list gives the Italian's name twice, both wrong. He is "Dorando, P." (bib number 19) and "Durando, P." (bib number 23). He ran with number 19. Another Italian, U[mberto] Blasi, is also given twice, with two numbers (20 and 21). Presumably there was some difficulty with the handwritten team declaration, and either the Italian management wrote the names the wrong way or British officials assumed that "Pietri" was an Italian form of Peter, and was his Christian name. Andrew and Dr. Bulger refer to him by "Dorando" as his surname throughout their official reports. Even when he was presented with his consolatory cup by Queen Alexandra, it was inscribed "To Pietri Dorando In Remembrance of the Marathon Race..." He was "Signior Dorando" when he appeared at the Hammersmith Palace theater. The name stuck. For many years he was always "Dorando" or sometimes "Durando" in the public mind, especially his fans in New York. He is only "Dorando" in Irving Berlin's song. A street near the former White City site in London has the name Dorando Close. Even Naples, Italy, has a Via P. Dorando, now mainly a road freight depot. There is still sometimes doubt which way round his names should go. Booth's biography of Conan Doyle gets it wrong, for instance.

The other persistent error started the day after the race when the *New York Times* called Pietri "a confectioner who resides on the Isle of Capri." A good many accounts perpetuate that mistake. His home was Carpi, not Capri. Few outside Italy have heard of Carpi, which is north of Modena, about thirty miles northwest of Bologna.

Dorando Pietri baked his cakes in Carpi, and by one version his running career began there at age 17, when his baker boss gave him a letter to mail to Reggio Emilia. Four hours later the blistered apprentice returned, having misunderstood, and delivered the letter in person, running fifteen miles/24km each way. Another tradition has him spontaneously joining in a race in 1904 that featured the greatest Italian runner of that date, Pericle Pagliani, and staying with his pace. More verifiable as fact, at age 19 he was second in a 3K race in Bologna. It seems likely that he was one of many young Italian men who were inspired by the prospect of the 1908 Olympic Games being hosted by their new, struggling, and impoverished nation, so found a sport which enabled them to aspire to compete at Rome, much like the fifty young Greeks who had lined up for their trial marathons in 1896. Running required no money, and even under amateur rules could bring quite significant rewards to a young man as poor as Pietri, with prizes like china or clocks.

Pietri was born on October 16, 1885, in Mandrio, a suburb of Correggio, and spent his youth in Carpi, leaving school early to work as assistant or apprentice to a baker and confectioner. Without running he would have stayed there. But he quickly gained some national fame as a long-distance runner, although many of his successes seemed qualified by some misfortune. When he won the Paris Marathon (30km), he lost the title over an entry informality. When he broke the Italian one-hour record, he found a rival had lowered it the previous day. When he ran in the "Intercalated Games" in Athens in 1906, stomach problems or a cramp forced him out of the marathon, though he never had the five-minute lead that Wikipedia claims; ominously, dehydration may have been a factor. And when the Italian trial was held for the 1908 Olympics, now transferred from Rome to London, he failed to qualify and had to be granted a solo time trial.

It's little exaggeration to say he became world famous as the hero of that disastrous Olympic hour on July 24, 1908. He was immediately recruited for professional races in New York, which will make him one of the stars of the next chapter. Now in his mid-twenties, he interrupted that hectic series of professional races to visit home and marry Teresa Dondi. He won seventeen of twenty-two professional races in America, although, typically, the song Irving Berlin wrote about him was about another humiliating collapse ("Dorando he's a-droppa" – see Chapter 8).

After 1909, he was based back in Italy, but running internationally; his last marathon was in Buenos Aires in 1910, and his last race in Gothenburg in 1911. He retired well placed financially, but that luck couldn't last: his first investment was in a hotel that went bankrupt. He eventually settled to work in the car garage business, in San Remo, on the sunny Mediterranean near the French border. He died there on February 7, 1942.

Even then, confusion and error could still follow him. At the time of the 1948 Olympic Games in London, six years after Pietri's death, an Italian who owned a café in Birmingham convinced newspapers that he was Dorando Pietri. He was showered with the publicity he sought, and arrangements were made to have him run a lap of honor at those post-war Olympics. Probably the British organizers were glad to have an Italian celebrity free of connection with World War II. But with no explanation offered, the arrangements were dropped. It's possible the imposter was in fact the Pietri half-brother who was living in England in 1908, and acted as interpreter at the height of Pietri's media fame. Perhaps something was again lost in translation.

A hundred years on, the fascination of the public struggle between the "set purpose" of this small, determined man and his "exhausted frame" has made him legendary, especially in Italy. In 2008, the town of Carpi put great energy into commemorating the centenary of his day of fame.

Only the Italians could orchestrate such a choric paean of triumph. In a commemorative version of Carpi's annual marathon, all runners wore his bib number, 19, and received a special T-shirt. At a prominent location in the town center, a specially commissioned statue was unveiled on July 24, 2008, a highly flattering representation, handsome and muscular, enlarged well above Pietri's actual skinny 5 ft. 2 in./1.55m, striding powerfully, showing no sign of tiredness, bare chested and bare footed, wearing only an orange cloth draped around his loins. Presumably the sculptor saw him as embodying the spirit of Pheidippides, perhaps influenced by the Steve Reeves pecs movie version. Members of the organizing committee for the Carpi celebrations were even granted an audience with Pope Benedict.

The 2008 London Marathon also commemorated the centenary, managing to borrow and display Pietri's gold-plated cup from Carpi, where it is stored. Re-enactments of the Pietri/Hayes finish were staged at the busy Expo, with a commentary that verged on the satiric. There was also a re-enacted run by two runners dressed as Pietri and Hayes from Windsor to the site of the White City on July 24, 2008.

Johnny Hayes

"Everyone in sport remembers Dorando, but no one remembers the winner Hayes," Ivano Barbolini, coordinator of the Carpi centenary committee, told Reuters in 2008. Hayes was not a self-promoter. Under 5 ft. 4 in., and a slight 125 pounds, he was usually described as quiet and mild-mannered. He was born April 10, 1886, probably in New York. His parents' previous home, Nenagh, Tipperary, makes some claim to him as a native son, with a bronze statue, running alongside two definitely Nenagh-born Olympians, a hurdler and a hammer thrower. There is no reference to the fact that Nenagh and Ireland were part of Great Britain in 1908.

Like Pietri, Hayes started as young as nineteen or twenty as a long-distance competitor. A member of the Irish-American A.C., he was also captain of the athletic club at Bloomingdale's Department Store in New York, where he worked. Usually he is described as a shipping clerk there, and supposedly trained on a cinder track on the roof of the Bloomingdale Building, specially installed to save interfering with his work in the store. Martin and Gynn question this true-blue amateur version, saying he did no active work for Bloomingdale's, but drew a salary that enabled him to train, most of which he did outside the city. If that is true, it is still an open question whether it made him more professional than Pietri, who ran for the Italian army for some time after 1904, or Tom Longboat, who reputedly was financed by patrons, and was established at one point as nominal manager of a Toronto tobacco store. Earlier, Hayes had done literally backbreaking work as a "sandhog," digging New York's subway tunnels, so he can be forgiven for enjoying whatever luxuries came with his Bloomingdale's employment. He became openly professional as a runner during the lucrative years of "Marathon Mania" (Chapter 8).

Hayes must have been a man of some intelligence and communication skills, since he was appointed a trainer for the U.S. team at the next Olympics, in 1912, despite strong prejudice in the sport's establishment against professionals. Later he taught physical education, as well as working in the food industry. He died in Englewood, New Jersey, on August 23, 1965, soon after Billy Mills and Bob Schul had become the first Americans since him to win Olympic gold medals in distance running events. The first American after Hayes to win the Olympic marathon was Frank Shorter in 1972. The Shore Athletic Club in New Jersey holds a collection of Hayes's memorabilia, which has enabled his Olympic gold medal to be on view on significant occasions, as when Hayes was inducted posthumously into the National Distance Running Hall of Fame in 2008. Material from this collection is available through www.runningpast.com.

The important thing in any account of Hayes is to give him credit for his astute pace judgment and strong finish in that London race. He deserves credit also for his calm and modest demeanor through all the hullabaloo and controversy that followed, including his VIP visit the next day to Britain's Parliament ("walking somewhat stiffly," reported the *New York Times*). Pietri's heroic status is assured; but there were two heroes that day.

Arthur Conan Doyle

A popular false belief is that Arthur Conan Doyle, creator of Sherlock Holmes, was one of the officials who helped Dorando Pietri get back on his feet after he collapsed, and then assisted him across the finish line, thus causing his disqualification. The error has been around for many years.: "Four times Dorando collapsed and each time helping hands – including those of Sherlock Holmes creator, Arthur Conan Doyle – reached out to rescue him from his sea of despair" (Giller, 1983).

Even more authoritative endorsement came in the biography of Conan Doyle by Martin Booth: "Some spectators, Conan Doyle amongst their number, guided and helped the exhausted and confused runner to the finishing line." In his picture caption, Booth then identifies Doyle as the burly man in a peaked cap and with an armband who is alongside Pietri in the famous finish-line photo (Booth, 1997). The story is repeated by such good running histories as Rob Hadgraft's life of Alf Shrubb, and David Martin and Roger Gynn's great work, *The Olympic Marathon*. They include a different photograph, showing Pietri in a state of collapse, with the burly man with the armband kneeling "to assist him…to his feet." Their caption again identifies this man as Doyle, "noted writer and creator of detective Sherlock Holmes" (Martin & Gynn, 2000).

And so history happens. Google "Pietri" with "Conan Doyle," and many websites include this specific identification, while most retell the story that Conan Doyle was one of those who lent a helping hand to the suffering Italian, thus causing his disqualification.

In age (Doyle was 49 in 1908), and build (Doyle was big, and a good boxer and footballer), and in facial appearance (Doyle wore a scrubbing-brush moustache, similar to that of the man with the armband), there is some resemblance, and as a famous British author, patriot, and sportsman, and as a qualified physician, Doyle might well have been among the Olympic officials. But Sherlock Holmes would not be satisfied with such first impressions. I decided to check further.

In the official Games report, an appendix lists each day's officials at every venue. Doyle is not among them. Nor is he listed anywhere as a "medical attendant." Most of the officials for the marathon were provided by the Polytechnic Harriers Club, which was delegated to take full responsibility for the marathon race by the Olympic Organizing Committee. The club's Honorary General Secretary, J.M. (Jack) Andrew, headed the marathon team. Doyle was not a member of Poly (as the club is known), nor of any running club. He had no status that would have given him access to the stadium and an armband to wear.

Since Doyle was a writer, I checked on what he might have written. Elementary. There he is, present at the Pietri incident, not as an official but covering the Marathon for the *Daily Mail* as a special celebrity correspondent. He makes a fine sports journalist, too, as you might expect, since he wrote excellent sporting short stories, about boxing, hunting and cricket.

Doyle's report on the Pietri marathon is the most compelling and convincing I know among the thousands of accounts of that memorable race. It employs the strong physical language that makes the Sherlock Holmes stories so vivid. He writes of Pietri's "haggard, yellow face" and "glazed, expressionless eyes." He captures his stumbling movement in phrases like "furious yet uncertain gait," or "the red legs broke into their strange automatic amble." He writes in a dramatic present tense, like a live broadcaster: "Surely he is done now. He cannot rise again." And Doyle perfectly summarizes the visceral appeal of the episode in the phrase I have taken as the title for this chapter: "It is horrible yet fascinating, this struggle between a set purpose and an utterly exhausted frame."

So where, exactly, was Doyle at the time? In his little-known autobiography, he says, "I do not often do journalistic work...but on the occasion of the Olympic Games of 1908 I was tempted, chiefly by the offer of an excellent seat, to do the Marathon Race for the *Daily Mail*" (Doyle, 1924). One sentence in his report confirms his location during Pietri's heart-rending last collapse.

"He was within a few yards of my seat. Amid stooping figures and grasping hands I caught a glimpse of the haggard, yellow face, the glazed, expressionless eyes, the lank black hair streaked across the brow."

So Doyle had an excellent seat in the stand, with a close-up view of the beginning of the short final straight (where Pietri fell for the last time). He wasn't jogging alongside Pietri's final staggering steps to the finish. In the photograph of the last fall, the burly chap with the cap and the armband who has so often been identified as Doyle was actually holding and lifting the collapsed runner. He was one of the "stooping figures" who almost blocked Doyle's view.

A wedding photo from 1907 shows Doyle as a well-built, upstanding man, but not as broad and bulky as the man with the armband, nor as heavily jowled, and probably taller. His eyebrows are fine and high-arched, not bushy. His moustache is trimmed differently, too, into sharp downward points, probably waxed – and later photos show he retained that style. The two are similar at a quick glance, but they are not the same man.

Turning my Holmesian magnifying glass to the big man's armband, I was excited to discern the first letters on the lower line as "ATTE... " which Sherlock Holmes fans will instantly remember as the beginning of the mysterious message sent by candle-flame in "The Adventure of the Red Circle," the Italian warning "Attenta." But Pietri was not victim of a Mafia revenge squad. On the upper line of the armband you can pick out "ME," the beginning of the humble English phrase "Medical Attendant." The burly man is without doubt Dr. M.J. Bulger, the marathon's medical officer, who was there helping Pietri throughout. In the photos he holds a roll or tube of paper in his left hand, possibly (though this is my speculation) shaped into a long funnel through which a restorative powder could be administered. The official race instructions state "stimulants will be available in case of collapse," although otherwise, "No competitor may take or receive any drug."

The other man, the thinner one, wearing the straw boater (hat) and carrying the megaphone is Jack Andrew, the race director or "chief clerk," although Martin and Gynn, or their caption writer, identify him wrongly as Dr. Bulger. A sash diagonally from across his right shoulder suggests he is a senior official, and the ribbon around his hat is not just a decoratively speckled band, but identifies him as "Chief Clerk," or officially "Chief Clerk of the Course."

Case solved. Since I published an early form of this Holmesian investigation in 2007, David Davis reached the same conclusion in his meticulously researched *Showdown at Shepherd's Bush*.

Doyle did go on to play a more active role in the Pietri story. He used his *Daily Mail* column inches to initiate a subscription for the unfortunate near-winner. Doyle's collection raised three hundred pounds, mostly from Italians in London, supposedly enabling Pietri to open his own baker's shop back home in Italy. In fact, Pietri promptly turned professional and made a lot more than three hundred pounds.

It's almost certainly another error, however, to claim that it was Doyle who "prompted" Queen Alexandra to present Pietri with an inscribed "replica" of the winner's gold cup, as is stated by Martin and Gynn, in their *The Marathon Footrace*. Doyle was not an aristocrat (he was knighted in 1902), and came from an Irish Catholic family. The rigidity of the English class system makes it unlikely that he could have access to the Queen within the few hours before the announcement that she wanted to make a special award. And the engraved gold cup she gave Pietri was not a "replica" of the winner's award.

I must add a new literary discovery. Doyle did one thing for Dorando Pietri's memory that only a best-selling writer could do: he paid tribute by using his name in a story. At exactly the time of the Olympic marathon, July 24, 1908, Doyle was working on the last stages of the Sherlock Holmes story, "The Adventure of Wisteria Lodge." It was first published in *Collier's* magazine in America on August 15, and in U.K. in *The Strand Magazine*, in two installments in September and October. In book form, the story was included in *His Last Bow: The War Service of Sherlock Holmes* (1917); the American edition was sub-titled *Some Reminiscences of Sherlock Holmes*.

Holmes and Dr. Watson investigate a "grotesque" murder, which turns out to be consequent on a failed revenge attempt against Don Murillo, whose evil past life was as the "bloodthirsty tyrant" of a small Central

American state. When Don Murillo's brutalities are explained, Doyle needed a name for a tragic victim of political murder, whose death in San Pedro has prompted his widow, an Englishwoman, to enter Murillo's employment and guide the would-be assassin to him. The name Doyle chose was "Victor Durando." As explained above, Pietri was then known only as "Dorando" or "Durando."

What is significant is that when Doyle needed a name for a man who displayed courage under suffering, it was the gallant hero he had so recently watched at the Great White City who came into his head. From the publication date, he must have written that last part of the story only a day or so after covering the marathon.

And the name "Victor" of course means exactly that: the winner. Doyle used a Sherlock Holmes story to make a coded affirmation of the British view that Dorando Pietri, not the American, was the true winner.

The Fascination of the Horrible

Newspapers were unanimous about the high excitement of the end of that marathon, "the most thrilling athletic event" since the death of Pheidippides, claimed the *New York Times* next day. As Doyle shrewdly identified, it had the dark fascination we all feel in watching the struggle of the human will to overcome physical exhaustion. The drama accrued significance because it was played out in front of the biggest roadside and stadium crowds in sports history to that date, and received the full attention of the biggest ever gathering of the world's media.

There was the added appeal that endurance athletes at that time were venturing into the unknown. Knowledge of what causes a runner to collapse was primitive, and included a good measure of sheer superstition. Dehydrated runners were given champagne or strychnine, in attempts at stimulation. One report said that Pietri took tablets of atropine and strychnine while crossing Wormwood Scrubs, not far from the stadium. Dr. Bulger declared Pietri to be "quite pulseless" the first time he collapsed, which seems unlikely. The official report quoted another doctor, who examined Pietri at the hospital, as pronouncing,

"His heart had been more than half an inch displaced." How did he know exactly where it had been to begin with?

It didn't dawn on any of them that on such a hot day the runners simply didn't drink enough water.

Alongside the thrill, some found the whole spectacle so "horrible," "painful," or "deplorable," that they questioned "whether so great a trial of human endurance should be sanctioned" (Daily News). The horror of Pietri's supposed near-death lay behind many such calls for sanctions throughout the early history of the marathon.

Postscript

That 1908 race is one of the greatest stories in sport, and quickly became almost mythic. The word "marathon" entered the English language (and other languages, of course). After the Greek victory of Spyridon Louis in 1896, the phrase "marathon race" (soon just "marathon") denoted the new sporting event, with added associations of long and heroic effort. After Pietri, it took on the extra meanings of a struggle against exhaustion, or gallantly surviving long-term difficulty. The word was applied outside running for the first time only four months later, when the London *Daily Chronicle* reported a potato-peeling contest named "The Murphy Marathon" (Nov 5, 1908). It entered literature the next year, in England and America. In H.G. Wells's novel *The History of Mr. Polly* (published in 1910), a criminal called Uncle Jim warns Mr. Polly off his patch, appearing one evening while Polly is taking his walk. Wells spares the reader Jim's more colorful adjectives.

> Mr. Polly…quickened his pace.
> *"Arf a mo'," said Uncle Jim, taking his arm. "We*
> *ain't doing a (sanguinary) Marathon. It ain't a*
> *(decorated) cinder track. I want a word with you,*
> *mister. See?"*

If the low-life Uncle Jim, or the non-sporting H.G. Wells, knew about the marathon, and could use it as a joke that would be picked up by a wide readership, it had arrived. The American usage was a topical reference to the marathon craze of 1908-1910, and came in another 1910 novel, *The Fortune Hunter* by Louis Joseph Vance, based on a Broadway play by Winchell Smith (1909): "I feel like a two-year-old. I could do a Marathon without turning a hair."

The public therefore knew about marathons and their demands. The controversial rivalry between Pietri and Hayes was too compelling to let go. Both were quickly signed by an enterprising New York promoter for a head-to-head race in November 1908. Pietri gave up his amateur status and endorsed Bovril (a beef tea drink) as the secret of his rapid recovery. That was another shaft for the Olympic race organizers, who had sponsorship from the rival Oxo. Tom Longboat, the native Canadian Boston record-breaker, who had a bad day in London, also declared himself available for prize-money racing. So did England's Fred Appleby, another star who had failed in the Olympics. So did an exciting new name to the marathon, Alf Shrubb of England, multiple world-record holder on the track and the world's greatest cross-country runner.

The author of the official report on the 1908 Olympics, still displeased by the marathon's outcome, grumpily dismissed what he called "the epidemic of 'Marathon Races' which attacked the civilised world from Madison Square Garden to the Valley of the Nile" (Cook, 1909). He could have added Milan, Cape Town, Melbourne, and Invercargill. The "epidemic" was in fact the first great running boom. For three years, it enthralled huge crowds and played out as one of the most colorful stories in sports history. By November 1908, Pietri, Hayes, Longboat, Appleby and Shrubb were all in New York. An all-star cast was ready for the greatest show in town.

Chapter 8

Marathon Mania – New York 1908-1911

800 BC   100 AD   1719   1896   1908   1928   1936   1964   1984   2021

For the great majority of adults . . . to take part in a Marathon race is to risk serious and permanent injury to health, with immediate death a danger not very remote...

New York Times, February 24, 1909

The world was fascinated by the near-death drama at the Great White City on July 24, 1908. Foot-racing (and the associated betting) was already big spectator entertainment, but Dorando Pietri's heroic struggle in front of that huge London Olympic crowd made the marathon a new kind of gladiatorial spectacle. The story could not end so tamely, with Pietri getting a consolation cup, and Olympic champion Johnny Hayes being carried off on a table.

Within days, an Irish American entrepreneur named Pat Powers made Pietri and Hayes offers they couldn't refuse to give up their amateur status and stage a re-run for New York's betting-crazy crowds. Being Italian and Irish-American made them doubly attractive in a city whose immigrant workforce was drawn largely from those two groups, often as rowdy rivals.

Bloomingdale Brothers did their best to retain their famous employee, Johnny Hayes, the new Olympic marathon champion. They resplendently decorated their huge department store building for Hayes's return to

Manhattan, and announced a sinecure promotion for him to be "manager of sporting goods." But neither that lure, nor the funds raised by Conan Doyle to help Pietri to a life of cake-making in Carpi, could stand against Powers's offer. The two runners accepted the challenge, the fame, and the money. That decision marked the beginning of three years of high-profile marathon racing, focused on the East Coast of America, arousing huge public interest, and spurring an upsurge in standards among elite runners. It was also the last flourishing of professional running until the 1980s.

First, as soon as it could happen, the public wanted Hayes and Pietri, racing head-to-head, over the exact marathon distance. ("Exact" was a new concept.) Powers staged the rematch indoors, with spectator tickets at a premium, more like a boxing world championship than what we think of as a running event. Hovering in the wings, ready to challenge whoever emerged as champion, were Tom Longboat, with the exotic appeal of being indigenous (a Canadian Onondaga Indian, "a Redman"), and Alfred Shrubb, the greatest runner of the decade from one mile to fifteen miles, who had dominated the American/Canadian professional circuit over those distances for two years.

It's hard now to realize that running at that time was mass-scale entertainment. Even before the London Olympics made the marathon into the glamor event, the big star races, usually man against man, often nominally amateur, were promoted with the kind of celebrity sensationalism that these days boosts the fame of rock singers, movie stars, and British royalty. Rob Hadgraft's book on Alf Shrubb recounts how Tom Flanagan, Longboat's creative Irish-Canadian manager, entered Longboat for an officially amateur race in Montreal called Round the Mountain, and stirred up publicity and the betting with a story of how Shrubb was going to run the course an hour after the amateurs and beat their time. Shrubb went along with the fiction (he never revealed whether he was paid) but had no intention of running. After the race, he met Flanagan by arrangement in a bar, where Flanagan first winked and then slapped his face in feigned anger about his being a professional. Later Flanagan had a cartoon on his office wall that read "Flanagan hits Shrubb in the interests of amateur sport."

Now Power was chasing the ultimate promoter's dream: the race to settle all the arguments about who really deserved to win in London. With luck, the loser would collapse in exhaustion. That's what the punters wanted, the fascinating struggle again, and near-death collapse. For maximum gate money, Power booked Madison Square Garden, then a splendid classical building with columns like an Italian palace, at Fourth Avenue and 27th Street. It had vast spectator space, holding an estimated 16,000, many in standing room, with trackside boxes for the wealthy. But it provided only a tiny, dusty indoor track 176 yards/161 meters around, ten laps to the mile. That meant 262 dizzying laps for the magic 26 miles, 385 yards.

The posters called it "America vs. Italy" as well as Hayes vs. Dorando. Part of the poster was in Italian. Turbulent crowds jammed the hall to the roof, waving Italian, Irish, and American flags and making the air thick with pungent tobacco smoke. Rival bands tried to make themselves heard, an Italian group pumping out rollicking and romantic tunes for Pietri, and the stirring brass band of the 69th Regiment thumping out military marches and Irish melodies for Hayes. The crowd was in a frenzy, especially the Italians, exuberantly chanting "Dorando! Dorando!" and "Viva Italia!" It was, the *New York Times* reported, "the most remarkable exhibition that Madison Square Garden has ever witnessed in all its years as the greatest show place in New York." That is saying a lot, for two small slight men side-by-side in their baggy shorts, ready to run 262 laps in a smoke-filled arena.

It was November 25, 1908, four months almost to the day after the London Olympic Marathon. The era of Marathon Mania was about to begin.

****

The Most Spectacular Foot Race Ever: Hayes versus Pietri, Madison Square Garden, November 25, 1908

"It was the most spectacular foot race that New York ever has witnessed," declared the *New York Times* next morning (November 26). It progressed as a battle of attrition. For twenty-four miles, Pietri led by a stride. Hayes doggedly followed. Lap after lap, they tried to wear each other down. The tension was sometimes broken by an occasional tactical burst, a surprise surge, as one man or the other tried to force a break, or at least grab the psychological initiative – always unsuccessfully. Each time, like cyclists slotting back into the orderly peleton, they quickly resumed their positions, Pietri pattering on relentlessly in front, Hayes treading in his fresh footprints in the dust, round and round and round and round. Both seemed to look only inward.

The atmosphere grew suffocating as the dust and tobacco smoke swirled. The crowd watched and murmured and tried to sustain some cheering through the gray haze. Each attacking surge was greeted with rapture by the Italians or the Irish, and the suspense never lagged. After they passed twenty miles (two hundred laps), Hayes was perceptibly tiring, but hung there, and increasingly threw in spurts to try to break Pietri. Each was short-lived, and Hayes dropped back to one stride behind the pattering Italian. A bit before twenty-five miles, with twelve laps to go, Hayes surged again, and he was in front across the finish line for the first time, after following Pietri across it 249 times.

But they had to pass it seven times more. However vehemently the Irish-American crowd tried to lift him, it was Hayes's last gasp. He faltered. It was only half a stride, but Pietri sensed the weakness (competitive runners are like hunting cheetahs in that ability). He picked up the pace, and opened the first real gap. Hayes was two yards back, then three. After two and a half hours of simmering suspense, the stadium erupted into five minutes of bedlam.

Now Pietri had the race won, exuberantly racing, moving always farther ahead of the struggling Hayes, clicking off the laps. Yet disaster tried to strike him again. As in London, the extra 385 yards were nearly

Pietri's undoing. At twenty-six miles (260 laps), he was in front by thirty yards and running strongly. But his Italian fans, believing the race was ending at 26 miles (and why not?), scrambled in chaotic triumph out of the stands, and surged on to the track to surround him, pat him, embrace him. Police and officials desperately tried to keep the tiny circuit clear, blows were struck (as the *Times* discreetly put it), and the whole place was on the edge of a full riot as the little hero wove and dodged his last two laps through a precarious narrow lane cleared by fist-swinging police. He made it, finishing in 2:44:20.4. Poor weary Hayes had to push through the full dense mass of the crowd as it closed in behind Pietri, and made it in 2:45:03.2.

Those times, over the now-accepted marathon distance, eleven minutes faster than they ran on the hot and dusty roads of London in July, are worth pausing to consider. On the tight curves of a 176-yard circuit, a surface of loose dirty sand and in a haze of smoke and dust, they are very impressive: 6 min 16 sec per mile. The skeptic in me wonders about the rigor of track measurement at that date; one yard short per lap would amount to 276 yards. But how accurate was Jack Andrew's measuring of the London course? How did he measure it? In those days, it's all a gray area.

But even allowing that it has to be called approximate, a time of 2:44 was mighty impressive in those conditions. And there was nothing uncertain about the quality of the race, or the commitment they both gave to it. These two small, determined, and very fit men were the real thing by any marathon standards. They ran to their strengths, they judged it right, they threw every tactic at each other, and overall they put on a wonderful contest, as great as you could hope to see at any time in marathon history. The outcome seemed just revenge for Pietri, perhaps proving him the true winner in London. His fans thought so. Many a poor Italian immigrant was lifted by his victory. Many staked their savings, perhaps their barber's shop, on his next race.

****

Dorando He's a Drop! Pietri versus Longboat, Madison Square Garden, December 15, 1908

Pietri had only three weeks to recover. No one then understood the long-term effects of hard marathon racing, the microscopic muscle damage, the glycogen loss, the battered immune system. Tom Longboat was ready, the crowds were eager, and champions in those days were there to be challenged. So Longboat challenged, and Pietri defended.

It was this next race, not the London Olympics or the vengeance over Hayes, that inspired the popular comic vaudeville song, "Dorando." It is sung in the supposed voice of a poor stage-Italian barber, who is so patriotically passionate for Pietri that he "sell da barber shop, And make da bet Dorando he's a win." Among the frenzied Italian crowd in Madison Square Garden, the song's character cheers for his hero, who carries the barber's entire savings on his back. The fan's hopes are high as "He run-a, run-a, run-a, Run like anything. One-a, two-a hundred times around da ring." But he can only watch in despair, as "Just then, Dorando he's a-drop! Good-bye, poor old barber's shop."

The song capitalized on the huge public interest in the continuing story of the marathon, and the colorful characters who were enacting it. The words and music were by a little-known thirty-year-old composer, born in Russia, named Isadore Baline. Two years later he wrote "Alexander's Ragtime Band," under his better-known pen name, Irving Berlin. "Dorando" is not as memorable as Berlin's "White Christmas" or "God Bless America," but it's evidence of the impact Marathon Mania made on popular culture.

Like the Pietri/Hayes contest three weeks earlier, the race for almost all the distance seemed too close to call. Pietri again led, staying there for twenty-five miles/250 laps. Several reports describe how smooth and controlled Longboat looked, and how confidently he seemed to choose the moment to strike, with eleven laps or just over one mile to go. Much taller than the Italian, with a loping stride, often smiling as he ran, Longboat liked to play the innocent, but he was an astute tactician who had come down from Ontario to win the Boston Marathon at age nineteen. He was exceptionally well prepared for the marathon in those light-training days, logging long runs alongside the Grand River on the Six Nations Reserve near Brantford. He had been unwell at the London Olympics. Now was his moment.

Pietri clung for three more laps, but it became futile. His energy reserves, depleted by two hard marathons in twenty days, ran out, and he staggered, then stumbled, and finally fell to the track exhausted. "Dorando he's a-drop!" Dismay spread among the Italian supporters, and the Indian war whoop of triumph from Longboat's fans drowned out the fading cries of "Viva Italia!" Longboat, who after his failure in London had been scorned as the "tottering Indian," and his defeat taken as proof of the unreliability of his race, was now "the stout-hearted redman," and "the greatest distance runner of the age."

The crowd had enjoyed another dramatic race. But they also wanted public suffering. Even the *New York Times* wrung the utmost sensation from Pietri's exhaustion.

"There was a glassy stare in Dorando's eyes as his brother and a trainer rushed to the track to help him to his feet. He fell back helpless... too far gone to speak...As he was carried to his dressing room he fainted, and was unconscious for some time."

Journalistic exaggeration, yes, but isn't there also, though I hesitate to suggest it, a possibility that Pietri was a bit of a thespian? In London there are those scraps of evidence that he was never as totally unconscious as he looked. He kept hold of his grip and handkerchief through all the collapses, and in hospital later he was only "almost" incapable of answering questions. Next day he was sprightly. However exhausted, it's just possible, especially this time in front of his fans, that he made the most of it. Whatever the truth, it was great theater.

There was just as much drama that night off the track. Swindlers took advantage of the throngs of Italians desperate to get into the Garden, many with limited English, and sold them thousands of phony tickets, mostly for a roller-skating event held the previous month. Disappointed Italians do not go quietly. Angry crowds clogged the gates, refusing to accept that the tickets they had paid for were worthless. Masses more, with fake or genuine tickets, fought to get past them to reach the entrance. People were wedged so tight that it was impossible to raise an arm, said the *New York Times*. Just as well, perhaps, when the fights broke out. It took an hour, police reinforcements, and finally the mounted squad, to restore order.

There was no television coverage or live streaming. The public without tickets had to gather in Times Square to follow the progress of the race on the newspaper's bulletin boards. People pouring out of Broadway theaters got some free extra drama, joining the cheering throng in front of the bulletin window just as the runners entered their sensational last mile. The streets and sidewalks were jammed, streetcars and all traffic halted, and only the final bulletin of Longboat's winning time (2:45:05) enabled police to clear a narrow lane to let passersby move along.

As with Irving Berlin's Italian barber, this public interest was not entirely purist. There was heavy betting. Pietri started as very much the favorite after his victory over Hayes. Longboat perhaps conspired to preserve his outsider status, and his racially stereotyped reputation for unreliability, by losing a race against obscure opposition in Philadelphia a few days beforehand.

But if the odds were manipulated, the race itself was for real. The first two indoor challenge marathons had deepened the grip of Marathon Mania, which was enthralling the public and the media, and producing its celebrities. Three very different men in four months had in turn proven themselves king of the marathon, each attracting their own fan-base: the New York Irish sandhogger Hayes, the valiant-against-disaster Italian Pietri, and the amiable but enigmatic First Nations "redman" Longboat.

And now, looking for even more sensation, and yet another challenger to seize the crown as king of the marathon, Pat Powers signed up Alf Shrubb.

Marathon Mania Afloat: On Board the USS Wyoming, Christmas Morning, 1908

History's first Christmas Day marathon, and first marathon afloat, was run when eleven American sailors set out to race the full 26.2 miles

144

around the deck of the warship Wyoming, at anchor at Mare Island, near San Francisco. The ship was being refitted to be powered by fuel oil, and was about to be renamed the Cheyenne.

The lap round the deck was 130 yards, making a mind-numbing 355 circuits. Understandably, only two men finished, and the winner, who deserves to be recorded, was J.P. White. No rank or time is given, but he somehow managed to shine again in other festive shipboard contests during that Christmas afternoon.

Bishop's Move: Tom Longboat's Wedding, Toronto, December 26, 1908

The marathon, although it took a while to welcome women, has from the start been open to all comers, whatever their social status or ethnicity. Not always so the church. Native Canadian Tom Longboat's hope to marry Lauretta Maracle, a white schoolteacher of Indian children, in a Christian Anglican service, was blocked by the archbishop on the grounds that the runner's "change from heathendom to Christianity at Deseronto last week was not sincere" (*The New York Times*, December 27, 1908). It sounds racist, or at the very least demeaning. Tom Flanagan, Longboat's inventive Irish-Canadian manager, protested loudly.

Even Flanagan could not have set up an archbishop, disappointed a bride, and arranged the media coverage, for the publicity. Could he?

The marriage went ahead later, was successful, but ended sadly: see Longboat note below.

Ice, Slush, Crowds, and a Record: Rye to Columbus Circle Marathon, December 26, 1908

The marathon returned to the roads, a point-to-point course, and amateurism, on the same day that Tom Longboat hoped to be married. The record for 26 miles, 385 yards was taken under 2:40, in an extraordinary run by Matthew Maloney of New York's Trinity Athletic Club.

Despite roads deep and slippery in slush and mud, and for the greater part covered by frozen snow, Maloney won by nine minutes in

2:36:26.2. It was an amateur race from Rye that came down Seventh Avenue, crossed on 110th Street, and finished down Central Park West at Columbus Circle, at the office of the *New York Evening Journal*, the race sponsor. So 1976 was not the first time a marathon was run through the midtown streets of New York. The "immense crowds" also matched today's. They lined the entire route, many chased in pursuit of the runners in newfangled automobiles, and they arrived so early and in such numbers at the best viewing positions in the last five miles that the police had difficulty keeping streets open. Even the field, 109 starters on a cold day, was large by any standards pre-1976. It could have been much larger, as more than four hundred would-be competitors were excluded on grounds of "physical fitness." There is no record of how that was ascertained.

The course was "carefully measured by a corps of civil engineers, accompanied by representatives of the AAU," reported the objective *New York Times*, which expressed confidence that the distance was legitimate. Others were dubious, and I'm with them, as I am about all course measurements in this era.

Maloney's performance, if over the full distance, would represent a remarkable improvement, especially on such bad footing. His marathon debut had been disastrous, in a fog-shrouded Yonkers race a month earlier, November 26, 1908, ending with him collapsed (yet another) on the track. An Irishman (yet another) who emigrated from County Clare three years earlier, Maloney was a "mild-mannered youth of 21," popular with his club, a non-drinking bartender who had given up his job to train for the marathon after a career as a strong but never a star runner. Six weeks earlier he had run well in a junior cross-country championship, which probably helped him in the December 26 marathon, when the snow and slush were sometimes almost ankle-deep.

Maloney took the lead at nine miles from his only serious competitor, James (misreported as being named Mike) Crowley of the Irish-American A.A.C.. Maloney dropped him at the Harlem River, and finished well. Crowley struggled to keep moving, barely able to stay on his feet, staggering unsteadily through the crowd at the finish. Maloney meanwhile "capered about," posed for photographs and waited to encourage many of the finishers.

Once again the marathon displayed its hallmark, the fine line between triumphant achievement and despairing collapse, the public's eager interest in the juxtaposition of victory and failure. Once again, crowds were enthralled by "the fascinating struggle between a set purpose and an utterly exhausted frame." And once again, new standards were set in human capability. In exactly one month, from November 26 to December 26, three great marathon races, all in New York City, had made the new distance one of the world's great sporting challenges.

Footnote: After the Rye to Columbus Circle race, there were angry protests when the "cup trophies" that the race had advertised for the first fifteen home were replaced, except for first and second, by medals, not even inscribed. The change aroused "bitter comment," and the athletes (all pure amateurs) at first refused to accept the medals until reassured that the AAU would provide the missing cups. Race directors take note: come not between runners and their bling.

And Maloney, loyal club man and amateur though he was, promptly turned pro and won a well-paid match-race marathon against the champion of Ireland, Patrick White. Amateurism (as Oscar Wilde said about truth) is rarely pure and never simple.

Dorando's Double: January 11 and 22, 1909

His latest collapse did not deter the irrepressible Dorando (as his fans and the newspapers invariably called Pietri). Four weeks after the defeat by Longboat, he was back on an indoor track to run a full marathon, and yet another only eleven days after that. His Italian devotees wanted to see him win, and were not too critical when he was matched with relatively weak opponents. He now seemed immune to the draining effects of running top-level marathons. He beat Percy Smallwood of Philadelphia in 2:44:32.4 and Albert Corey of Chicago in 2:56:00.4. Corey limped off the track, "distressed and labored," at nineteen miles. Pietri was described as "seemingly fresh and strong."

There was another good amateur marathon, too, when Robert Fowler won the Yonkers Empire City Marathon on the roads on January 1 in 2:52:45. But the marathon was waiting for Alf Shrubb.

Grim and Gritty, Stirring and Heart-Throbbing: Longboat versus Shrubb, Madison Square Garden, February 5, 1909

Alf Shrubb was Pat Powers's greatest coup since Marathon Mania began. A rural builder from Horsham, south of London, Shrubb was the world's greatest runner. A contemporary account called him, "the most extraordinary athlete the world has ever seen, a slight, almost flimsy-looking little fellow...the mystery is...where he packs all his lung power away...he must be the most scientifically-trained runner who has ever taken to either the track or cross-country" (Murray, 1908). He dominated amateur competitions on track and cross-country in the first few years of the twentieth century, though as a mere builder he was disapproved of by those who tried in that era to limit amateur athletics to "gentlemen," and exclude working men. Thanks to intelligent training far ahead of anything being done in the universities, Shrubb won the first two International Cross Country Championships, in 1903 and 1904, and in those same years set at least fifteen world records on the track, from one and a half miles to one hour. He was so far ahead of his time that some of his records lasted for decades. His six miles in 29:59:04, for instance, stood as the world record for twenty-six years, and thirty-two years as the British record; and his ten miles in 50:40.6 lasted twenty-four years as the world mark. Few runners today can match those times.

In 1905, at the peak of his success (and probably because of that) Shrubb was suddenly banned as an amateur, for receiving excess expenses. He was exposed and condemned by the same officials who had paid him the money, an act of mind-boggling duplicity equaled only by the similar disqualification of Wes Santee in America later in the twentieth century – see Chapter 11.

Defiantly, Shrubb took himself to America and its thriving professional circuit, where no one worried about your accent or pedigree. He quickly triumphed at every distance from one to fifteen miles. In 1908, he took on a relay of five top American runners over ten miles at Boston's Park Square Coliseum, and beat them in 51:33.4, still a time that would win many ten-mile races, and even more impressive on a tight indoor track with no banking against opponents running only two miles each. His only loss was in Winnipeg, Canada, over ten miles, against a horse called Patsey, the top local trotter, who beat him "in a desperate finish, by 15 yards."

Shrubb was a pioneer of twice-daily training, and author of a coaching book that was influential for half a century. He belongs with Paavo Nurmi and Emil Zátopek as one of the true greats of early running history, and only his exclusion from the 1908 London Olympics left him unrecognized as that. He could have won five gold medals (1500m, 5 miles, steeplechase, and 3 miles individual and team). When Marathon Mania broke out soon after those Olympics, he was a paid coach at Harvard University. Unbeaten by all comers up to fifteen miles, the greatest runner the world had seen at those distances, he felt confident, at age twenty-nine, about triumphing in the new phenomenon, the marathon. Like many before and since, he was to learn how very much longer it is than fifteen miles, and what different skills it requires.

Well capable of running fourteen miles in training at 5:30/mile pace (he did exactly that on February 2, 1909), Shrubb's insistence on going out fast in every race undid him in the marathon. This time he had to go on into what we now know is glycogen-deficiency territory. We find it utterly predictable that to run your first mile in 4:52, as Shrubb did against Longboat at Madison Square Garden, will lead to disaster after twenty miles if you haven't done extended endurance training. Round tight bends and on a surface of crushed cinders, he was running 2:09 marathon pace in days when the best ever was 2:36, and his own longest run was an hour short of what was needed. We call it "hitting the wall," that moment when the glycogen goes empty, and we have learned the hard way that we must train the body beforehand to cope with depletion, by switching to burning fat, among other conditioned responses. Teddy Flack had suffered under the same harsh realities in 1896 (chapter 6).

Shrubb's book was written before his chastening experiences on the professional marathon circuit, before Dorando Pietri shocked the world by showing how exhausting the marathon can be. Shrubb was disparaging about the marathon, writing that "the course is much less severe than many people imagine," and the current amateur record of 2:51:23 is "nothing so wonderful." His advice is to develop "staying power" by "a sixteen-mile walk three or four times a week," with eight-mile runs, and one sixteen-mile run. Not a bad formula for a beginner's half-marathon, perhaps, but it lacks any practice in depletion, any real endurance miles, and looks a perfect plan for even the greatest runner in the world to hit the wall at about 20 miles.

Shrubb also badly misjudged his pace. His chapter on the marathon sensibly advocates "a long, steady stride – one that you can keep up indefinitely," but he failed to follow that good advice in the fervor of Madison Square Garden. Shrubb ran the intermediate splits, up to twenty-three miles, faster than anyone had ever done in a marathon. It's testimony to his quality that he lasted so far. But winning a race isn't about leading for nine-tenths of the way. He was never credited with those split times because he failed to finish. It was Longboat, scorned for being erratic, who understood that the marathon distance is a far horizon and requires calm patience, not aggressiveness. Longboat logged training runs up to fifty miles, and when he won Boston in 1907, he didn't take the lead until after seventeen miles. And the marathon now was more than a mile longer than Boston in 1907.

This time Longboat wasn't even sticking close behind Shrubb, as he did with Pietri in December. He had to endure the wrath of the Madison Square Garden crowd as he plodded unexcitingly along while Shrubb zoomed confidently farther and farther ahead. Even when a lissome Indian squaw in full fringed costume appeared alongside to urge him on, he declined to respond. Lauretta, described as "his little white wife," appeared at the side of the track to inspire him, but he still didn't attack. The crowd wanted action.

Nevertheless, even as Shrubb kept adding to his huge lead, lap after lap, Longboat was winning the race. That's how the marathon often works. At seventeen miles, the Canadian had been eight laps behind, four-fifths of a mile. On a road course, Shrubb would have been well out of sight. Longboat waited. After twenty miles, when Shrubb finally began to falter, Longboat got hissed and booed because he still refused to do more than what looked like jogging. But the gap now whittled down relentlessly. At twenty-one, Shrubb had trouble with his shoes, and lost more than a lap; at twenty-two, he had trouble keeping running; and at twenty-three, he was alternating walking with "running very feebly." The gap was down under two minutes.

Only a half mile later, after Shrubb had shuffled painfully forward at a slow walk, Longboat sailed past, and Madison Square Garden erupted. The crowd was "whooping and howling," now wildly encouraging the Indian underdog, rejecting the pre-race favorite, the seemingly arrogant Brit who had set out so ostentatiously to destroy him. The uproar was a mix of excitement and relief, after two hours of prolonged suspense. The great Madison Square Garden arena had seldom witnessed the like, "famous as it is for stirring and heart-throbbing events," reported the *New York Times* (February 6).

Shrubb's heart was throbbing pretty feebly. Only half a lap after he was passed, he slumped "limp and worn out" into the arms of his supporters. "I lay gasping on my back for four hours with two doctors in constant attendance. They told me afterwards I nearly pegged out." Longboat strode the last two miles at the same deceptively loping pace, reaching the line in 2:53:40.4.

Once more, a race between two excellent runners, "one of the great historic contests" (*The Times*, London), had revealed the two contrasting faces of the marathon. It was, wrote the *Evening Journal*, "a race that had sensational features and grim, grueling grit." Spectators once again witnessed triumph and despair in vivid close-up. The elemental struggle between those two human extremes sustained Marathon Mania into the next decade.

Fast Amateur Time by Crowley: New Haven, Connecticut, February 7, 1909

James Crowley was yet another Irish New Yorker who had tested Longboat in Quebec, when Longboat was still amateur, and placed second to Maloney on December 26. He briefly usurped the rapidly-moving crown of greatest marathoner with a spectacular 2:38:48 in an amateur indoor marathon, in the New Haven Armory. If the track was "found to be accurate, Crowley will indeed be regarded as the most wonderful middle-distance and marathon runner of the day," said the *New York Times* (February 8). He didn't feature again.

Police Swing into Action Against Reservoir Runner: New York City, February 8, 1909

S. Levy was arrested in New York "for using the Central Park Reservoir for cross-country running." (Presumably that means the path around the reservoir.) The previous year Alf Shrubb had a similar encounter while training there but used his speed and cross-country skills to elude the mounted cop who pursued him. These are the first known recorded instances of runners training in Central Park. These days the Reservoir path is one of the most heavily used running routes anywhere in the world.

Debilitation, Danger, and Death: The New York Times, February 24, 1909

In modern life, you don't often get the buzz of watching someone stagger helplessly about in advanced exhaustion, especially with the added interest that you may have staked your life's savings on whether or not he falls over. Every race in these first two epic months of Marathon Mania had the appeal of dicing with death, or at least extreme exhaustion,

Atalanta stoops,
Melanion runs on.
Guido Reni 1625.
Alamy

Wet ditch where Sam laid the
trail, 1852.
Courtesy of Roger Robinson

Edward Poynter, Atalanta, 1876.
Alamy

Paul Manship, "Running
Atalanta" Gilded bronze, 1958.
*Smithsonian American Art Museum:
Bequest of Paul Manship*

Peru: Inca messenger,
carrying information on
knotted strings.
Alamy

Thomas Yeates,
illustrations for Atalanta:
The Race Against Destiny,
by Justine and Ron Fontes.
Courtesy of Thomas Yeates

Japan: Running messengers.
Hokusai, One Hundred
Views of Mount Fuji, 1834.
Alamy

I Am The Only Running
Footman. Signboard,
1700s/1800s.
Alamy

James Steventon, British artist,
creates running performance art
in authentic footman costume.
Courtesy of James Steventon

Foxes or hares lay the trail,
late 1800s.

Alamy

Marathon village, second Greek
Trial, March 24, 1896. Spyridon
Louis in white in doorway.

Alamy

Samuel Butler, age 18,
stands alertly among friends.

*By permission of the Master and
Fellows of St John's College,
Cambridge*

Earliest image of cross-country
by schoolboy Sam Butler, March
1852. Never before published.

Courtesy of Shrewsbury School

Pietri, semi-conscious, supported
by Dr Bulger, 1908.

Alamy

Henri St Yves, surprise star
of Marathon Mania, 1909.

Alamy

Earliest image of cross-country by schoolboy Sam Butler, March 1852. Never before published.

Courtesy of Shrewsbury School

Olympic Marathon, 1896, probably Lermusiaux (France) leads Blake (USA), Levantris (Greece). Mounted, Colonel Papadiamontopoulos.

Alamy

Before the start, 1908 Olympic Marathon, Princess Mary and royal grandchildren.

Alamy

The famous finish: Race director Andrew supports Pietri, Dr. Bulger in attendance, 1908.

Alamy

Hayes finishes strongly, ignoring Andrew's proffered support.

Alamy

The Great Marathon Derby: Genial Tom Longboat, watchful Henri St Yves (striped gown), Dorando Pietri (spotted gown).

Alamy

World's six best marathon runners: (left to right) Shrubb, Pietri, St Yves, Longboat, Hayes, Maloney.

Alamy

Start of women's 800m, 1928 Olympics, nine fit and focused athletes.

© *Hulton Archive / Getty Images*

Midfield friendship of Long and Owens. Berlin, 1936.
Alamy

The "artistic creation" of Jack Lovelock (467), one lap to run, poised between Ny (575), Cunningham (746), and Beccali (331), 1936.
Alamy

Lina Radke leads Kinue Hitomi and Inga Gentzel, all under the world record, 1928.

© *Underwood Archives / Getty Images*

Bonding by competing: Sohn Kee Chung, 21, and Ernie Harper, 34, Olympic Marathon, 1936.

Alamy

Sohn Kee Chung as Korean national hero, Olympic Games, Seoul, 1988.

Alamy

Bannister's last stride into legend at 3:59.4, 1954.

Alamy

The second shove: Gammoudi pushes Mills, Clarke off camera, Temu being lapped, 1964.
Alamy

Roe, the new Atalanta, takes a corner, Auckland, 1984.
Courtesy of Tony Scott

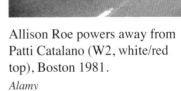

Out of the tunnel: Joan Benoit Samuelson wins first women's Olympic Marathon in 1984, Grete Waitz follows.
Alamy

Allison Roe powers away from Patti Catalano (W2, white/red top), Boston 1981.
Alamy

a two-hour-plus suspense drama climaxed by a sensational last act that set triumph alongside tribulation.

The *New York Times* decided to take a tone of moral disapproval toward the whole craze, which it had reported up to that point with such hyperbolic gusto. On February 24, 1909, it ran an editorial expressing "considerable apprehension about the sudden popularity of the so-called Marathon race" and its physical consequences ("serious and permanent injury to health...immediate death a danger not very remote.") "The chances are," the editorial intones, "that every one [who runs a marathon] weakens his heart and shortens his life." We know now that such warnings are mostly superstitious hooey. Unfortunately, six weeks later, on April 4, the *Times* was able to gloat that a successful English marathon runner, Frederick Rumsby, collapsed and died during a twenty-mile track race at Hull. His was, so far as I can establish, the only death in these years of frenzied Marathon Mania, despite the fact that none of the competitors could have experience of the weird new distance, and few were by modern standards sufficiently trained.

The *Times* followed up on April 6, 1909, with the dismissive comment, "they will all kill themselves if they run many Marathon races...every one in which they take part cuts off several years of their lives." But these editorials probably helped promote the horror-show appeal of marathon races, which touched some of the same death lust as public executions.

Pietri's Whirlwind Finish: Pietri versus Hayes, Madison Square Garden, March 15, 1909

The Native Canadian Longboat against the dapper Englishman Shrubb was good sport, but what New York crowds really yearned for was a rerun of the conflict between their own immigrant cultures, Italy vs. Ireland. Pietri and Hayes had become like the Yankees and the Red Sox – no one would tire of watching them try to thrash each other. So Pat

Powers provided. Pietri vs. Hayes again. More bands, patriotic tunes, flags waving from floor to ceiling, more "joyous enthusiasm," more throngs clamoring to get in, two celebrity runners idolized by their passionately partisan fans, "no wonder the marathon still holds a firm grip upon a large proportion of New York's sports-loving public," remarked the *New York Times* (March 16, 1909), forgetting in the heat of the moment to disapprove of the health risk. Dorando was adored by every Italian immigrant, a belief untroubled when a fully recovered Shrubb totally outran him in a fifteen-mile race in Buffalo on February 26. Johnny Hayes, in addition to his devoted Irish following, was the chosen idol of New York's masses of boys, who packed the cheap standing area. Fifteen-year-old John Donnelly broke his ankle trying to get in free by climbing over the Garden's high iron fence. "I won't mind the broken bone if only Hayes wins," he said gallantly.

That sacrifice was in vain. Despite "a wild outburst of cheers when he appeared on the track," Hayes seemed to have lost his spark and could only follow Pietri's pace. The Irish were briefly hopeful when Hayes managed to take the lead in the thirteenth mile, but it was only for one lap. Two miles later, Pietri put the race away with a burst that took him two laps clear. With that lead safe (about 350 yards), he ran again with Hayes until twenty-five miles, when he gave the night some excitement with "a whirlwind finish," again the skilful showman. Italians rejoiced. The London Olympic debate was surely settled now, with the New York score two races to nil to Pietri. Meanwhile, Hayes quietly and slowly made it to the finish, with no crowd invasion this time, and did not collapse or die. The marathon was beginning to mature. But as a spectacle to thrill the crowds, something new was needed.

The First World Marathon Championship: "The Great Marathon Derby," Polo Grounds, New York, April 3, 1909

A stroke of promotional genius supplied that new spectacle. Powers staged the Great Marathon Derby, the marathon of winners, a race between "the six most famous runners in the world, each a champion in his own country," effectively the first world championship of marathon running, for the richest prize purse ever offered, $5,000 for the winner, worth approximately $150,000 in 2021 terms, close to the listed prize money for winning a major marathon today. The Great Marathon Derby deserves to be much better remembered in sports history than it is.

In six sensational months of Marathon Mania, five colorful celebrity stars had emerged who could draw and entertain the crowds, who had their followers and their betting odds, whose times were consistently well inside three hours, who for six months had rejoiced and conquered and collapsed in public view: Dorando Pietri, Johnny Hayes, Tom Longboat, Alf Shrubb, and Matthew Maloney. Added to them was one unknown, a little French chauffeur (or waiter, according to your source) called Henri St. Yves, who qualified by winning a fast marathon that ended in Edinburgh, Scotland.

It was the dream field, and a whole new concept. You can't have a championship boxing match between six challengers at once, but in running you can, and it was promoter Pat Powers, of course, who thought of it, made the investment, and put it together. Maybe his inspiration was horse racing, as he called his race the Great Marathon Derby. Maybe it was Roman gladiators, fighting to the last man standing. The East Coast was hot with anticipation, gossip, and gambling.

Longboat started favorite in the betting, at 6-to-5. He had won both his New York marathons, at a seemingly easy lope, looking well in charge as he beat Pietri and then Shrubb. Pietri was at 11-to-5 and Shrubb 3-to-1. Boston put its money on Shrubb, at 8-to-5. He was coaching Harvard, after all. The Irish money was on Hayes or Maloney. They were still outsiders, with St. Yves. The unfancied Frenchman had trained for three weeks at Princeton University in New Jersey with the student cross-country team, who ran with him in relays. Loyally, they backed him at long odds.

To accommodate bigger crowds, the Great Marathon Derby was staged at New York's famous baseball venue, the Polo Grounds in Upper

Manhattan, north of Harlem, which squeezed in 25,000, with more overflowing to every vantage point. They were clinging in their hundreds to Coogan's Bluff, and perched six deep along the Speedway and the heights above it. Boys beyond number, nearly all Johnny Hayes devotees, prowled the adjoining Manhattan Field searching for illicit ways in.

The setting for this battle of the six heroes was an outdoor grass track, five laps to the mile. In the tradition of the Pietri-Hayes contests, Viola's Italian Band and Bayne's 69th Regiment Band were hired to "alternate in a concert," which continued throughout the race. (And when track meets today add recorded music to long-distance races, they think they are being daringly inventive.) The crowds stacked the stands and clung to every ledge and branch and chimney that offered a glimpse of the track. The bookmakers smirked. Everything was set for one of the most spectacular sporting entertainments since the Coliseum in Rome was closed.

And then it rained.

The baseball field was so soggy that the size of the track was reduced to improve the footing, making it six laps a mile, marked with little stars and stripes flags. Six men running 158 laps on wet grass means churned up mud. It means difficult, slippery bends for tiring legs. On April 3 in New York, it means a dank kind of cold. It did not mean an unhappy crowd, who arrived hours early, sat intrepidly on open banking, got soaked, and "cheered madly" as the competitors one by one made theatrical entrances, all wearing dressing gowns like boxers. Pietri trotted over to the Italian block and bowed operatically; Longboat beamed a big amiable grin, his gown open to show the maple leaf on his chest; Shrubb was stiff with English restraint; St. Yves, short and unnoticed, astutely eyed the bigger stars; and Hayes entered last and got the loudest and most Irish applause as he posed at length for the photographers.

A pre-race photo suggests it was misty drizzle rather than heavy rain, and there are no gloves or ear-warmers, and the runners wore short sleeves, so it was April cool and damp, not serious New York winter cold. In these conditions, the crowd expected a good race but a slow time. They prepared for two hours of tactical caution, with the familiar stars in control. They were wrong. After Pietri and then Shrubb had led briefly, the foolish little St. Yves surprisingly took over on the fifth lap. The crowd laughed in derision. He was setting a pace they knew was utter folly. A mere beginner among celebrities, a Frenchman and so by definition mercurial and given to short-lived gestures, with an unpronounceable name, almost wholly unsupported in the betting, running at the front of such a famous field with a pattering stride and low knee-lift, St. Yves made it look like a French farce. He set off faster than even the notoriously fast-starting Shrubb was willing to contest. St. Yves (pronounced "Sant Eve") ran 5:14 for the first mile, and well under six minutes per mile from then on.

The crowd knew he would kill himself at that ridiculous pace on sodden grass. Shrubb thought the same, running cautiously for once, keeping company with Pietri. Further back came Hayes, again using the negative-split tactics that won him the Olympics, and Longboat, whose patience had paid off in his duels against Pietri and Shrubb. Maloney also watched and waited. St. Yves lapped them all as early as lap eight (in the second mile).

To everyone's surprise, and reluctant admiration, tiny St. Yves stayed in front, lap after pattering lap. His action, said the *Times*, "seemed to glide rather than run over the grass track." Still, they had seen Pietri and then Shrubb run in front like this for twenty miles, and still end on the doctor's table, while Longboat plodded home the winner. So this time they kept their eyes on Pietri and Longboat, three yards apart. Surely both would come through late in the race. Or it could be Maloney, or the boys' favorite Hayes, who was smilingly refusing to be more assertive, even when the band played "The Star-Spangled Banner" to stir him.

The real race had to start soon. It came in the tenth mile, when Shrubb, who had never been behind in a race for so long in his life, grew impatient, reeled St. Yves in, and took over the lead just on the ten-mile mark. The crowd whooped. They wanted action, aggression, tactical change. St. Yves, unperturbed, tucked in behind Shrubb. Longboat stayed cautiously fifty yards back, with Pietri another fifty behind him, and Hayes and Maloney trailing, all awaiting their moment. Ten miles is still early in a marathon. The over-eager ones would burn out. That was how it was supposed to go.

But it didn't. Shrubb led, as he usually did, but this time St. Yves stayed right there, sitting for eight miles. Everyone in the ground expected both to fade, especially the impudent little outsider. But at eighteen miles, the unthinkable happened. St. Yves slipped past Shrubb and was in the lead again. With his quick, low stride, he looked effortless. Even the increasingly sloppy mud didn't seem to trouble him. The rain had stopped, but the track was getting churned.

It became more incredible. St. Yves moved away from Shrubb, still setting world marks for every intermediate distance. Pietri and Hayes looked more focused now, but never came close. Longboat was in trouble at eighteen miles. He stopped to change his shoes (which were like light boots, ankle-high), but he was done, and walked off the track before twenty miles. The other excitement came at about the same moment, when St. Yves lapped Shrubb. Now he was at least a lap clear of the entire field, and he looked a lot better than those who should have been threatening him.

Shrubb was drifting, and by 22 miles he was paying for that reckless mid-race surge, when his patience had cracked and he tried to break St. Yves. He slowed to a walk, then staggered. Once again Shrubb learned that the marathon is different from ten or fifteen miles. Once again he lost what Conan Doyle called the fascinating struggle between weakness and will. The great Alf Shrubb was again forced to quit. Yet the irrepressible St. Yves scampered on. A pistol shot announced the last mile, and the little Frenchman responded by picking up the pace, lapped several of his famous rivals yet again, charged briskly around his last lap, and finished with a splendid flourish of a sprint, pure French panache. The crowd wildly acclaimed St. Yves, even though he had cost most of them a lot of money. Both bands, after some hasty research, broke into the "Marseillaise." St. Yves had run 2:40:50.6, the fastest at that date for these multi-lap marathons.

While there has to be doubt about the exact accuracy of a track that was reconfigured in the rain just before the race, there's not a shadow of doubt about the brilliance of the victory. St. Yves had surely run the greatest marathon ever. It's still one of the best and most significant. In what was equivalent to a modern world championship, with the best in the world all there and highly motivated, with big money at stake, he had dominated them. He controlled the whole race in a way we associate with Paula Radcliffe or Eliud Kipchoge. Pietri was nearly five minutes back (2:45:37), Hayes and Maloney another five. Longboat and Shrubb were in the dressing room of despair.

In Times Square, there was a huge gathering around the *Times* bulletin board, the biggest assembled there for any event except a national election. Race progress was shouted by those closest to the notice boards, who had claimed their spots hours beforehand, and was passed back through the massed crowd that filled Broadway and Seventh Avenue. Even the streetcars and taxis slowed down to hear progress reports. Half-heard news was garbled, rumors flew and grew. All was consternation and confusion. They expected to hear about Pietri, Longboat, Hayes or Shrubb, the celebrity names. The unexpected race leader was shouted out as being Spanish, Mexican, Hungarian, before being finally identified as French. No one had heard of Henri St. Yves.

No one, that is, except the Princeton University cross-country team, who had trained with him, and won a great deal of money. They were reported to be "jubilant."

"Dorando's Chauffeur Arrested"

William McCarthy of the New York Taxicab Company was arrested after the race for speeding, reported the *New York Times* the next day (April 4). He protested that Dorando Pietri and a party of friends had asked him to make fast time from the Polo Grounds into downtown Manhattan. Pietri refused to put up $100 as bail. The vehicle was doing 22 miles per hour.

$10,000 International Marathon, May 8, 1909

Six men racing for $5,000 had been a spectacular success for Pat Powers. He topped it by bringing ten men to race for $10,000, a sum beyond the dreams of any of them in any other possible way. Only five weeks after the Great Marathon Derby, Henri St. Yves, effectively the new world champion, was on the line at the Polo Grounds again, this time for the hastily convened $10,000 International Marathon, against a largely new cast of challengers. Pietri and Maloney reappeared, to draw the Italian and Irish fans, but seven fresh men now had their chance to do what St. Yves had done, and become the greatest, by one great winning race.

The buzz was about the Canadian, John Marsh, who had broken St. Yves's professional world mark in winning the Canadian championship in 2:39:47 on May 1, just a week before. Replacing Longboat was a new Native American, an Ojibwa with the non-ethnic name of Fred Simpson. Shrubb had wisely conceded that the marathon was beyond his range, so was replaced by another Englishman, Fred Appleby, who was eager to make up for a non-finish in the London Olympic marathon; and eager also to add the colorful life of professional running to his regular routine as a dentist in the London suburbs.

A new American, Tom Morrissey, helped the home betting. John Svanberg of Sweden was there to point to the Scandinavian future of the marathon in the coming decade; and two Frenchmen, Edouard Cibot and Louis Orphée, who had both beaten St. Yves at home, were there to do the same again.

This time the race had a classic simplicity. Pietri rushed out fast and then Marsh, who led through mile one in 5:02. That's 2:11:58 marathon speed, not quite Shrubb's pace, but foolishly fast. Marsh kept it quick until just after four miles (21:51). There, the moment the crowd was waiting for – St. Yves skipped past Marsh, and was away. He was back in charge again. *Plus ça change, plus c'est la même chose.* ("Different field, there goes Henri again.")

He slowed toward the end, but again his low economical stride showed uncanny aptitude for the narrow laps and grass surface. Being either a chauffeur or a waiter in Paris gets you used to tight corners. St. Yves won by a mile, in 2:44:05. Svanberg was second, finishing in some trouble, in 2:50:54. In five weeks, the swift little Frenchman had trounced the best fifteen runners the world could find.

And to complete the spectators' day, Tom Morrissey collapsed. He fell twice, was bustled back on the track by his handlers, the crowd screamed for him to be removed, an attendant ran alongside, he fell limp in front of the grandstand so that the other runners had to veer around his helpless body, and it took ten minutes before he regained consciousness and was carried off. Svanberg, too, was "dazed and staggering," and fell twice in his last lap. St. Yves trotted briskly off to collect his prize money.

The Story Continues

The headlines below are quoted from the *New York Times*, 1909-1910. The date given in each case is of the actual event. The print coverage is usually the next day.

Svanberg Wins Chicago Marathon
St. Yves is Forced to Quit
(May 29)

Orphée Scores Easy Marathon Victory
Frenchman Wins Brighton Beach Event
(May 31)

St. Yves Collapses
French Runner May Never Race Again
(October 3)

St. Yves In Form Again
Wins Guggenheim Marathon at Seattle
(October 17)

Marathon Victory for Harry Jensen
First in Yonkers Event (2:40:43)
(November 27)

Marathon Under Ban
Illinois A.C. Will Eliminate All Long-Distance Runs
(December 4)

Ljungstrom Wins Marathon Derby
New Mark of 2:34:08 2/5 Set by Swede in Capturing the Polo
Grounds Race
(April 2, 1910)

New Marathon Record
Svanberg Runs 26 Miles and 385 Yards in 2:29:40 at Lawrence,
Mass.
(August 26, 1910)

Thus the most intense period of Marathon Mania ended with the Scandinavians emergent as the new force, and with the world's best professional time under 2:30. It would be another fifteen years before Albert Michelson brought the official, amateur world best to that level. Yet the protective reaction against the "dangers" of the marathon was still strong enough for a ban to be officially imposed in at least one state, Illinois. Well into the mid-twentieth century, doctors and others would continue to call for the event to be banned.

Winning Time 2:02 as America Wins Marathon Team Race: Madison Square Garden, November 29, 1910

Another new idea to keep the crowds entertained and the betting profitable was an international two-man teams race, with a relay format, the two men running alternate laps. Hot favorites were St.Yves and Svanberg, as a French/Swedish team, but the Americans Hans Holmer and William Queal utterly outran them, winning in 2:02:16. An intense interval-session format requires a different specialization. Finland was third, with Britain and Canada both failing to finish. Shrubb was a notable casualty. The team dimension was new. It excited the reporters, but there is no mention of the crowd's response. It's significant that once again the total distance was the exact marathon. As would happen again after 1972, the very name "marathon" carried the magic.

Finale: Bronx to City Hall Amateur Half-Marathon, May 6, 1911

Then, to confirm that appeal, came the world's first half-marathon, fifty years before that event caught on. If there is little real reason to choose 26.2 miles/42.2km as your race distance, there is even less to race over 13.1 miles/ 21.0975km, except that to have "marathon" in the title makes everyone feel heroic and historic. This one in 1911 was strictly speaking not even a half, but a "modified marathon," about twelve miles. It was an open-entry amateur race. The story is too good to lie forgotten.

When the borough president's secretary gave permission for the finishers to "resume their street clothes" in a City Hall committee room, he thought there would be about twenty-five of them. He underestimated Marathon Mania. The turnout showed that the popularity of running went deeper than spectator fervor for a professional racing circus.

The race was won by Louis Tewanima, the Hopi Native American who had placed ninth in the London Olympic Marathon and went on to win an Olympic silver medal at 10,000m in 1912.

"Tewanina [sic], a ward of the Nation and a student at the Carlisle Indian School, yesterday demonstrated the superiority of the red man as a foot runner over a cosmopolitan field which numbered nearly 1,000 athletes of all sorts and conditions," reported the *New York Times* (May 7, 1911). "When it became known that Tewanina was the pacemaker the crowd bubbled over with excitement...the City Hall plaza re-echoed with the plaudits in his favor." The crowd seems to have been less preoccupied by Tewanima's ethnicity than the *Times*, which never gives him a first name (unlike the other leading runners), calling him only "Little Tewanina" or "the Indian," and describing him at one point as "the copper-colored youngster."

From our perspective, this race could be said to be historically significant, as the first evidence of a true running boom, presaging the 1970s upsurge in some key ways. It was the first instance of unexpectedly high participant numbers, a field drawn from "all sorts and conditions," a winner from an ethnic minority, large crowds lining streets and greeting the runners with an "ovation," high media interest, and a festive, exuberant post-race atmosphere.

The media at the time were more excited by what the *Times* called the "muss in City Hall" after the race. The field was bigger than officials could keep track of, and although many dropped out, at least five hundred reached the finish. Tired and scantily dressed runners overcrowded the City Hall committee room, and swarmed out over much of the building, looking for space to rub down and change clothes. One horde occupied the lavishly furnished Board of Estimates Room and used the solid mahogany table as a rubbing-down bench, smearing it with liniment and reportedly damaging the expensive carpet. Shouting and laughing, they ran from room to room, scattering orange and lemon peel, bottles, and towels. When one official of the Bureau of Weights and Measures refused them entry to his upper-story premises, they "made a rush upon his offices," filled the room with runners, splashed water about, overturned chairs and desks, "and general pandemonium reigned." Several meetings being held in the building were disturbed, and one conference of women schoolteachers, alarmed at the noise, left their meeting room only to find themselves trapped in the corridor in the midst of a cheering mob of men "in various stages of nudity" (probably baggy running shorts). The teachers were escorted out of the building, "hiding their faces as they went." It took cleaners two hours to put the building partly to rights.

Thus, with the biggest runner field known at that date, some endorphin-fueled high spirits after the race, and some suspiciously sensational reporting, the magnificent era of Marathon Mania came to a close.

****

Dorando Pietri won seventeen out of twenty-two professional races during Marathon Mania, but is really remembered only for his heroic failure in 1908.

Johnny Hayes stayed in shape well enough to look trim in a 1928 photograph where he is jogging with world heavyweight boxing champion Gene Tunney. For sketches of the lives of Pietri and Hayes, see Chapter 7.

Tom Longboat volunteered for the Canadian Army in World War I and served three years, partly as a running messenger in the trenches. Reported missing presumed dead, he returned home to find his wife had remarried. His second wife, Martha, was from his own Six Nations Reserve. After the war, he tried farming, without success, and later became a garbage collector in Toronto. But he was rarely unemployed, even during the Depression, owned a car at least at some point, and seems always to have been respected. He sustained a friendship with Alf Shrubb. He retired to the Six Nations Reserve. When he died at 61, Shrubb wrote a generous and affectionate tribute. Longboat's running medals had been pawned. He is commemorated in two biographies, by Bruce Kidd and Jack Batten, both rescuing him from the demeaning stereotype descriptions of journalism in his own time, and showing what an astute tactician, responsible citizen, and amiable individual he was. The annual Tom Longboat Awards recognize the outstanding First Nations sportspeople in each Canadian province, and Longboat Road Runners is a flourishing club in Toronto. He has also been commemorated at events like the Great Raisin River Run in Williamstown, Ontario, which began as a showcase for him in 1908.

Alf Shrubb was attracted to Canada, where he and Tom Longboat often raced each other, over distances shorter than the marathon, in the remaining years before World War I. Shrubb returned to England and managed a pub, also coaching at Oxford University, before choosing

Canada, and settling in Bowmanville, east of Toronto, where he enjoyed some recognition for his running achievements. He died in 1964 at age 84. He is commemorated by an indoor sprint facility in his birthplace of Horsham, England, an annual 8K race in his adopted Bowmanville, Ontario, a profile in Peter Lovesey's classic *The Kings of Distance*, and a biography by Rob Hadgraft.

Henri St. Yves achieved in the new profession of flyer as well as the new profession of marathon runner. His early life is briefly mentioned by Noel Tamini in *La Saga des Pédestrians,* but much additional information here comes (2010) from his grandson, Alain St. Yves, of Ottawa, who had previously interviewed his aunt, St. Yves's daughter, Jeanine Garcia, in Grenoble. Born January 17, 1889 in Mont au Malades (Seine-Maritime), St. Yves was apprenticed as a small-engine mechanic in a motor garage in Neuilly-sur-Seine at age 15. He became a chauffeur on an estate, but was soon working as a waiter, as his first known race was for the Café Monica against the Café Pagany, over three miles on September 6, 1908. He was a waiter in London when, according to Tamini, he ran the Windsor to Chiswick course on December 21, 1908, five months after the Olympic race, in 2:33.23, much faster than Hayes or Pietri. It could not have been the exact Olympic course, given the private status of the start on royal grounds exclusively for the Games. The whole story sounds dubious.

On January 2, 1909, St. Yves won a marathon from Falkirk to Edinburgh, Scotland, in 2:44:40, beating a strong British and Irish field, on a hilly course with slushy snow lying on the roads. He then returned to France and broke the world record for two hours, with 33.48km at Colombes, on February 19, 1909. Only nine days later, he ran a track marathon at Neuilly, then moving on to America. He established himself at Princeton, and became the sensational outsider winner in New York at the Great Marathon Derby, and the $10,000 International Marathon, each in front of more than 25,000 spectators. On October 18, 1909, he topped those two triumphs by setting a new world record of 2:32:39 on a reliably accurate 440yd track in Seattle.

He was not unbeatable, partly because they all raced so often, but he won when it mattered against the strongest international fields, so deserves to be regarded as the world champion of the era.

The ebullient and adventurous St. Yves then gave up running and became a test pilot. His daughter recalled that he built airplanes and motorcycles, which he also raced; and that he flew with the early "barnstormer" flying circuses in New Hampshire and New Jersey. He fought and was wounded in World War I, when his brother was killed.

"Running for my grandfather was always a means of making money, and he made a lot of it, most of which he blew on airplanes," said Alain St. Yves, in a private email in 2010. "He loved machines, engines, cars, and being a mechanic. When he came to Canada in 1954, he met a lot of old sports reporters who remembered him, and a lot more was written at that time. He had two children, my father Sernand and my aunt Jeanine. He died on March 31, 1961."

****

Footnote: Amateurs and Professionals

Supposedly intended to free nineteenth-century sports from the evils of gambling and race-fixing, the code of amateurism more insidiously also sought to perpetuate class divisions. New rules attempted to make organized sport a leisure activity for the moneyed and educated classes, by excluding those who worked as "mechanic, artisan or labourer" (in the terms of the original English Amateur Athletic Association). Most sports in their modern forms began in Britain with upper-class "gentlemen" wanting to continue the games they had played at their private high schools (in Britain called public schools). In cricket, the division between "gentlemen" and "players" lasted into the 1960s. In earlier years, the class separation was almost as rigid in the republican United States as in aristocratic Britain.

In running, this exclusiveness quickly began to break down, since good working-class runners, accustomed to sustained physical work and long-distance walking, could win victories and bring kudos. The U.S. team for the 1908 Olympics, for instance, with working-class Irish athletes like Hayes, and the Native American Tewanima, was demographically quite different from the 1896 team, which had been drawn wholly from universities and socially exclusive urban "athletic clubs." Under-the-table expense payments were soon common, and competitors from lower socioeconomic groups were admitted, provided they retained the appearance of amateur purity. The social acceptance was often partial. The great French-Algerian runner of the 1950s, for instance, Alain Mimoun, represented the Racing Club of Paris but was only allowed onto the premises to work as a waiter. Sometimes athletic or running clubs hired former runners like Shrubb or Walter George as "trainer," whose duties (I remember in the 1950s) included cleaning the changing rooms and filling the baths with hot water.

In 1908 in America, and in parts of northern England, Scotland, Ireland, and Australia, a separate sport of professional running continued to exist, if not often flourish, alongside amateurism, mostly on the track, where it is possible to attract paying spectators. Pat Powers's enterprise in 1908-1912 made professional running more viable than at any time until the 1980s. When Pietri, Hayes, and Longboat accepted payment, they were excluding themselves from the Olympic Games, and from the Boston and other amateur marathons, but they still had a flourishing professional athletics scene to be part of. But by the 1920s, the success of the Olympic movement made amateurism emphatically the dominant code. Jim Thorpe (1913), Paavo Nurmi (1932), Wes Santee (1955), and Gordon Pirie (1960) had nowhere to go once they were banned as amateurs.

The two codes were hostile. Where professionalism survived, as in Victoria, Australia, it was despised. See the Adrienne Beames story in Chapter 13. Any athlete tempted to defect was banned as an amateur for life, and dismissed almost morally, like some running equivalent of a fallen woman. The system kept power in the hands of the national and local federations and their officials, who often used it vindictively or to eliminate athletes who showed too much independence. That power structure persisted until the early 1980s. For the transition to an open system, and the story of "the Ghost Runner," John Tarrant, see my *When Running Made History*.

The dominance of the amateur code until then means that it also effectively wrote the history of running in its own image. The received narrative lurched in one giant leap from Ancient Greece to Baron de Coubertin. Important professional phases like the running footmen (Chapter 4), the eighteenth-century smock races for women (see my *Running in Literature*), and the Marathon Mania circuit were ignored, or rather suppressed, in the histories. Pietri, Hayes, Longboat, and Shrubb were recorded only for their achievements as amateurs, and the importance of St. Yves has almost never been noticed. Fortunately, the primary sources for my narrative in this chapter are American newspaper reports that are full of detail and make colorful reading. What a great story it all was.

Chapter 9

The First Great Women's Track Race: How Many Collapsed? – Amsterdam 1928

GREATEST EVER RACE BY WOMEN!!!
NINE SUPERLATIVE WOMEN. SEVEN BREAK WORLD RECORD
IN EPIC OLYMPIC TWO-LAPPER
NEVER BEFORE SEEN DISPLAY OF ENDURANCE AND SPEED

Amsterdam, August 2, 1928

Lina Radke of Germany powered two laps of the Amsterdam Olympic track today to win the greatest women's middle-distance race of all time. Shattering her own 800-meter world record, Radke gave her resurgent post-war nation its first Olympic track and field gold medal since 1912.

Despite hot and humid conditions, almost all the runners achieved new levels. The pace was blazing fast, with first Kinue Hitomi (Japan), and then Inga Gentzel (Sweden) threatening to command the race, as each took a turn in front. Their initiative was rewarded with the silver and bronze medals, and the honor of joining the winner in crashing through the world record.

This was a historic event in every way. In yesterday's qualifying races, 25 women stepped on to the track, in three heats, from 13 nations and four continents, an impressive affirmation of global support for the new event. The 800m was one of five included in these Amsterdam

Games, as the International Olympic Association's first recognition of women's track and field. The world has glimpsed the potential at the so-called Women's Olympic Games in 1922 and 1926. Amsterdam marks women's first appearance on the Olympic track. The athletes seized the opportunity. Yesterday, despite the high summer temperatures, the three heats were all won in times that would have been world records until 1927. That was the year that saw the emergence of Radke and Gentzel. Between them, in just over twelve months, those two took the record down from 2:26 to 2:19.6 (by Radke, in July 1928).

In this afternoon's even warmer weather – overcast, stifling, and clammy – the nine finalists toed the line looking serious and focused, several crouching forward in readiness for a fast pace. Hitomi the tall Japanese gave them one, starting like the sprinter she is, with the field following her intently in a close single file. It was not fast enough for Gentzel. Along the back straight of the first lap, the long-striding Swede moved quickly forward, passed the entire field, and hit the front just before 200m, looking eager to reclaim the world record she held at 2:20.4.

Gentzel kept up that pressure around the bend, with gaps now opening up in the field strung out behind her. But every competitor was fighting for every yard. Gentzel led past the clanging bell at the start-finish line in a remarkable 64.2 sec, with the crowd roaring. At that pace, the whole field might be expected to run out of steam, but very few did. If the pace up front slowed, no one in the stands guessed, so gripping was the contest.

Round the first bend of lap 2, it was still Gentzel, but suddenly, with 300m to go, Radke struck, and surged away to a lead that stretched from five to ten meters. The cheering stadium was amazed that she could find extra power when the pace was already so fast. On the final half lap, the runners were all at their limit, inevitably after two laps at such unprecedented speed. Radke's courage carried her through, as she held her form, and broke the tape in an epoch-making new world record 2:16.8, a magnificent break-through of almost three seconds. She became the historic first women's Olympic gold medalist in a middle-distance running event, and was rapturously acclaimed by the many German spectators.

Hitomi, who raced the 100m dash earlier this week, found that sprinter's speed again when it mattered, and despite being visibly tired, somehow held off Gentzel for second place, 2:17.6 to 2:17.8. Both were competitive to the last stride. Hitomi, a sprinter and long jumper who is a total novice at 800m, fell to the grass in weary relief after her closing effort captured the silver medal.

The rest of the field pressed eagerly for every place, several reaching the line on the edge of exhaustion, almost all having run significantly faster than ever before. One of those was the talented 17-year-old Jenny Thomson (Canada), who like Hitomi fell to the ground on the infield after giving her all to hold on to fourth place, four seconds back from Gentzel. Thomson led a closely competitive group, with Canadian teammate Bobbie Rosenfeld fifth in 2:22.4, Florence MacDonald (USA) sixth in 2:22.6, and Marie Dollinger (Germany) seventh in 2:23.0. Since the recent pre-Games world record times by Radke and Gentzel are still awaiting ratification, that means the first seven ran faster than the officially listed world record. That is an extraordinary transformation for any international track event in a single race.

Winner Lina Radke-Batschauer (24), was born Karoline Batschauer, in Baden-Baden. She has won several German championships at 600m and 1,000m, the standard women's middle distances until the Olympics chose 800m for these inaugural women's events. She is coached by her husband, Georg Radke, and both have advocated for women's track and field to be better supported and developed. Radke won the gold medal wearing a pair of lightweight spiked shoes specially designed for cinder tracks by shoemaker Adi Dassler of Herzogenaurach.

Runner-up Kinue Hitomi (21) is Japan's first woman track Olympian and medalist. She was born in Okayama, where she is employed by a major newspaper. Unusually tall for her nation (5 ft. 6 in./170cm), she is a talented all-round athlete. In the 1926 second Women's World Games in Gothenburg, Sweden, she won the long jump in a world record, and also won the standing long jump, and medalled in the discus and 100m. With no long jump here in Amsterdam, the 100m dash was her first choice, and she won her heat, but was narrowly eliminated in the semi-finals. She then made a late entry to the only other individual women's running event, the 800m, where despite her inexperience, she made a historic mark by leading the field for the first half lap, and taking the silver medal. Canada's Fanny (Bobbie) Rosenfeld ran the same double, taking silver in the 100m and sixth place in the 800m.

The only regret after a race of such quality is that the International Olympic Committee permitted only five women's events, cutting the original ten in half at a late point, and describing the reduced program as "an experiment." Today's fine race surely proved the experiment to be a success. The British women's team, which withdrew in protest against the belated reduction in the program, would have made the race even stronger, especially if the outstanding Gladys Lunn had been in the field.

Those lucky enough to be present will look back on this as an historic day, when nine strong and courageous women were given the opportunity for the first time to race over two laps for the highest stakes, and when they all pushed themselves to new levels of athletic achievement. These nine superlative women showed the world that women's middle-distance running is both a serious competitive sport, and a thrilling spectacle.

****

What History Believes: Not "Nine Superlative Women" but "Eleven Wretched Women"

That is what actually happened. The news report above is a 2021 reconstruction of how the 1928 race might have been reported, and deserved to be reported. I did not attempt to imitate authentic 1920s style or usages, such as giving every female athlete their title, "Miss," "Mrs." or even "Frau," as newspapers did at the time. But every fact reported is authentic. I included some that have been almost wholly overlooked, such as the high number of entries in the heats, the significance of the race for Germany and Japan, and the Olympic debut of adidas shoes. Every statement is based on verifiable fact or reliable reporting (the little there was). And my closing affirmation that the race was of such quality as to be historically significant is justified in the retrospect of more than ninety years.

Sadly, even disgracefully, no such report was published at the time. The world was not ready for what it saw. It was not willing to believe or celebrate the race that happened, the race that the report above describes. Instead of these facts and this assessment, the world's press produced a chorus of sensation, distortion, and disapproval. Instead of "nine superlative women," the world read about "eleven wretched women." The sloppy miscount of how many actually ran in the final is symptomatic.

Next morning, this is what people around the world found in their newspapers.

"Below us on the cinder path were 11 wretched women, 5 of whom dropped out before the finish, while 5 collapsed after reaching the tape" (John Tunis, *New York Evening Post*). Note: there were nine in the race, at most one dropped out.

"Women Athletes Collapse – Fierce Strain of Olympic Race – Sobbing Girls" (*Daily Mail*, London).

"...of the eight girls who finished six of them fainted exhausted – a pitiful spectacle and a reproach to anyone who had anything to do with putting on a race of this kind" (*Chicago Tribune*).

"The half-dozen prostrate and obviously distressed forms lying about on the grass at the side of the track may not warrant a complete condemnation of the girl athletics championships, but it certainly suggests unpleasant possibilities" (*The Times*, London).

The *Pittsburgh Press*, like Tunis in the *New York Post*, claimed that only six women finished the race, utterly indefensibly when the official results give finishing times for eight of the nine. Other journalists fudged the distinction between falling to the ground after the finish, and "collapsing" during the race. The *Montreal Daily Star*, like the *Chicago*

Tribune and London *Times* (above), struck a moral pose and asserted, "the disgrace...should be taken off any future program [as] obviously beyond women's powers of endurance, and can only be injurious to them." Other interpretations included "a massacre," "a terrible event," "ridiculous," and scene of "terrible exhaustion." Some of these quotations are drawn from Colleen English's seminal essay (English, 2015).

The chorus of condemnation drew support from people who might have shown more integrity. Harold Abrahams, the 100m gold medalist in 1924, who later became the most powerful man in British track and field, as well as dean of his country's track journalism, was present as a journalist in 1928. He joined the chorus, writing, "I do not consider that women are built for really violent exercise" (Ryan, 2011).

Later, Abrahams reversed his opinion. He looked back on the 1928 race and its impact, in a concise Olympic history that he wrote in 1960: "...the sensational descriptions of the terrible exhaustion which overcame the runners in this race, much exaggerated I can assure you, led to the abandonment of this event from the Games" (Abrahams, 1960).

That is valuable as an eye-witness response, although it came thirty-two years after the event. It is a pity it took Abrahams so long to see the reports as "much exaggerated." It's a pity, too, and that he did not have the grace to acknowledge that he had himself endorsed the event's abandonment. We can only wonder why.

Even the American 100m sprint gold medalist Betty Robinson, concurred:

> *"I believe the 220-yard dash is long enough for any girl to run...Imagine girls falling down before they hit the finish line or collapsing when the race is over! The laws of nature never provided a girl with the physical equipment to withstand the grueling pace of such a grind"* (Montillo, 2017).

As an athlete, Robinson might have been expected to focus on the competitive race and the world record. But in an atmosphere of righteous outrage, it's hard to step outside the framework of condemnation, set in place in this case by such a widely-shared interpretation from such a chorus of vigorous writers. Robinson seems to have accepted the consensus yet unfounded claim that some runners fell down "before they hit the finish line."

Later accounts accepted the fiction, and became more and more colorful: "the gals dropped in swooning heaps as if riddled by machine-gun fire," luridly wrote the *New York Times*. At the time, every report focused not on the race, but on the finish-line collapses and tears, all described through cheap hyperboles, like "massacre" and "sobbing girls."

Shamefully, no report alluded to the fact that most, if not all, competitors had run faster than ever before. Shamefully, none made allowance for the heat and humidity. None mentioned the short recovery time after they had all run demanding qualifying heats in hot weather the previous day. Most shamefully, not one deigned to acknowledge that athletes who have pushed themselves to the limit do often fall to the ground ("collapse") after finishing. Several men did so in these same 1928 Olympic Games, including the godlike Paavo Nurmi after he lost the 5,000m to Ville Ritola. The most famous photo of Murray Halberg's legendary Olympic 5,000m win in 1960 shows him lying on his back with the finish tape across his chest.

As well as distaste for a spectacle they found unseemly, most reports moved on to repressive advocacy, asserting that such physical distress was inappropriate and possibly harmful for women, and raising the issue of whether the event should therefore be struck from the Olympic program. The chorus was consistent, with no dissenting voice. Newspapers don't often all agree like that. Was this litany of disapproval orchestrated? Was this a campaign that was in some way being consciously promoted? Perhaps even paid for? Across so many newspapers on both sides of the Atlantic, it was strikingly harmonious.

A jeering consensus in the all-male journalists' bar is not an unthinkable scenario. Nor is the more insidious possibility that the IOC somehow made it known that they would welcome and reward attention to the negative aspects in reporting the race. We can never know the truth of how the chorus of inaccuracy was fomented, but it was a shameful episode in sports journalism.

Unfortunately, the outcry touched a chord in the age. The era in which women were finally winning the right to vote in many countries was not ready to change its attitudes with regard to their physical capacity and entitlement. Wretched women overreaching and sobbing and swooning in mass distress was a version the world wanted to believe, rather than the hard-contested and transformative race they had actually seen (seven under the listed world record).

Whether or not the IOC and IAAF initiated the distortion, they made good use of it. The Olympic President, Count Baillet-Latour, promptly declared "I do not think women should be allowed to do track and field," appealing to the ancient Greeks' all-male convention. Within a week, the federations acted on the journalists' proposition that women should be spared endurance sport, on the grounds that it is inappropriate and harmful, and that women had no place in the ancient Greek Games. On August 7, 1928, the two organizations formally agreed to remove the women's 800m. It's some consolation to know that it was a close vote, reached only after "a spirited debate." Some nations, led by Canada, wanted to delete the whole experimental limited program of women's track and field events, but a motion to retain them was passed 16-6. A counter-proposal to enlarge the program to ten events was defeated 14-8. The deletion of the women's 800m was agreed 12-9. (These details are from the *New York Times*, August 8, 1928.)

The influence of the chorus of misrepresentation perhaps explains why Great Britain voted against the 800m. That is a surprise, after the country was previously so committed to the women's program that they had withdrawn in protest when the Amsterdam events were cut from ten to five. Perhaps there was a division of opinion between the Amateur

Athletic Association, the Women's AAA (separate at that time), and the British Olympic Committee, who would control the vote. Something similar may explain the perplexing position taken by Canada in leading the move against all women's events, since their women athletes performed at Amsterdam better overall than any other nation, and were well placed (fourth and fifth) in the 800m final. Perhaps they simply had the most male-sexist, or most envious, delegates to the international meeting. Australia/New Zealand and South Africa will take some satisfaction in knowing that their delegates voted against Great Britain and supported the retention of the 800m.

The *New York Times* was impressed by the contribution to the debate of Lady Heath of Great Britain (an Irish-born athlete and intrepid aviator). She had been influential in the move to include women's events in the first place, and her eloquence in support of gender equality is worth recording: "We are now your comrades and co-workers, in industry, commerce, art and science, why not in athletics? Women need the stimulus of matching their prowess against others of the world's best athletes."

Challenged on the grounds that women's events were not part of the ancient Greek Olympics, Heath sensibly riposted, "Neither were the hop, step and jump, fencing, and pistol shooting." Neither were the marathon nor the men's 800m, she might have added.

And so, despite the obvious truth of Lady Heath's argument, the women's 800m was cut. It was not restored to the Olympic program until 1960. The litany of negative reporting of the 1928 race thus left an indelible mark on sports history. Even more seriously, the whole sensationalized fiction of massacre and collapse became accepted as truth. The belief prevailed for several decades that women were embarrassingly incapable of endurance running, and liable to collapse if they try. Until very recently, and still rarely, even the strongest supporters of women's running, those who have been most critical of the decision to cut the event, have not questioned the factual accuracy of the false version of the race that the journalists lodged in our shared consciousness.

Why were the IOC and many of the media so eager to misrepresent the truth? The background story provides one explanation. Women had been admitted to the Olympic Games since 1900, but only in sports deemed suitable for their skills and appearance – tennis, golf, archery, gymnastics (very different from today's version), skating, and swimming. The Olympics' founder and president, Pierre de Coubertin, had made his belief clear in 1912 that "the Games are a solemn exaltation of male athleticism, with female applause as reward."

Alice Milliat of France, one of the great activist leaders in sports and women's history, a rower, led the campaign to break away from that constrained view of women as suited only to the role of adoring applauders, or sweat-free participants in sports that showed them off as graceful and desirable. In 1921, after World War I, Milliat created and led La Fédération Sportive Féminine Internationale. Women's Games were held in 1921 in Monte Carlo and Paris, and in 1922 Milliat initiated the ambitious Women's Olympic Games, held in Paris. A one-day event, it attracted a reported 20,000 spectators. A second version, at Gothenburg in 1926, attracted large numbers of competitors, including, in track and field, Lina Radke in the 600m, Kinue Hitomi as winner of the long jump, and Sophie Elliot Lynn, later Lady Heath, in the javelin.

Milliat's ambitious and unprecedented series of international events succeeded in pressuring the reluctant IOC into including ten women's track and field events in their own 1928 Games, as a trade-off (it seems probable) for Milliat agreeing to drop the word "Olympic." She renamed her 1930 and 1934 gatherings "Women's World Games." At a later point, the IOC cut the added events from ten to five, a move that now looks devious. Great Britain's women's team thought so, and boycotted in protest. That sadly deprived the 1928 800m of some of the best middle-distance and cross-country runners, notably Gladys Lunn, a potential gold medalist.

Another explanation lies deeper, in the attitudes and impulses that underlie this story. One is the continuance of the Victorian male preference for women to be charming and decorative, and less than fully mature. The London *Daily Mirror* described how, before the race, the athletes "skipped daintily into the field," which seems unlikely. The phrase is revealing about why it then seemed inappropriate for these dainty skipping creatures to run themselves into a state of distress. Mark Dyreson has documented the era's typical sports reporting that sought always to present women as "objects of desire." Hence the press enthused over Gertrude Ederle's English Channel swim, still looking fresh and alluring as she emerged on the beach, but deplored the "terrible exhaustion" of Amsterdam. IOC President Baillet-Latour suggested that "aesthetic events" were the most appropriate for women (Dyreson, 2003).

The emphasis always is on a pleasing appearance, and even a lingering of the Victorian era obligation for women to appear as edifying moral paragons.

"It was not a very edifying spectacle to see a group of fine girls running themselves into a state of exhaustion," was the reflection on Amsterdam from the *Pittsburgh Press*, whose syndicated reporter was the Notre Dame football coach. He suggested a "six-day dance contest between couples" would be no less ridiculous (English, 2015).

The other undercurrent is concern that such extreme effort will impair women's reproductive capabilities. The London *Daily Mail* predicted that "feats of endurance" would make them "prematurely old." An earnest woman doctor wrote to the London *Times*, "Nature made woman to bear children, and she cannot rid herself of the fat to the extent necessary...for feats of extreme endurance," which sounds scientific, but isn't.

These attitudes are unacceptable now, but it's worth some effort to understand their underlying impulse. In Europe in 1928, that reproductive fear was a human anxiety so deep that it is best called sub-conscious. Eight and a half million young males had been killed in World War I, and an estimated fifty million people died in the influenza pandemic of 1918, the deadliest illness in human history (so far). Humanity's urge to compensate for that loss of reproductive energy drove many things in the next two decades, including the reporting of this women's 800m track race. (It also drove the representation of women in early Hollywood, the Nazis' *Bund Deutscher Mädel* (League of German Girls), D. H. Lawrence's *Lady Chatterley's Lover*, and much else). Pope Pius deplored a women's gymnastics competition in Rome in May 1928 in typical terms: "After twenty centuries of Christianity, the sensitiveness and attention to the delicate care due to young women and girls should be shown to have fallen lower than pagan Rome." As late as the 1960s, official medical opinion endorsed the prevailing anxiety. When the Surrey County Women's AAA asked for an expert opinion on adding the 880yd race for junior girls, the British Medical Council advised against it. This is not to condone the false reporting of the Amsterdam litany of lies, but to try to understand its deeper motivation.

As we attempt to understand how this kind of fear turns into disapproval, we should also remember that there was little understanding of the reasons why any runners collapse. From Dorando Pietri's exhaustion in 1908 (Chapter 7), men's marathon running attracted similar criticisms, and calls to ban it. The Illinois Athletic Association did ban it in 1909 – see Chapter 8 – and such demands were still being heard well into the twentieth century. One close in date to 1928 came from an Australian doctor and athlete, a former national 440yd hurdles champion, after some marathon runners became distressed in 1931: "... the most pitiable sight I have witnessed for some years...How can such a race be classed as in the best interests of sport? I express the hope that the Victorian AAA will ban marathon racing for all time."

The attitudes and the terminology there are strikingly similar to those that caused the women's 800m to be excluded.

What Really Happened?

The most luridly mendacious newspaper reports have to be discounted. They couldn't even be accurate about the number of runners in the race. Two accounts exist that can be taken as mostly valid. Wythe Williams, on the front page of the *New York Times,* although vocal among the chorus of condemnation, and giving only the most cursory report of the race before asserting that "even this distance makes too great a call on feminine strength," seems to have reported the finish-line scene with some, though selective, accuracy:

> At the finish six out of the nine runners were completely exhausted and fell headlong on the ground. Several had to be carried off the track. The little American girl, Miss Florence McDonald, who made a gallant try but was outclassed, was in a half faint for several minutes, while even the sturdy Miss Hitomi of Japan, who finished second, needed attention before she was able to leave the field (August 3, 1928).

Another on-the-spot report came from Dr. Fr. M. Messerli, a supporter of women's sport, a track judge at the event in Amsterdam. Like Williams, he is more specific than the norm of "eleven wretched women," although clearly his interpretation is tilted in the other direction:

> When reaching the winning post, two Canadians and one Japanese competitor collapsed on the lawn, the public and the journalists believed them to be in a state of exhaustion. I was judging this particular event and on the spot at the time. I can therefore testify that there was nothing wrong with them, they burst into tears betraying their disappointment at having lost the race, a very feminine trait (Montillo, 2017).

So the probability is that Hitomi (second), the two Canadians, Thomson (fourth) and Rosenfeld (fifth), the American MacDonald (sixth), and two others, fell to the ground in some degree of tiredness, disappointment, or distress. Those lying on the grass did not include Radke (first) or Gentzel (third), who would surely have been mentioned. Significantly, they were specialist middle-distance runners. So was MacDonald, but she was only 18 and had run over her head. Hitomi, Thomson and Rosenfeld were all-rounders in sprints and field events. Total novices in the newly available two-lapper, it's no surprise they lacked the key ability to distribute their effort over the whole distance and suffered accordingly from oxygen debt.

Film footage and photographs ought to resolve what happened, but in this case they have increased the problems. The moral is that with film and photographs, beware of what you think you see. Some brief footage obtained from the IOC Museum in Lausanne has been included in, for instance, high-quality documentary movies like *Spirit of the Marathon II- Rome,* and *Free To Run,* in their sympathetic treatment of the history of women's participation.

The footage, which is of course silent, first shows the start, very briefly; then a sequence with Hitomi leading the single-file field in the first lap, as Gentzel moves up to take the lead at 200m; then a glimpse of the pack at the bell; and finally some runners finishing, one of them leaning forward and falling, and being helped back to her feet by an official. This brief moving image of a single falling finisher, a four-second glimpse that is hard to interpret, has been taken as visual endorsement of the united journalists' narrative of a debacle of mass collapse.

On careful analysis, the glimpse does little to support that narrative. The runner who falls does so because she is leaning eagerly forward in a tight finish; she is helped back on her feet in 3.2 seconds, and walks away without signs of "exhaustion." We do not see the first three finish. Radke and Hitomi can be identified, inside the track, near the judges' stand, on their feet, Radke back view, walking, Hitomi standing wrapped in a blanket, being escorted by an official. The runner falling, I thought for some time, must be Jenny Thomson of Canada, in fourth place, but there were problems with this reading. How did Hitomi get so comfortably wrapped in a blanket in the mere 3.6 seconds she had between her crossing the line and Thomson's finish? With Hitomi visibly on her feet, what do we make of the reports by Williams and Messerli (cited above) that name her as one of the athletes who needed attention? Why do we see only one woman fall on the track, instead of six falling on to the grass? Why is the woman who falls in a desperate dead-heat, when the official times for the final put Thomson one full second ahead of fellow-Canadian Bobbie Rosenfeld? Where is MacDonald, specifically named by the *New York Times* as being in "a half faint" and receiving extended attention?

The clue is in another question that had troubled me. One or other of two different pictures of Radke and Hitomi are often reproduced as the finish. In one, both look tired, Radke is several strides clear, about right for a one-second gap, and Genzel can be seen in third, probably finishing faster than Hitomi, to judge from the small time-gap at the line. That's clearly the final. But another photo is more often published as if it were the final, with Radke leading Hitomi by barely a stride, and the two both looking unstressed as Radke slightly lifts her hands to break the tape. That makes sense only if it is not from the final, but the previous day's heats, when Radke and Hitomi were first and second in heat 2, close to each other in 2:26.0 and 2:26.4.

So what if the film finish-line scene that we're trying to decipher is also not the final?

It's a leap, since it has been edited in as the finish, immediately following three short sequences that irrefutably show the final. It has always been taken as the final, and as evidence, however skimpy, that some women collapsed. But the facts don't fit. We're not watching the same finish. On the other hand, the film clip could fit heat 2. Radke and Hitomi, who were first and second, are visible on the infield, Hitomi wrapped in her blanket. The film cuts in as one woman falls, alongside another. If it's heat 2, they are placed somewhere towards the back of the field, well behind Radke and Hitomi. No official times below third place are given for the heats, but the gaps were bigger than in the final. If the falling runner is, say, ten seconds behind Radke and Hitomi, that would allow them time to be exactly where they are, among officials alongside the finish line. Three more runners are seen in the film clip finishing, behind the one who falls. That identifies her (Daniel Justribo kindly suggested to me) as probably Sébastienne Guyot (France), or possibly Juliette Segers (Belgium), since those two finished together. That solves all the problems. A scene from heat 2 on August 1 has been edited in, without explanation or apology, as the final clip of the footage of the final on August 2. That misleading mix has presumably been the IOC's film version of the race for a long time. Again, it's possible to theorize conspiracy. There was motive to show women falling over. If the film camera missed those who fell to the ground after the final, they may have chosen to borrow a glimpse of at least one woman falling in a heat, to endorse the preferred account of the finish as a disaster zone. It is certainly suspicious that the official film footage of the final does not show the finishes of the gold, silver or bronze medalists, especially as all three broke the world record. So, please do not be misled into believing that the last brief clip of the one woman falling forward is the finish of the final, or that she is evidence of women in the final "collapsing."

****

The story of that 1928 race is a sad one, a story of prejudice, sexism, and dishonest distortion of the facts. I tell it in full in the hope that the long dominance of the distorted version might now end. I decided against giving this chapter an attention-grabbing title taken from the hostile headlines, like "Eleven Wretched Women" or "Women Athletes Collapse." That would have been complicit with the negative sensationalism that my chapter refutes. I chose a chapter title that highlights the positive truth. I decided to write the report that should have been written, one that is accurate and approving about a major break-through in women's running.

My report is in no way over the top or even selective. It is celebratory, because there is plenty in the real history to celebrate. Women from Australia, Austria, Belgium, Canada, France, Germany, Italy, Japan, Lithuania, the Netherlands, Poland, Sweden, and the United States, thirteen nations on four continents, participated in the new event, confirming that women runners around the world were ready and eager for the opportunity. The standard achieved in the four races was unprecedented, both at the top and in depth. The final was a great leap forward in every way – except the way it was perceived and interpreted and turned into reactionary fake history.

The women's Olympic 800m at Amsterdam in 1928 has been seen for almost a hundred years as the day when elite women's middle-distance racing was tried, and failed, the day when it ended. My purpose in this chapter is to affirm that in truth it was the day when elite women's middle-distance racing really began.

Chapter 10

Three Heroes of Berlin – Olympic Games 1936

800 BC   100 AD   1719   1896   1908   1928   1936   1964   1984   2021

The Olympic Games of 1936 were awarded in 1932 to Berlin, a gesture of international support for Germany, which at that moment seemed to be a democratic nation emerging from the humiliation of World War I. The Berlin Organizing Committee held its hopeful first meeting on January 24, 1933. But six days later, the National Socialist Party headed by Adolf Hitler thrust their way into power in Germany. Soon after, the Organizing Committee chair, the highly respected Dr. Theodore Lewald, was threatened with dismissal because one of his grandparents had been Jewish. Pressure from the International Olympic Committee saved his position, but he was mostly sidelined.

Hitler had raged against Berlin hosting the Olympics, "an invention of Jews and Freemasons," and he was still lukewarm about the Games when Lewald and the Mayor of Berlin formally met with him in March 1933. Preparations proceeded on a financially small scale. That summer, Joseph Goebbels, in the new post of Minister for Propaganda, began to persuade Hitler of the potential of an international sports festival to show off the aspirations of the new Reich. On October 5, 1933, Hitler visited the site, a stadium built for the canceled 1916 Games. On the spot, he ordered the plans for modest renovations to be thrown out and replaced by an ambitious 100,000-seat new stadium "built by the Reich." Over the next months, his vision for the Games became more and more grandiose, with a magnificent Roman-inspired stadium rising to seventy-one tiers of seats, and an adjacent open-air theater and vast assembly area that would enable the whole complex to hold half a million people.

Under Goebbels, the grandiose vision became cultural as well as architectural, with "culture" now synonymous with "propaganda." The torch run from Olympia in Greece was conceived, an Olympic hymn was composed by Richard Strauss, with a literary prize awarded for the words, an Olympic magazine was published monthly, a giant bell was installed, reproduction Greek sculptures of imposing size were commissioned, and the celebrity filmmaker Leni Riefenstahl was selected to direct the official Olympic film, fresh from her success in propagandist film art with *Triumph of the Will*.

The opening ceremony was, of course, stupendous, and was, of course, conceived to glorify the triumph of Hitler and the Third Reich. The gigantic Graf Hindenburg airship, the world's biggest and most advanced aircraft, cruised overhead. The *Lustgarten* assembly area outside the stadium came into its own when the torch was carried across its vast space, between acclaiming ranks of 28,000 young Germans in semi-military uniforms. Twenty thousand carrier pigeons were released in a huge moving cloud. The Olympic ideals of peace, youth, and endeavor as morally superior to victory were communicated again and again through a pageant promoting power, militarism, and nationalistic arrogance. A sad human moment came when poor naive old Spyridon Louis (see Chapter 6) was brought out of his quiet retirement in Amaroússion, to carry the Greek flag around the track, and present Hitler with an olive branch from the sacred grove at Olympia, putting a timeless symbol of peace and spirituality into the hand of that nasty little warmonger.

Hitler and Goebbels scripted the Olympic Games – brilliantly, to give them credit – to glorify Germany made great again, militaristic, racist, and triumphalist. But sport never conforms well to a script. As it turned out, the three greatest heroes of Berlin, in their different ways, all subverted Nazi pretensions, Nazi inhumanity, and Nazi lies.

The unpredictable truthfulness of sport means that those Berlin Games are valued now not for Hitler's Germany, not for the ranks of obedient youth, or the swastika-emblazoned banners that festooned the streets and stadium, but for Jesse Owens, Jack Lovelock, and Sohn Kee Chung.

Jesse Owens - Beauty of Mind and Body in a World of Ugliness

To start with something that has never been said about Jesse Owens, and crucially resets our understanding of him: in Jesse Owens's running and jumping, there was a dimension of inventive intelligence. Commentators galore have praised Owens's perfection of beauty in motion, but none has praised the equal quality of his mind. That overlooked dimension is what made him most special, and most potent as a subversive symbol, in the dire context of history in which he was placed.

The extreme in praise of his physical quality came from the Nazi hosts for the 1936 Games, who sought to appropriate even Owens's beauty of movement for ugly racist propaganda. A supposedly scholarly book on high school science curricula published soon after the Berlin Games included an analytical comparison of long jump images of Owens and the German silver medalist, Luz Long.

> For the Nordic-like people, a deliberate style, a systematic approach...complete control of the body. With the Negro, it is an unmethodical soaring of the body, almost like the...leap of an animal in the wild (Dobers, 1936).

As analysis, that's spectacularly wrong. Owens's jumping seemed gravity defying, yet look closely, and it is disciplined, economical in effort, and precision-controlled. The demeaning comparison with an "unmethodical" wild animal perfectly illustrates the racist context in which he had to perform. I also wonder what wild animals would say about being called unmethodical. If there is anything brutal in this story, it is racism posing as science.

Medium height, and ordinary build (180 cm, 75 kg), Owens was not exceptional to look at, especially in the context of Olympic 100m champions. He was not strikingly tall and long-striding like Usain Bolt, not heavily muscled and powerful like Bob Hayes or Alan Wells, not blazingly competitive like Harold Abrahams or Armin Hary, not silkily elegant like Carl Lewis. Owens looked an average man – until he rose to the set position, and moved. Then his lithe fluidity, swift flickering stride, controlled composure, and precision pace judgment became poetry in motion.

Or for 1936, a solo jazz piano is a better analogy – dazzling fast, deeply rhythmic, flowing with an inward joy, expert, controlled, with not a note wasted, and wholly creative. Inventive, that's the key word. Owens embodied form that matches function, poise of mind and body, the perfect balance that philosophers have always extolled.

Only 22 (born in 1913), from a poor family of ten, midway through college, Owens had never before left America. Yet in Berlin, he found himself the center of attention for a huge fervid public gathering that seethed with controversy, and was calculatingly designed to shape world ideology and politics. It was a lot to ask of a shy, inexperienced young man.

It's to the credit of the German people that despite all their leaders' bragging about Aryan supremacy, the official disparagement of America's "negro auxiliaries," and Chancellor Hitler's unwillingness to congratulate the African American winners in person, they took Owens to their hearts. The stadium crowds idolized him. They picked up a chant from American fans, so that when you watch old film, you can hear the rhythmic Germanic "O – venz! O – venz!" rising above the voice of the commentator. Admirers pursued him, pushing autograph books through his dormitory window as he tried to sleep. Women cried "Wo ist Jesse?" ("Where's Jesse?") and tried to snip at his clothing with scissors.

Owens had to cope with that frenzy of attention, as well as the stress of a messy pre-Games controversy over whether the USA should boycott the Games because of Germany's repression of Jews. Berlin was full of reminders of racism, and his own team management was far from free of it. It would be hard to devise a more difficult international debut for an inexperienced Black athlete. It's greatly to his credit that he rose so superbly to the big occasion, not once, but every time. Repeat: every time. Look at the full record. It's almost flawless. Counting qualifying rounds and jumps, Owens in Berlin had to perform nineteen times in events that demand intense effort and split-second judgment at a level of near-perfection. He fulfilled the very different demands of the 100m, 200m, long jump, and 4 x 100m relay. He was unfazed by drawing the loose churned cinders of the inside lane for the 100m final; and by rain that fell during the 200m final; and by getting put into the relay squad at the last minute without practice; and by a dramatic challenge when Luz Long came level in the fifth round. His only error in those nineteen trials was one misjudged long jump.

It takes versatile skills to win those four gold medals. Owens showed good planning, self-discipline, craftsmanship, calm temperament, competitive focus, and the ability to utilize what he had learned from his coaches. Yet it's impossible to find any report of his events that pays him the compliment of looking closely at how intelligently he won them. Merely to rave about his unbeatable natural talent is to underrate him, and is near to that Nazi pseudoscience. Jesse Owens was not a good-looking primitive animal, but a well-prepared and intelligent athlete with excellent judgment and the ability to perform at his absolute best when it mattered most.

Yes, he arrived in Berlin as favorite. He was the legend who on May 25, 1935, at age 21, at Ann Arbor, Michigan, had set six world records in four events in a space of 45 minutes (100yd, long jump, 200m/220yd, 200m/220yd hurdles). But at the Olympics no victory is inevitable. Legends often lose. The different stories of how he won the four gold medals reveal four key things about the man.

First, he knew how to hit his peak on the day that matters. Despite his 100 yards world record in 1935, Owens was only the number 3 sprinter in the USA through most of 1936, losing several times to Eustace Peacock and Ralph Metcalfe. Then, at the U.S. Olympic Trials, with Peacock absent, Owens outraced Metcalfe in the 100m, and comprehensively won both his other events, the 200m and long jump. He nailed Metcalfe again in Berlin.

Second, he had creative tactical judgment. Watch the Berlin film footage. In the 100m and 200m prelims and semi-finals (eight races in all), he is relatively slow away, and comes smoothly through in the final third of each race, scarcely using his top gear. He saved that for the two finals.

In the 100m, knowing that he faced the fast-finishing Metcalfe, and having drawn the slow cut-up inside lane, Owens leaves nothing to chance, perfectly poised (look at the film) at the starter's "Fer-tig!" ("Set!"), and is leading from the first step, his stride flickering at the highest cadence in the field. Metcalfe closes near the finish, but Owens has it won. He equaled the Olympic record with 10.3, on loose uneven cinders.

Same pattern in the 200m. In the final, Owens accelerates around the bend, hits the straightaway two meters in front, and wins by 4 meters, in a 20.7 Olympic record that would stand for 20 years. That was 0.4 sec faster than any other performance in the four rounds. It's another sprinting masterpiece. What a joy it would have been to see Owens skim over a smooth modern all-weather track, coming off fixed starting blocks instead of digging little holes for his toes in the loose ash with a trowel, and then having to push every stride off rain-sodden cinders wearing rigid leather shoes.

Third, he could handle a setback. In the long jump, scheduled immediately after his Round 1 200m heat, he took a practice jump in his tracksuit, only to have it recorded by unbending German officials as a foul. Not surprisingly, he misjudged the takeoff for his second, and fouled again. Now everything depended on his third, the last chance to get a qualifier for the final three rounds. He stayed calm, played safe, moved his take-off marker, and narrowly qualified.

It may be a myth that his German rival Luz Long gave him friendly technical advice, telling him to move his take-off marker, but Owens told that story over and over. It is indisputable that Long quieted the crowd before Owens's crucial fifth jump (just after Long had come level) and that he warmly congratulated Owens after he won. Film shows indisputably that he went over as soon as Owens stepped out of the sand after his winning jump, in full view of Hitler and the massed German crowd, and put his pale Nordic arm around Owens's black shoulder in genuine sporting friendship. Their warm comradeship is immortalized, too, in emotional photographs of the two lying side by side on the infield, and walking off the arena arm in arm.

Long must have known what he was doing. It's worth pausing to pay tribute to him, for once, for the courage it took to make such a public display of comradeship in defiance of state-imposed white supremacy. It was a political protest as strong and as visible as the black-glove gesture of 1968. Long died fighting for the German Army in Sicily in 1943, at age thirty (he had been married for two years), but he is a reminder that the Germans who fought were not all nationalistic racists.

"It took a lot of courage for him to befriend me in front of Hitler...I would melt down all the medals and cups I have, and they wouldn't be a plating on the 24-carat friendship I felt for Luz Long at that moment," Owens wrote later (Baker, 1986).

That's his fourth strength – his generosity. It emerged also from the way he gained his fourth gold medal. Owens had not been selected for the USA 4 x 100m relay team, which reserved places for American Trials finalists not competing in individual events, who were thus free to practice relay skills without distraction. The night before the relay final, the American team coaches called a meeting. They presented the squad with a concocted story about how the Germans were supposedly concealing a star sprinter. Therefore, they announced, Owens and Metcalfe were being brought into the USA quartet to replace two "less experienced" runners, Sam Stoller and Marty Glickman – who both happened to be Jewish.

It's more than likely that the motive for the late change was to placate the Nazi hosts' anti-Semitic preference. After high placings in the U.S. Trials, and a month when relay practice was their only business, Stoller and Glickman could hardly be called "inexperienced." Yes, Owens and Metcalfe were faster, but not more experienced, and it was a very risky change to make, against agreed policy.

That dark story has become known recently. I told it in 1990, after becoming friends with Glickman, and in my 2018 book *When Running Made History*, and it is part of the script in the Jesse Owens feature film *Race*. But for many years it was almost disregarded. It made no impact in American media at the time. The fourth gold medal for Owens overwhelmed any concern for the disappointed Jewish athletes.

Glickman became a distinguished sports broadcaster in New York, but the experience of being rejected by his national team, probably for anti-Semitic reasons, remained a source of profound pain. His telling of the story gave an insider's view into the courage and generosity of Owens.

"Definitely they did it to please the Nazis. Everyone at the meeting went quiet. The only person who spoke up for us was Jesse Owens. He said, 'Coach, Sam and Marty have earned their places. That's why they're here. They've practiced the baton. Let them run.' Yet Jesse was the one who gained most. The switch would give him his historic fourth gold medal. That didn't matter to Jesse so much as being fair to us. I've never ceased to feel grateful" (Personal conversation, 1985; Glickman, 1999).

That's how Glickman always told it. He died in 2001.

Did Hitler snub Owens? Did he refuse to shake the hands of the Black winners, as the disputed story goes? Did he leave the stadium in a huff and arrange to congratulate the German medalists in private? There are many versions, and many historians of the Berlin Games have obsessed over getting it right. Who cares?

Owens was much the better human being. He gave priority to justice and friendship. His courageous protest on behalf of Glickman and Stoller, and the image of him lying side-by-side on the grass infield with

Long, rivals relaxing in harmony after a fierce competition – those say more about the Olympics and their contribution to humanity than the sulks of a petulant sociopath. The sadness of the Jesse Owens story is that he is doomed forever to be trapped in that historical context, so alien to his own fundamental decency.

The rest of his life was also shaped by the forces of context. There was no escape for most of his lifetime from being an African American from a poor family in the mid-twentieth century. At Ohio State University, he was a sports star who was not permitted to shower or eat with the team. When he arrived at the Waldorf Astoria Hotel in New York for a banquet in his honor as the American Olympic hero, American law enforced that he had to ride the freight elevator to reach the banquet floor.

He had his faults, like all humans. He made the most of his sexual allure, and did not treat his wife well. He could be less than straight financially. But his situation was not easy. There was no money. None. Today, such a superstar would have elite performance contracts, become a corporate spokesperson, an endorser of products, a media personality, the figurehead of a foundation, a social media phenomenon. Owens was left in limbo. He was a celebrity and a pauper. He was given track shoes in Berlin by the first specialist manufacturer, the German Adi Dassler, thus making another contribution to history (like Lina Radke in 1928) as one of the first to promote the brand that became adidas. But if he received some under-the-table Deutschmarks for the deal, the payment was trivial.

The USA's Amateur Athletic Association, rigorous guardians of the amateur code, used that power to exploit their athletes as unpaid sources of gate-money. When, soon after the Games, Owens declined to join an exhausting American team tour of Sweden designed to make money for the Federation, they declared that he had broken the amateur rules, and banned him. That appalling decision, after all he had done at the Olympics, came from class-conscious contempt for the athletes whom the Federation was supposed to represent.

Back in the USA, with a wife and child, desperate for income, Owens was the target of scams seeking to exploit his celebrity. He became financially involved in a Baseball League for African Americans, but that soon foundered. He was paid to endorse the 1936 Republican Presidential candidate, Alf Landon, but that also proved a mistake, as it meant he received no recognition from the Democratic sitting President, F.D. Roosevelt. Owens's often quoted statement that "Hitler didn't snub me – it was our President who snubbed me," has to be read in the context of an election campaign, most probably with someone else writing the quotes.

Always, these bigger historical forces shaped Owens's life and reputation, though not his personality or values. He was harassed by those wanting to use his name and voice. In 1936, the young Owens was at first pressured into supporting the protest movement that demanded an American boycott of the Berlin Games; then he retracted on the advice of his coach. In middle age, he criticized the Black Power salute of John Carlos and Tommie Smith at the 1968 Olympics as ineffectual, later changing his views on that, too. Don't dismiss him as naive, or politically inept. He was man who liked to think through his positions, not instantly leap aboard what was fashionable. His values were not political. It was naive and inept to speak up for Glickman and Stoller, but it made him the best man in the room.

It's a wonder he kept his fundamental decency. No one offered to pay for him to complete his college degree. He tried sports promotion. He became an entertainer, racing against horses or motorcycles.

"What was I supposed to do? I had four gold medals but you can't eat gold medals," he said. He ran a dry-cleaning business, and filed for bankruptcy. Further ahead, in 1966, he was found guilty of tax evasion.

Then at last the tide of history changed to his advantage. As the Civil Rights movement gathered momentum, the United States government needed African American role models, and appointed Owens as a goodwill ambassador. He used his celebrity in Germany well at the time of the Munich Olympic terrorist crisis, calming the irate German organizers after American coach Bill Bowerman called in the Marines to protect his athletes.

At this better time of his life, Owens found his other great skill, after running – he became an outstanding motivational speaker.

"He projected a modest sincerity, and told his story eloquently and very movingly. He was well-dressed, with no flashiness, and in person was a quiet, dignified, seemingly sweet-natured man, with a strong sense of responsibility, but not comfortable with activism or protest," said women's running pioneer Kathrine Switzer, who was a co-speaker with Owens at an event in 1973.

So his last years brought Owens some calm of mind, and fame uncomplicated by politics. He was awarded the Presidential Medal of Freedom, America's highest honor, in 1976, and died, of lung cancer, in 1980, at age 66. Owens wasn't the first Black athlete to win an Olympic gold medal – that honor went to Eddie Tolan in the 100m and 200m in 1932. But Owens's foursome of medals, his world records (his long jump mark lasted 25 years), his high profile, and the dignity and decency of his conduct, even as he dominated the Olympic Games, made him an important pioneer and role model for African American runners like Ted Corbitt.

"My father began as a sprinter, and was deeply influenced by Jesse Owens. He always talked about May 25, 1935," Gary Corbitt, son of the marathon pioneer, told me.

Owens has twice been on U.S. postage stamps. Schools, parks, and running tracks bear his name. A street leading to the Olympic Stadium in Berlin is named Jesse-Owens-Allee. Soon after his death, he entered a higher level, when a newly discovered deep-space asteroid was named "6758 Jesseowens." No runner's story has ever ended on such a height.

Jack Lovelock – Artist of the Track

One little-known story about Jack Lovelock is that while he was marching at the head of the New Zealanders during the militaristic grand entrance of teams in the Berlin opening ceremony, he ordered the "eyes right" salute and dipped the New Zealand flag not to smirking Chancellor Hitler, but to a minor uniformed man standing before they reached Hitler, with a mustache like Hitler's. In one version it was a small mustached cleaning attendant who stood on the stadium steps with a broom. Lovelock was confused, reported his teammate Cecil Matthews, and whispered over his shoulder, "Who's Hitler?"

"He made a stab. We all took off our boaters, clasped them over our chests and went eyes right. It was the wrong man. We were premature. By the time we reached Hitler we were looking straight ahead and had our hats on again" (Matthews MS).

Confusion or mischief? A roguish protest is credible, as Lovelock was a man of individual spirit and impish humor, as well as a strong aversion to what in one published essay he called "the nations where dictators have recently taken command over all departments of their peoples' lives." In the same essay, published in 1935, he affirmed that the role of sport "is to engender a spirit of congeniality and initiative...and all who have its interests at heart cannot help deploring any influence which may take away from the individual's freedom of expression and action."

It's worth unearthing that unknown essay, in a book called *Growing Opinions: A Symposium of British Youth Outlook,* because it shows how fearlessly Lovelock expressed his condemnation of the dictatorships, only a year before Germany was to host Games that were the pinnacle of his aspirations as a runner. The essay reveals him as a man openly committed to "the individual's freedom" in a way totally contrary to the zealous nationalism of the Reich (Lovelock, 1936). It is clear evidence to refute any suggestion that Lovelock had Nazi sympathies, which is among other inventions in James McNeish's novel *Lovelock.*

Lovelock's own achievement was essentially individual. He won the Olympic 1,500m gold medal in a world record time – the ultimate double – by running a race of such tactical perfection that he could justly describe it in his private journal as "an artistic creation." The world's media agreed, poetically lauding his run as "the greatest footrace of all time," "perfect," "marvelous," "faultless." "It was a race magnificent beyond all description...And it was Lovelock's day...He was running in a rapture, and no human being could live with him today...There never was such a race nor such a runner," wrote Evelyn Montague in the *Manchester Guardian* (Colquhoun, 2008).

Lovelock was a subversive, non-conformist hero in another way, in the context of the power hierarchies that defined Fascism. Like Owens, he came from modest origins. When he was born, his father was manager of a gold-crushing facility at a remote and tiny settlement on the West Coast of the South Island of New Zealand, the outermost fringe of the world's outermost fringe, a place called, appropriately, Crushington. Later, in declining health, Lovelock Senior managed a small garage in a very small rural township. Lovelock's distinguished academic career, at Timaru Boys' High School, Otago University, and Oxford University, was financed one hundred percent by scholarships. "I haven't any money," he told his training partner Harold Pollock at Otago University in 1930, as motive for bidding for a Rhodes Scholarship. He went on to become accepted by the Oxbridge elite of British athletics, yet outside England, when not representing Oxford, he always raced in the defiant black with the big silver fern of little egalitarian New Zealand.

None of the leading Berlin 1,500m finalists, in fact, came from the privileged backgrounds we associate with 1930s Olympic sport, except Lovelock's Oxford friend and mentor Jerry Cornes. The Americans Glenn Cunningham, Archie San Romani, and Gene Venske had rural beginnings best described as poor or dirt-poor. The Italian Luigi Beccali really wanted to be a race cyclist but couldn't afford a bike. Phil Edwards, representing Canada, though not born in poverty, was from a Black family of thirteen siblings in what was then British Guiana, and suffered racial exclusion, despite qualifying as a specialist doctor. It's one of the strengths of distance running, that most demanding of sports, that so many of its best exponents come from humble beginnings, even in a constrained era like the Depression, even at a time of rigid amateurism.

Lovelock was one who found a vehicle for achievement in running. His ailing father died when Lovelock was only thirteen, a loss that may have given him the deeper determination that he somehow summoned on crucial occasions. A perfectionist, he had a combination of aesthetic and scientific skills, experimenting while still a student with photography to perfect his fluid and springy running style.

Beneath his beguiling, mischievous charm, he was quietly competitive and determined. After finishing a disgruntled seventh in the Los Angeles Olympic 1,500m in 1932, he wrote in his private journal that he hoped "for a chance to square my account with Beccali & Co." The top five that day – Beccali, Cornes, Edwards, Cunningham, and Erik Ny (Sweden) – all made the final again in 1936. Lovelock more than squared his account.

Between those two Olympic races, Lovelock was the leader of one of the finest of all sporting vintages, the 1930s milers. "Conquerors of time," one journalist called them, and Lynn McConnell took that as the title of his seminal study of the era. Lovelock's individual story is also the story of their international union of rivalry. Lovelock began the story in July 1933, in an inter-Universities match at Princeton, with "the greatest mile of all time," a world record 4:07.6, almost two seconds under the old mark, his impeccably timed sprint defeating the powerful American Bill Bonthron, on his home track. Told he also had run under the old world record, Bonthron remarked, "Aw, nuts. He beat me." Beccali, the 1932 Olympic champion, riposted by beating Lovelock in the International Student Games in Turin, Italy, equaling the world 1,500m record, and then breaking it a week later.

As the clock ticked towards Berlin, the top Americans kept improving. In June 1934, Bonthron set a new world record for 1,500m, and Cunningham for the mile. Lovelock out-raced Bonthron again in London in July 1934, and in August added the British Empire Games gold medal, beating the rising Sydney Wooderson and the British Number One, Jerry Cornes, in 4:12.8 with a sixty-yard burst, in a style one writer called "melodious prose."

The highlight of these between-Olympics years of dramatic contest came in June 1935, when American entrepreneurial flair assembled the best mile field ever for the proclaimed "Mile of the Century" at Princeton. It was promoted as the "4:00 minute mile cocktail." Lovelock, facing

Cunningham for the first time since the Los Angeles Olympics, peaked to perfection. Strong winds enforced a tactical race, and he brilliantly outthought and outraced Bonthron, Cunningham, and Gene Venzke.

Lovelock went to Berlin as one of the most globally famous sportsmen the world had ever known. That's not an exaggeration. This was an era when the media were rising to a new place and power in the world, thousands of newspapers with huge circulations co-existing with the emergence of radio and film. Newspaper writing and news photography were at the height of their entire history. Sound radio commentary was a powerful new form. So was film. The feats of the 1930s milers were witnessed through more audio and visual forms than any human achievements before them. After the Games, Riefenstahl chose Lovelock's Olympic race as a centerpiece of her documentary tribute to sporting contest and the human body.

By August 1936, all the media and all the people were hungry for good international sport with big supporting crowds, just as Goebbels had recognized. Perhaps by intention, Hitler entered the Berlin stadium just as the 1,500m finalists were lining up. He received titanic acclamation, and their start was delayed. But Lovelock stole the show.

Cornes did the early leading, and then Cunningham and Ny took over. Lovelock looked boxed after one lap, but slid neatly out to sit watchfully in third, watched in turn by Beccali, who was looking to repeat his 1932 win. There was tension and some jostling – Cunningham had to take a step inside the track as they entered the straight with just over a lap to go. Lap three in 61 seconds was the fastest third lap Lovelock had ever run, but he wrote "it was easier for me than the first half." (All Journal quotations, Colquhoun, 2008.) Approaching the bell, again there were men outside him, but again he slid between them and was ready, poised in third. Round the first bend of the last lap, he sensed the moment.

"Just before entering the back straight I felt the tension of the field relax, and realized, subconsciously perhaps, that everyone was taking a breather – ready for a hard last 200." He moved past Cunningham into second, slipping into a space behind Ny. Seeming to hesitate, Lovelock paused there for a brief moment, but only a moment, just enough for Cunningham and Beccali to be deceived, and as they came off the bend, suddenly he picked up his cadence and surged to the front, seizing a crucial few strides. "I struck home, passed Cunningham and gained a 5-yard break before he awoke." (Lovelock seems to have forgotten Ny. The gap over Cunningham was probably three yards rather than five.) Cunningham and Beccali had to go around Ny to give chase, and never closed. The strike came earlier than anyone expected, yet Lovelock with his quick light stride sustained it for a last 400m of 55.5, and time of 3:47.8, a full second under the world record.

"It was as usual a case of getting first break on the field, catching them napping," he wrote. Years later he spoke to Roger Bannister about the need "to choose the moment for the unexpected finish." That's understating it. The moment he chose was the one that exactly fitted his strengths in relation to his rivals. All his key opponents possessed better basic sprint speed. Lovelock's asset was his ability to sustain a pace close to his maximum, and yet accelerate with dramatic suddenness, and then hold it for an unpredictable period at the finish.

He wrote in his journal that night:

"I finished in perfect form, relaxed and comfortable...It was undoubtedly the most beautifully executed race of my career, a true climax to 8 years steady work, an artistic creation."

Lovelock died accidentally, not beautifully, at age 39. He was living in New York, married happily to an American, with two small daughters, and was developing a successful career in medical practice and research, specializing in rehabilitative surgery. His only problem was his eyesight, which had been damaged in a fall while horse riding in England during World War II, when he was serving in the Medical Corps. In December 1949, suffering from flu, he was traveling home to Brooklyn by subway, after phoning his wife to say he was feeling unwell and dizzy. He stumbled off a curving New York subway platform, and fell under an incoming train.

Lovelock, like Owens and the third hero of this chapter, Sohn Kee Chung, has inspired a rich cultural afterlife, initially in the key roles they all play in Riefenstahl's *Olympia* (1938). Ironically, those images chosen for a propagandist interpretation of sport, have immortalized their individual artistry as runners, in lasting counterpoint to the mass regimentation of the context. Lovelock's Olympic race has another dubious distinction, in its famous radio description by Harold Abrahams, the 1924 100m gold medalist and hero of *Chariots of Fire* but in 1936 a part-time BBC commentator. As commentary, it is incompetent ("The time at 800 I missed, sorry, excitement") and full of errors and misidentifications ("I'll let you know who's leading in a moment"), yet it is so babbling and boyishly partisan that it has become legendary on its own right:

"Lovelock leads! Lovelock, Lovelock! Cunningham second, Beccali third. Come on, Jack! A hundred yards to go. Come on, Jack! My God, he's done it! Jack, come on! Lovelock wins, five yards, six yards, he wins, he's won, hooray!"

Abrahams, in his own way, was like Riefenstahl, seeking to appropriate Lovelock, to make him into a symbol, in Abrahams's case for Great Britain, or rather elitist Oxbridge, doing it by the insider upper-class schoolboy idiom of his language ("hooray!"). But New Zealand knows its own. That cold late winter night (August 6, 1936) they gathered before dawn outside small-town post-offices to see the telegram from Berlin pasted to the window. Lovelock's understated smile for the camera as he sat on the grass after his victory belongs with the down-beat summary of conquering Everest by Ed Hillary, another pioneering New Zealander: "We knocked the bastard off." Only in the privacy of his journal did Lovelock write of perfect form and artistic creation.

He was his country's first Olympic gold medalist in track-and-field athletics, the second in all sports. He has become a figure of almost mythic standing and complexity. The New Zealand Ministry for Culture and Heritage now refers to a "Lovelock legend." His life and somewhat elusive personality have been reinterpreted in four excellent biographies, all by New Zealanders, in essay-length studies, and in fiction, drama, television drama, and sculpture. Novelist McNeish deserves credit for fanning the embers of the legend, but none for the irresponsible sensationalism of claiming that Lovelock was neurotic, narcissistic, fascist, and suicidal. The real Lovelock has full entries in the *Dictionary of New Zealand Biography* and the *Oxford Companion to New Zealand Literature*. His own journal, edited and published by David Colquhoun in 2008, is one of the best of all books from inside the life and mind of a famous runner.

Some writers have presented Lovelock as highly strung or "brittle," but in his forthright personal journals and all the reports from those who knew him, I can't find evidence of anything beyond the anxieties and self-doubt felt by any athlete, or any human facing a major test, however supremely talented. Rather than a victim to nerves, Lovelock seems in his private journals a man of unusual self-control. He wrote, "on the day, I go in a little nervous always, but determined to hide those well-known symptoms, to try to force or bluff the enemy into...doing what he really does not want to do."

The mind and personality we meet in that sentence sound like those of an interesting man – strong, original, and pragmatic, competitive without any arrogance, confident yet conscious of the pressure, and able to make it into a strength, fully knowing his own fallibility but also subtly aware of how to expose the fallibilities of his rivals. It sounds like a considerable intelligence, a well-balanced mind touched with quiet humor, brought to bear on the complex challenges of world-class competitive running.

Those who knew him remembered intelligence and mischievous charm, not neurosis. Lord Arthur Porritt, his team manager in Berlin, told me in 1986 that Lovelock was genuinely perplexed about whether to compete in the 5,000m before the 1,500m, and placed unquestioning trust in Porritt's decision. For many years, Porritt and Abrahams met every year on August 6, the anniversary of Lovelock's gold medal win, to commemorate the friend they had so much admired. Another perspective came when, after giving a talk about him in New Zealand,

I was approached by a very elderly lady who told me, between small happy giggles of reminiscence, that she had been head girl of Timaru Girls' High School when Lovelock was head boy of Timaru Boys' High, "and we organized the schools' dance together." And enjoyed the last waltz together, I thought, but that is pure speculation.

In the races that really mattered, Lovelock was the greatest of a great generation. He was exceptionally finely attuned to the tensions and tactics of a race, his perceptions working at what he called a subconscious level. At his best, he was sublime. He carried his wit, his intelligence, and his commitment to "the individual's freedom of expression and action" into the very fortress of Fascism, and brought light to the darkest Olympics.

Sohn Kee Chung – A Happy Ending

Kitei Son, a lithe 21-year-old wearing the colors of Japan, ran into the 1936 Olympic Stadium in Berlin as winner of the marathon, a Japanese national hero, acclaimed by a crowd of 100,000 people, and by global audiences for the radio and film coverage.

Sohn Kee Chung, a vigorous 74-year-old wearing the colors of Korea, ran into the 1988 Olympic Stadium in Seoul as the honored bearer of the Olympic torch, a Korean national hero, acclaimed by a crowd of 80,000 people, and by global television audiences.

Son and Sohn were the same man.

As a television commentator working in the stadium in 1988, I can affirm that Sohn's appearance as Korea's Olympic torch-bearer in his own capital city had professional broadcasters on the edge of tears. That elderly man's zest as he almost danced along the track was one of the most positive moments I have experienced in a lifetime in sport. Sometimes a story really does have a happy ending.

Sohn Kee Chung's story began less happily. He was born in the north of Korea in 1914, four years after Korea was annexed by Japan, following decades of struggle between China, Russia, and Japan for regional dominance. For thirty-five humiliating years, Korea endured repression, as something between a colony and a minor province of

Japan. The Koreans' own term for that period, 1910-1945, is "the forced occupation." Sohn's youth coincided with Japan's industrialization and exploitation of Korea. His birthplace, the obscure northern river town of Yeng Byen City, was developed as a modern industrial center, and in 1925 renamed Sinuiju. It is a border town, with Dandong, China, visible on the opposite bank of the Amnok River.

Sohn was not a primitive peasant child scampering up and down mountains, the version that has been widely accepted in the West, but was from a riverside family with its own land, able to send him to Yongchang (or Yangjeong) High School in Seoul. There he was taught well, though wholly in Japanese. There also he revealed a talent as a runner that could bring credit to the imperial government.

My source for some of his story is Alex Kahng, grandson of a fellow-student of Sohn, a businessman and runner in Vancouver, Canada, with thirty-five marathons and sixty half-marathons behind him. Alex discussed Sohn with me when we met at the Toronto Marathon Expo, and he has since helpfully amplified some details with his mother.

"My grandpa Ahn Joong Hee grew up with Sohn Kee Chung in Sinuiju, and with several other friends they were sent away to Seoul to attend high school. Sohn became a prominent distance runner and my grandpa a national level speed skater (5000/10,000 meters), who narrowly missed selection for Japan at the 1936 Winter Olympics. Sohn ran 1500m and 5000m, and with some of his Yongchang High School teammates started to be noticed by Japanese sports authorities when they won Ekiden relays against some of the best Japanese high school and university teams. My understanding from my mom is that all the best Korean athletes went to this high school. From there, Sohn and my grandpa and two more of the best Koreans were enrolled at the elite Meiji University in Tokyo, which was usually restricted to the top families in Japan. My understanding is that the Japanese were obsessed with sports at that time, aiming to reflect their cultural superiority in the region. So they brought the top Korean athletes to study in Japan, treated them very favorably, and required them to compete under the Japanese flag" (private email, 2019).

The success of Yongchang High School runners was in part due to the notable coach, Lee Sun-il. According to the hagiographic life story of Sohn Kee Chung that is now part of the curriculum taught in Korea's schools, Lee's training regime for the teenager included long runs with stones strapped to his back and sand stuffed in his pockets, designed to build running strength and endurance. That could work. Stories of runners carrying added weight in training go back to the "cunning footmen" wearing "shoes made of lead" in 1620 London (see Chapter 4), and include Emil Zátopek running in army boots or carrying his wife on his back.

Whatever his exact training, Sohn did enough of it to become a successful marathon runner by the age of nineteen, when he won his debut marathon race in Seoul in 1933. By the end of 1935, when he was just twenty-one, he had run ten marathons, winning eight of them, with one second and one third. His last win, in Tokyo on November 3, 1935, was a world's best performance, 2:26:42 (no "world record" was yet recognized). He compiled this vita of victories in an era when Japan, or, to be accurate, Japan and Korea, were the world's strongest marathon nations by every measure. By the beginning of 1936, their elites filled seven slots out of the world's ten fastest ever marathons. Even more ominously for the rest of the world, with Berlin imminent, in the pre-Olympic year of 1935, eight Japanese (again including Koreans) were among that year's ten fastest marathoners. Two Americans, John A. Kelley and Patrick Dengis, in eighth and ninth, were the only intruders in the list. Only Kenya in the next century has ever come near to such dominance.

Sohn, with his name now in Japanese form as Kitei Son, was forged in this blazing cauldron of competitive excellence. He made sure of his world-leading ranking by winning Japan's first Olympic trial in 2:28:32. In hot conditions for the second trial a month later, he settled for ensuring selection without much damage by a controlled second place.

Marathon running in this era became almost a religion in Japan. The spiritual Zen of long-distance running had a long history there, in the reverence for *hikyaku* messengers, and the adoption of running as a religious ritual by Tendai Buddhist monks of Mount Hiei (see Chapter 3). Ekiden Relays became popular after the first was held in 1917, and were important in developing modern distance running in Japan. The name Ekiden means "mail-service by stages," and links road relays with the traditional *hikyaku*. Japanese culture, and perhaps Korean, is attracted to the concept of enduring to exhaustion, the element of total commitment to the point of self-sacrifice that is implicit in the marathon. As late as the 1960s, European runners visiting Japan reported that their routine training runs would be applauded by the passing public. "That never happened to me in Liverpool," said my source.

A digression, but the story is too good to leave out, in a book of running's great stories:

Japan had athletes at the Olympic Games for the first time at Stockholm in 1912, with one sprinter and one marathon runner. Shizo Kanakuri as a young man was one of the first in Japan to try the new sport of marathon running. He had real ability, as at age only twenty he ran 2:32:45 for the 40km/25 miles Japanese trial. (That was also the Olympic distance that year.) In cool conditions for the trial, he had only minor problems from his belief that it was harmful to drink water before and during the race. That notion, somehow imagining that water or perspiration cause weakness, was common worldwide until the 1950s. Kanakuri would pay for it.

Kanakuri travelled from his home in Tamana, in the south of Japan, to Stockholm, by ship and train, an eighteen-day trip, accompanied on the Trans-Siberian Railway by his sprinter teammate, Yahiko Mishima. He kept some vestige of fitness by running up and down the station platform whenever the train stopped. (I once did the same when crossing America by train.) By some accounts, he also had to care for Mishima, who fell ill. With limited sleep and strange food, it was not an easy journey.

The Olympic race was unusually hot for Sweden, close to 90° F/32° C. Eventually thirty-four runners, half the field, dropped out, and one died, the only death in an Olympic marathon. Kanakuri was among the DNFs. He had problems with his frail Japanese shoes, but more seriously his refusal to take water left him severely dehydrated, though it's unclear whether he actually collapsed. By his later account, he gate-crashed a garden party in the yard of a rural house alongside the course, lured by the sight of people drinking orange juice. The kindly family cared for their exotic uninvited guest in singlet and shorts until he had recovered enough to take a train or tram back to Stockholm.

Ashamed at his failure, he decided against reporting back to the stadium. With no team manager, language would have been a deterrent, and probably he did not want to lose face. Whatever the reasons, Kanakuri took himself home to Japan. He sent his kindly garden party hosts a Japanese scroll, which is still extant. With the Swedish authorities, however, he was listed as a missing person, probably because of concern that he might be another Olympic death. He remained on those police books for half a century.

Unaware of his strange status, Kanakuri continued to run, as well as playing a major role in laying the foundations of Japan's successful marathon tradition. He was selected for the 1916 Olympic marathon, but those Games were canceled by World War I. He competed in the next two. In 1920, on the long Antwerp course (42.7km, 26.53 miles) he placed sixteenth in 2:48:45, with two other Japanese close behind in twentieth and twenty-first. In Paris in 1924, when it was again warm, he failed to finish, as did his two teammates.

But in Sweden, Kanakuri still counted as missing. He stayed missing for another forty years. In 1967, looking forward to the 1968 Olympics, a Swedish television crew tracked him down in retirement at Tamana, and invited him back to Stockholm. On March 20, 1967, now age 75, in his overcoat, he completed the 1912 Olympic course. Or to be precise, he ran through the finish line. Whether he covered the entire distance on foot from where he stopped in 1912 seems a gray area. But no one minds. His final time of 54 years, 246 days, 5 hours, 32 minutes, 20.3 seconds (the point three is nice) is accepted by the *Guinness Book of Records*, with its tongue slightly in its cheek, as the world's slowest marathon time.

"It was a long trip. Along the way, I got married, and had six children and ten grandchildren," Kanakuri told the media at the finish line. He was also a geography teacher, so his Olympic travels probably proved useful.

The world's slowest marathon record will keep Kanakuri as a half-comic celebrity internationally, but in Japan he is increasingly revered for his leadership in the development of athletics and marathon running. Among other innovations, in 1917, he gave runners a sense of belonging to a great tradition, by initiating the first Ekiden relay, celebrating the long history of the running messengers. Being a teacher, he established some Ekiden for students, as a way of introducing them to long-distance racing. By the 1932 Olympics, the Japanese team was good enough to place three in the top ten, and by 1935, with Koreans now included, they led the world.

So Kanakuri, who died in 1983, age 92, deserves his fame. The awards in the Hakone Ekiden are now named after him. He features as the hero in a 2019 Japanese television historical drama, part of a series created to build interest for the (postponed) 2020 Tokyo Olympic Games. Rather than being merely "the Missing Man," Kanakuri is known in his marathon-loving country as "the Father of the Marathon."

Sohn Kee Chung is connected to that story, as one beneficiary of Kanakuri's developmental work, and the near-cult of Japanese marathon running excellence that Kanakuri helped create. The Japanese made no secret of their ambition to finish in the top three nations in the unofficial Berlin medal table. The marathon would be key in achieving that goal. With an embarrassment of riches to select from, they ran two trials, in April and May 1936, and sent four athletes to Berlin, leaving the choice of the final three to the coach. He chose one Japanese (Tamao Shiaku, who would DNF) and two Korean-Japanese (Sohn and Nam Sung Yong/Shoryu Nan) to go to the start-line in the Berlin Olympic Stadium on August 9, 1936.

They lined up among fifty-six athletes from eighteen nations, mostly European. Sohn had the fastest time with his 2:26:42, but had lost to Nam in the second Japanese trial. The local favorite was Juan Zabala of Argentina, the gold medalist from the Los Angeles Olympics in 1932, still only 24, who had been training and racing in Germany. In that time, he had broken the South American 10,000m record, set a world record for track 20,000m (20km), and placed sixth in the Olympic 10,000m a week before the marathon. The Americans had John A. Kelley and Ellison "Tarzan" Brown, the 1935 and 1936 Boston winners. South Africa's Johannes Coleman was a factor after an African continental record of 2:31:57 in April 1936. Finland and Great Britain had strong teams, without obvious medal prospects, although Ernie Harper, 34, had twelve years of successful all-round experience to draw on, including top-six placings (10,000m and cross-country) in the 1924 Olympics, a win in the 1926 International Cross-Country Championship, a solid twenty-second in the 1928 Olympic marathon, a 25K track world record in 1929, and a silver medal in the 1930 Empire Games six miles.

Zabala had led the field out of the stadium on the way to his victory in 1932, and he did the same again in Berlin, prancing zestfully away from the start, already fifty meters in front as he crossed the Olympic Park assembly area in front of the orderly ranks of applauding youth lined up there. They were the first of what the *New York Times* estimated as more than a million spectators along the route. The ardent Argentinian built a lead of 1 min 40 sec by the 15km mark (49:45). It was a mostly flat course, smoothly paved, partially shaded by forest, but sometimes exposed to the warm (74° F/23° C) afternoon sun, giving the runners elongated shadows that occupied Leni Riefenstahl's attention in the film coverage. More prosaically, the temperature and the ambitious early pace began to be factors in the race. None of the eventual top six featured among the three leaderboard positions until just before 15km, when Sohn and Harper, running together, moved up to third and fourth.

Those two ran together most of the distance, forging one of those strange bonds, random yet intense, that marathon runners know, supporting and encouraging each other without ever being less competitive. That bond, as is often so, was in spite of their being wholly unknown and seeming alien from each other. Sohn had never before been outside Japan or Korea, so Harper was his first close-up European; and although Harper had run in two Olympics, the nearest Asians he saw then were two Japanese who finished ten minutes ahead of him in the Amsterdam marathon.

Sohn and Harper contrasted in many ways as they worked through the field together. The lean, boyish-looking Sohn was not yet twenty-two, yet a specialist marathoner, and the world record-holder, with a youthfully floating stride. Harper the sturdy Yorkshireman had a hawk face hardened by twelve years of intense international racing, yet he had less marathon experience than Sohn. He looked at least his thirty-four years, with a precise parting in his light brown hair, and a running action that was efficient rather than lithe.

Harper had earned a reputation for resilient consistency in all events and all conditions, and was also admired for his sportsmanship. Once in a big cross-country championship, he stopped and helped a fallen teammate, who then outkicked him for the title. In the Berlin Olympic race, he seems to have quietly offered advice and reassurance to Sohn, rather as a battle-hardened sergeant will support a novice officer. At one point in the Riefenstahl film, Harper can be seen signaling and speaking to his younger rival. It seems he was advising that there was no need yet to chase down Zabala. After the race, Sohn asked a journalist, "Please say Mr. Harper is very fine man for telling me about Zabala." Coming from a tough Yorkshireman like Harper, the advice would probably have gone, "Take tha time, lad, no rush, he'll blow oop, 'e will that."

Zabala's lead fluctuated. Sohn and Harper cut it to fifty seconds at 20km, but the turn-around came just after that, and Zabala got a good look at the impending double threat, enough to scare him to a ninety-two-second lead again by 25km. Ellison Brown was also coming on strong on this stretch, moving up to fourth. In both cases, it was too much too soon. Harper and Sohn kept it steady, and benefitted later.

The next five kilometers was when the real action happened. Zabala began to struggle. Sohn pressed the accelerator and edged away from Harper. Three Finns running almost in lockstep moved up from outside tenth to equal fifth. Brown drifted back. Nam moved up into the top ten. Zabala tripped and fell. Sohn and then Harper passed him as he struggled to regain rhythm.

After 30km, that picture was confirmed. At 32km, Zabala shuffled exhausted out of the race, and Sohn had twenty-five seconds over Harper. Then came the three Finns. Brown stopped. In the last six miles, there was only one more major change, as Nam capitalized on his intelligently cautious start, and kept moving unstoppably through to third. At 10km, he had been thirty-third; at halfway, fifteenth.

Sohn sprinted along the stadium straight to win by two minutes in 2:29:19.2, and kept going so vigorously past the finish line that the two blanket men had trouble catching him and wrapping him up. Harper, always resilient, despite blistered and bleeding feet, held second, finishing strongly, although Nam had closed to only nineteen seconds behind him. Nam's caution got him the bronze medal, and showed the effectiveness of even pace running, but also showed its limitation. He was never in the chase. With a little more aggression a little earlier, he might have taken second. It was Sohn who got it impeccably right, always in contention for the win, always ready for any move, but without risking any error. He had made the key decision, to let the impetuous Zabala go away, by his own judgment, before Harper offered whatever advice passed between them. He timed to perfection his other key decision, the move away from Harper at 31km, and he did it emphatically, gaining forty-five seconds in five kilometers. He made that winning move, by the way, at pretty much exactly the same point as Eliud Kipchoge in the 2016 Olympic Marathon in Rio and in Tokyo in 2021.

I hope these details are forgivable. The Riefenstahl film ought to make them unnecessary, but she was really much more excited by camera angles than marathon tactics, and about halfway through the race her coverage loses the plot. The remainder conveys no sense of how the race progressed, apart from showing Sohn in the lead, and lots of others suffering in various inelegant ways. Her interpretation seems to be that the marathon is about survival through suffering, about strong and beautiful males becoming enfeebled and pathetic. Her marathon runners have endurance and courage, but no minds. The later part of the marathon segment in the film lapses into an over-contrived near-abstract montage of fragmented figures and shadows, much of which was in fact reconstructed by bringing the runners back several days after the race for fake footage to be shot. Did Ellison "Tarzan" Brown really take his USA singlet off during the race? Or did he forget to bring it to the re-shoot session? Or did the body-conscious Riefenstahl stipulate and contrive those shots? The "naked native" aspect anticipates her later work photographing Nuba tribespeople.

Was there really an enormous Japanese flag above spectators near the stadium? Or did Riefenstahl introduce that prop, and linger on it with her camera, for political reasons, as Germany maneuvered toward the wartime alliance of the two nations? The Nazis didn't believe in subject peoples having rights or identities, and needed this Korean victory to be a triumph of the Japanese will. The movie renders Sohn entirely as Son, entirely Japanese. When I first watched it as a teenager, it never occurred to me that he was anything else. As in 1928 (Chapter 9), film is not always as accurate as it pretends.

As the world's politics changed, the image that became dominant from that 1936 marathon is of Nam, Sohn, and Harper on the victory dais during the Japanese national anthem, Nam and Sohn both with bowed heads, in what they many years later said was "silent shame and outrage." Sohn holds his potted oak seedling close to his chest, perhaps to conceal the Japanese Rising Sun on his tracksuit. Reportedly, he took every opportunity in Berlin to describe himself as Korean, signing his name in Korean characters, and trying to elude the censorship of his translators. He is said to have dodged a Japanese team party held to celebrate his victory, and gone to the house of a prominent Korean nationalist. There, the story goes, he saw a Korean flag for the first time

214

in his life, and broke down in shame at having been forced to wear the Japanese Rising Sun emblem in the Games (Bull, 2011).

That account, or Sohn's personal later interpretation of events, may include some revisionism. At the time, at home in Korea, Sohn and Nam were ostracized, criticized as "traitors," Alex Kahng told me, because, officially and willingly, Sohn ran for Japan. His name is engraved as "Son Japon" on the giant victors' slabs at the top of the stadium, and the world remained convinced until well after World War II that Japan had placed two in the top three in the Berlin Olympic marathon.

Not Korea, however. The daily newspaper *Dong-a Ilbo* ran a sketch on its front page, showing Sohn on the dais with the oak seedling held away from his chest to show his track top with the Japanese icon conspicuously absent, and an image that I think could be the Korean flag added to the Greek wreath on his forehead. The Japanese government, in retribution, closed down the paper for several months and arrested some of its journalists.

As Korea established itself after the Korean War as a significant modern nation, history was revised, Sohn's Japanese affiliation was presented as enforced, his Korean name was written into history, and in due course he became a Korean national hero. The process has continued since his death in 2002. His old high school site in Seoul is now the Sohn Kee Chung Athletic Park and the school's main building houses the Sohn Kee Chung Memorial Hall, which opened in 2012. At the World Athletics Championships in Daegu, Korea, in 2011, his story was central to the whole event's branding:

"There is a Korean hero at these championships. His face is plastered on posters around the city, and his life story is written down in leaflets piled up at the information booths. The opening ceremony included a film of his life story... His autobiography is part of the school syllabus in South Korea. His life is already part of the national mythology," wrote Andy Bull in the *Guardian* (Bull, 2011).

A statue funded by the Sohn Kee Chung Memorial Foundation was installed in 2017 alongside the marathon course in Berlin, with the

Korean flag now securely set in bronze on the bronze runner's chest. A movie of his life is portentously titled *The Run: A Symbol of Resistance. One Man's Race for Korea's Freedom.*

The forced occupation of one nation by another is never acceptable, and the compulsory imposition of the invader's nationality is worse. But to call Sohn's win a "Race for Korea's Freedom" is another kind of imposition, a retrospective politicized caption. It's as well to remember how complex and shifting the issue of nationality can be. For simplicity, I'll stay with winners of the Olympic marathon. Of the first twelve champions, seven had a national affiliation that was less than straightforward. Michel Théato, who won in 1900, was from Luxembourg, but lived in Paris, and ran in the colors of his French club, so his win has always been attributed to France. Johnny Hayes the 1908 winner (see Chapters 7 and 8) is still claimed by both the USA and Ireland, and it's far from certain in which of them he was born. If he was truly Irish, his gold medal would need to go to Great Britain, as Ireland was not yet independent. The 1912 winner Kennedy McArthur represented South Africa, but he for sure was born in Ireland, County Antrim, and South Africa had been separate for only two years, as technically a Dominion of Great Britain. The British national anthem was played for him.

Hannes Kolehmainen moved to New York right after he won the Olympic Marathon for Finland in 1920, and quickly became a U.S. citizen, though in 1924 he represented Finland again, because of an IAAF rule at that time against switching allegiance. The closest to Sohn's situation was Boughera El Ouafi, who won in 1928 for France, but was born in the French colony of Algeria, and lived there most of his life. Algeria is now independent, and by Korea's precedent could reasonably describe El Ouafi's run as a "race for Algeria's freedom," and demand a statue alongside the Amsterdam marathon course with the Algerian flag on the bronze chest. Alain Mimoun, also Algerian, who won in 1956, would have indignantly resisted any such proposal, as he voluntarily took his French name in place of the Arabic Ali Mimoun Ould Kacha, and when he was honored as France's Athlete of the Century, proudly insisted to President De Gaulle that he was "Alain Mimoun, toujours Français" ("forever French").

It might also be said in fairness that it was Japan that gave Sohn the opportunity to become effectively a full-time runner, and thus Olympic champion. He benefitted from Japan's adulation of the marathon, the culture of running excellence that Kanakuri had created, the educational openings it provided, and the highly efficient competitive and coaching structure it created to produce good marathoners, who were selected for the national team without prejudice as to their ethnicity. Yes, of course the IOC should at least restore Sohn's Korean name to its records, but the full story should be known before a revised political interpretation is accepted. Especially in the context of the 1936 Berlin Olympics, I prefer to see Sohn's victory not as propaganda for a nationalistic cause, but like Owens's and Lovelock's – an artistic creation.

I wish we knew what Sohn was thinking as he ran those last miles. Was he truly already full of "shame and outrage" at being acclaimed as Japanese? When he saw the Japanese flags waving in triumph, did he consider throwing the race as a public protest against the oppressors, like the anti-hero of Alan Sillitoe's novella "The Loneliness of the Long-Distance Runner?" Was he racing for Korea's freedom, or betraying that cause by his complicity? Most young top runners I know mainly want to race. Nationality is not their main concern. On the film Sohn looks calm, intent, focused. He runs with zest and concentration. I have written elsewhere that the secret of running a good marathon is to balance cool judgment with hot passion. Sohn found that balance, and ran at the high-crest pace that it supports. Perhaps he was embarrassed by the flag on his chest, but more likely he was focused on keeping clear of Ernie Harper, and getting to the finish.

Sohn graduated from University in 1940. There is no indication of wartime military service. After the war, with the Japanese defeated and departed, he was appointed national marathon coach, and had conspicuous successes. He took a winner to Boston, Yun Bok Suh, as early as 1947, and was in fact himself entered that year as a competitor, but didn't run. Tom Derderian in his history of the Boston Marathon speculates that Sohn needed to withdraw to enable Suh to win, as "the student would never be so disrespectful as to overtake the teacher" (Derderian, 1994). Suh won by four minutes in a course record 2:25:39. Coach Sohn had three runners in the 1948 London Olympic marathon, all with "Korea" in a large crest on their chests. He was waiting for them at the finish and can be glimpsed in the Olympic film.

In 1950, Sohn had a coach's dream day at Boston, with his Koreans sweeping the top three places. His other major triumph was coaching the 1992 Barcelona Olympic champion, Hwang Young-Jo. And not merely coaching. Hwang had to win a wire-to-wire battle against Koichi Morishita, who was seeking to be the first ethnically Japanese male Olympic marathon champion. Hwang needed inspiration.

"At the press conference, Hwang emotionally related that he had absolutely no choice but to be supreme. His mother was back home in a temple praying during the race, and his idol, Sohn Kee-Chung, was watching him" (Martin and Gynn, 2000). However we interpret his 1936 victory at age 22, Sohn served Korea well in later life, and earned his legendary status.

We can know quite a lot of the personality of Owens and Lovelock, but what manner of man was Sohn? His university degree and coaching career suggest that he had considerable intellectual ability as well as the capacity to instruct and inspire. From photographs, he seems to have been a lively, warm, and perhaps emotionally extroverted man. His high-spirited cavorting at age 74 in the 1988 Olympic stadium was light-years from the inscrutable calm of his manner at Berlin. That may have been simply racing discipline, or perhaps acquired from the Japanese culture he lived in, and the fellow runners and teammates one hopes he made friends among. More recently, Japan-based Kenyans like Douglas Wakiihuri and Eric Waina acquired a similarly distinctive samurai imperturbability.

For the rest of his life, Sohn received, and seems to have enjoyed, many moments of honor, especially at most Olympics. There is a photo of him with 1948 winner Delfo Cabrera as happy VIP guests at the 1952 Helsinki Games. He also served for several decades on the Korean Olympic Committee.

"I had an opportunity to personally meet Sohn Kee Chung at the 1976 Montreal Olympics where he was a delegate. He would often send our family Christmas and greetings cards from the Korean Olympic Committee," Alex Kahng told me.

His was not an obscure life story, even though it took years for the world to interpret its significance in the same way as in Korea. That finally happened in 1988, when the Olympic Games were awarded to Seoul, and Sohn was active on the Organizing Committee. When it came to selecting the bearer of the Olympic torch at the climax of its long journey from Greece, he was the clear and proper choice. And so, fifty-two years after he sprinted to the finish at Berlin, came his apotheosis, that perfectly symbolic moment when a historical injustice was set right, and Sohn Kee Chung ran once more into an Olympic stadium, this time as an acclaimed and very happy Korean.

Epilogue

In his much-admired book on cricket, *Beyond a Boundary*, the Trinidadian author and activist C.P.R. James said that he chose to write about great batsmen because they are so remarkable as individuals.

"I believe that every great batsman is a special organism. It must be so, for they are very rare, as rare as great violinists" (James, 1963).

I believe the same is true of great runners. As evidence I offer Jesse Owens, Jack Lovelock, and Sohn Kee Chung, three rare runners, as exceptionally good at their vocation as great violinists. Very different in origin, character, and their subsequent lives, those three took the 1936 Berlin Olympic Games away from politics and propaganda, and gave to the world individual achievements that were, in Lovelock's phrase, pure artistic creations.

Chapter 11

The Story of the Four-Minute Mile

800 BC   100 AD   1719   1896   1908   1928   1936   1964   1984   2021

The first distance running race at Ancient Olympia, the dolichos, was introduced in 720BC. Later it was added at other Greek Games festivals. It was probably about one and a half or two miles, or two to three kilometers. The measurement of distance by miles came much later, when Roman legions marked out conquered territory in multiples of one thousand marching paces: *milia passuum.* "Milia" (thousand) came into English as "mile." Milestones were placed on roads in England, as measures of the distance between towns, from about 1700.

The first journalistic reference to a one-mile race came in 1719, when two running footmen went head to head on Newmarket Heath – see chapter 4. Later "pedestrian" events often made use of the tempting roadside milestones. Thomas Hughes in *Tom Brown's Schooldays* has a scene derived from his own experience, where boy runners at Rugby School run a time-trial between milestones, alongside the stagecoach. The guard calls out "4:56" and explains that the coachman slows the horses to avoid disappointing the "'mazin' fine runner" (Hughes, 1857).

James Metcalf, tailor and professional runner broke four and a half minutes for the first time in history in 1835, running between two milestones on a dirt road, and won one thousand guineas. The first gentleman amateur to get there was Walter Chinnery, resplendent in mustache and striped long johns, on a Cambridge, England, university track of just over three laps to the mile, in 1868 (4:29.6). His time was overtaken by the great Walter George, with 4:18.8. When George, a pharmacy assistant, gave up his amateur status in 1885 to face the professional record holder, William Cumming (4:16.5), they raced the "Mile of the Century," to such mass acclaim that fences around the stadium were broken down and crowds surged close around the track (Lovesey, 1968). George won with an epoch-making 4:12.75. The mile was now nearer to four minutes than 4:30.

It came no nearer for thirty years. The amateur code was now dominant, and few yet understood the training work required for distance and middle-distance racing. It was 1915 when Norman Taber (USA) at last broke George's thirty-year-old record with 4:12.6, the first time the amateur mile record was the best ever run. The man who did most to change preconceptions about the total of training that can be beneficial was Paavo Nurmi (Finland). In his decade of never equaled dominance, he left the mile world record at 4:10.4 (1923).

The early 1930s brought a generation of great milers, as Jack Lovelock, Luigi Beccali, and Americans Glenn Cunningham and Bill Bonthron traded the world records for the mile and 1,500m in a high-profile series of races. (See chapter 10, "Lovelock.") Track and field was attracting big crowds. Tracks became standardized at 440 yards or 400 meters. The appeal of four laps in four minutes began to take hold. Now the talk began of a four-minute mile, and a "four-minute barrier," and those words took on an almost mythic resonance. The "Mile of the Century" at Princeton in June 1935 was promoted as the "4:00 minute cocktail." Glenn Cunningham's 4:06.8 in 1934 was actually 4:06.7, but only fifths of a second were recognized for records at that time. That was where the record rested before the 1936 Olympics. Lovelock's world record victory in Berlin was of course over 1,500m, but his 3:47.8 converts to a 4:05 mile. The next year, Britain's Sydney Wooderson, whose Olympics ended early with injury, edged the mile record down to 4:06.4.

From time to time, potential four minute milers were well publicized. In 1941, the *New York Times* announced that America had found "the man who is going to run the mile in four minutes," when Leslie MacMitchell, an NYU sophomore, set an indoor record of 4:07.4. The author Laura

Hillenbrand made a similar claim retrospectively in her book about Louis Zamperini, *Unbroken*, on the basis of his good collegiate 4:08.3 in 1938. Those who have no idea of what a seven or eight second difference means in a track mile can enjoy such optimism.

In reality, it took four years of dedicated training and racing by effectively full-time runners, Arne Andersson and Gundar Haegg in neutral Sweden from 1941 to 1945, to trim and retrim the mile record, and bring four minutes almost within reach, with Haegg's 4:01.3.

At racing speed on the track, 1.3 seconds is still a big gap, more than double the convincing gap (say) by which Lovelock beat Cunningham at Berlin in 1936. And a generation or more of runners had been excluded in various ways by World War II. As the world struggled to recover, the mile record stayed in Sweden. But in 1952, John Landy, an Australian too young to have fought, ran in the Olympic 1,500m at Helsinki, and, after being eliminated in the heats, spent time with Emil Zátopek. The thoughtful Landy took home a new belief in intensive interval training, a pair of European track spikes (with a heel), and his own quiet determination. The race for the four-minute mile was about to reach the bell.

****

As the world grows hazy about who first reached the South Pole or flew faster than the speed of sound, anyone will tell you that Roger Bannister broke the four-minute mile, even people who could not guess another track world record or name another record breaker. Although few now survive who were there that night, those mere 3 minutes 59.4 seconds on an old-fashioned university sports field lie deep in the collective consciousness. The image of Bannister breaking the tape is one of the most familiar pictures of the twentieth century or the whole modern age.

The magic lies partly in the numbers, four laps in four minutes, a seeming perfection that makes us forget how arbitrary are human ways of measuring distance and time, and how recently running tracks had been standardized. Partly it is the four-act four-minute dramatic structure, and the ideal poise that the mile distance demands between speed and endurance. And partly it is the age-old semi-divinity accorded to the pioneer or inventor. The ancient Greeks revered "The First One," those who achieved new things in human knowledge and achievement. Bannister lives on with Prometheus, Columbus, Edison, the Wright Brothers, and Hillary. Whether that is a just way of telling the history is a question I will consider.

His achievement came at a time and place when it was deeply needed. In the 1950s, a battered generation was struggling out of the devastation of war. Bannister, tall, young, amateur, and dressed in white, ran himself to exhaustion on crushed cinders not for money, nor for any kind of warlike victory, but simply because it seemed worthwhile, because the challenge, as mountaineers say, was there. With the Cold War gripping that era, he embodied what seemed a reprieve from belligerence, a more innocent kind of contest. He did it, in fact, with the help of friends, not the threat of immediate rivals. I was just short of fifteen, and I won't claim to have understood or articulated all that at the time, but at some level I know that's how I felt. Bannister, like me, was a child of blitz and food shortages, who had grown to manhood, and the excellence he attained was a symbol of renewal and progress.

****

That post-war English interpretation was important, but Roger Bannister was also a hero for the world. In truth, he was one of three heroes – the lucky one of the three. The race for the first four minutes was international, before a global audience. Any one of three might have claimed the semi-divinity of being first and each could justly be said to have deserved it. This is the story I want to tell, the full story, not only recounting what happened but trying to understand what might have happened. Bannister was the most skillful planner, and the most personally driven of the three. But character is not always destiny. Any of the three might have been the one to break the barrier if circumstances had been different. Sometimes history is made by weather, or a fallen football cleat, or the lust for team points of American college coaches, or the time it took in 1954 to sail from Melbourne to Scandinavia.

After the War, the world turned thirstily to sport. It provided cheap and accessible crowd entertainment, and had a human reality, immediacy, and significance beyond the movies. Sport gave us a sense of communality, loyalty, challenge, and striving for excellence without the taint of war. Improving newspaper and radio coverage, and the beginnings of television, added to the importance of major events. It wouldn't be true to say that every mile race seemed like an attack on the four-minute barrier, because Haegg's 4:01.3 remained out of reach. Yet we were always conscious of how close each race came, and it didn't take much for the newspapers to write of breaking four.

I'm still writing of things as they seemed in England as we moved into the 1950s. The main events I remember were the sudden death of King George VI in February 1952, and Emil Zátopek's Olympics in July-August that year. It was a while before we were aware that on the other side of the world, a new mile talent had emerged, and it was much longer before we could piece together a life that is as essential as Bannister's to the bigger story. That's the one I'm now telling.

John Landy's quiet manner and genuine modesty were his way of expressing his deep inner resolve. He had played Australian Rules football at first, because, "I didn't think I had the ability as a runner to compete at the Olympics." When he was finally lured into athletics, he benefited from the colorful (some said fanatical) coach Percy Cerutty, who extolled Ghandi, Christ, H.G. Wells, and the human spirit, at his legendary "conditioning centre" in the sand dunes of Portsea, near Melbourne. Herb Elliott was another superlative athlete to benefit from the Cerutty credo of natural living and diet, and "suffer to succeed." Landy's other influence was Emil Zátopek, who shared his zestful wisdom with Landy at the 1952 Helsinki Olympics, and gave him inspiration that overcame his disappointment at his failure in those Games. Landy had been eliminated in the first round of the 1,500m, finishing some yards behind one of the favorites, Bannister of Great Britain. They had no personal contact.

Back in Melbourne, Landy did four months of the most intensive training any runner had done, even Nurmi, primarily high-volume Zátopek-style intervals, with a big increase also in his weekly mileage. That took courage at a time when beliefs about "staleness," and "straining your heart" were still prevalent. His aim was (modestly as always) to race well in the 1952-53 Australian summer season, with no thought yet of the four-minute mile, which was an unthinkable eleven seconds faster than the best he had ever run.

The work paid off, as it usually does. In December 1952, on a grass track in his home city of Melbourne, Landy ran 4:02.1. That slashed nine seconds from his personal best. It was the fastest anywhere in the world since Haegg in 1945, seven years earlier. Whether Landy was aiming for it or not, suddenly the four-minute mile looked possible. The news trickled through to Britain, probably via the invaluable *Athletics Weekly*. Landy brought a new continent and its ardent sporting culture into the race. And he was in Australia's high summer racing season while Europe and America were enduring winter, and no track running was possible. On January 3, 1953, Landy was under four-minute pace until the final twenty seconds, ending that race with 4:02.8. That began a year of heroic failures.

Now a strange kind of contest developed, between three competitors in different seasons, different hemispheres, and different sports cultures, racing separately, often effectively solo, in different conditions, yet essentially racing each other. Since the Covid-19 pandemic we might call it "virtual miling." Landy's 4:02.1 was the first target as the 1953 northern Spring came. On May 2, in Oxford, England, Roger Bannister sprinted past his pacemaker Chris Chataway to record 4:03.6, and (with measured English understatement) "realize that the four-minute mile was not out of reach." The British media acclaimed him. On June 5, in Compton, California, Wes Santee of the University of Kansas ran a negative splits strategy, with two flying sub-sixty-second final laps for a 4:02.4 finish. Four-minute fervor came back to America.

Always media-shy, Bannister chose an obscure high schools' meet at Motspur Park, near London, on June 27, 1953, for an all-out paced effort. On the same date, five hours later, Santee was racing a mile in Dayton, Ohio, with the American press predicting sub-four. Bannister was paced first by Australian Don MacMillan, then by Chris Brasher, who had jogged very slowly for one and a half laps, waiting to be caught, and then paced Bannister's last one and a half, shouting encouragement over his shoulder. Bannister responded with 4:02.0, the best in the world since 1945. The British Federation didn't like the flagrant Brasher pacing device, and rejected Bannister's time as a record "because it does not consider the event was a *bona fide* competition according to the rules." Bannister took note that any record would need to be set in a race "in which all runners set out to finish" (Bannister, 1955).

Now it stood at Bannister 4:02.0 (paced), Landy 4:02.1, Santee 4:02.4. Scandinavia rejoined the challengers on August 7, at Gavle, Sweden, when Sune Karlsson ran 4:04.4.

The barrier stood. The American and European seasons in those days were over by early September. The northern winter came, and indoors Wes Santee ran 4:04.2, and a relay leg of 4:02.6. Allowing for the tight bends and jostling elbows of indoor racing, Santee was clearly capable, in the right outdoor race, of what was now being widely spoken of as a lasting place in history. But the long summer of the four-minute mile moved south to Australia again.

****

John Landy thought he might break Haegg's world record, but remained consistently modest about breaking the four-minute mile. Australian fans disagreed. Crowds of up to 30,000 urged him around the country's bumpy grass tracks.

"People got carried away. I guess it was exciting. At times I found it worrying. I felt I was carrying a big burden, and once or twice I didn't run well. I remember running 4:05 in Sydney before a big crowd who, I am sure, expected a world record. The cricket ground was very wet, and I found it difficult to run on the spongy grass," Landy recalled. He dismissed talk of a "barrier."

"It was simply a barrier in terms of conditioning by runners at that time, the track conditions, and the competition...I was essentially trying to break the world record and to win the Empire Games mile at Vancouver. The talk about a psychological barrier was nonsense."

Yet even Landy acknowledged that for the public, the four-minute mile had become "the Mount Everest of track and field." Edmund Hillary and Tenzing Norgay had conquered the summit of Everest on May 29, 1953. The news reached London and elsewhere on June 2, the morning of the Coronation of Queen Elizabeth II. (Some believe the news was held back to ensure that happy timing.)

Time after time, Landy set out from base camp towards the summit. Through that too-hot Australian summer of 1953-54, the crowds roared him on four times around the grass track, held their breath as he reached the tape, then beat the air in disappointment. That season Landy ran 4:02.0, 4:02.4, 4:05.5 (on the wet track), and 4:02.6. There are still elderly Australians who hold among their most vivid memories the image of that slight, lonely, dauntless figure walking across the grass to prepare for the next time. Then came the last chance of the dying Southern Hemisphere summer, April 19, 1954. In a cold spring on the other side of the world, Bannister's May 6 date with destiny was less than three weeks away. The American college season was in full swing and Santee was in form, coming off an intense indoor season. The groundsman at Bendigo had carefully rolled his grass track.

The conditions were right. The track was smooth and firm, and at last it was a day without wind. A pacemaker helped Landy to halfway. But on the first lap, as Landy skimmed along in his frail racing spikes, with one fatal step he picked up an unseen football cleat from the rolled grass, fallen from a boot months before. Its sharp nails pierced his foot. It stayed in his foot for nearly four laps, a significant and distracting pain, if not debilitating. Finishing fast, Landy ran 4:02.6 again. He would never discuss the cleat incident. The same was true of the cut foot that he suffered just before his Vancouver "Miracle Mile" against Bannister in 1954.

For the want of a nail, the battle was lost, the saying goes. Without being overly dramatic, that small stray cleat may have changed history. Landy would be the last to say so, and the last, it seems, to care. "Buzz Aldrin, Norgay Tenzing and me," he chuckled in August 2002. "They should have given us our own private club."

****

Wes Santee in his later years was less relaxed about missing immortality, and justly so.

"Every time I tried to set up a pacer, the AAU would throw a fit. Often others would not run against me because they feared they might lose. We missed a golden opportunity back then. If we'd have put all our best together in one race, I think we could have done it."

With his obligations in the American collegiate system, Santee was less free to focus than Bannister. Bannister was able to choose his date, his coach, his pacers, and his venue, and could take five days off for refreshing recreation, planning every necessary detail to take the tide of fortune at the flood. American college track had other priorities. On April 10, 1954, nine days before Landy's Bendigo football cleat race and less than four weeks before Bannister's quietly and meticulously planned first mile of the year, Santee had to run three events for the University of Kansas against the University of California at Berkeley. He won the half-mile in 1:51.5, won the mile in 4:05.5, and ran a 440 relay leg in 48 flat. It was probably the finest one-day achievement ever recorded by a middle-distance runner to that date. It won a pile of points for his college team and their coach. But Santee's image breaking the mile tape is not among the "one hundred photographs that changed the world."

Meanwhile, in late April, after his near-miss at Bendigo, John Landy embarked from Melbourne on a passenger ship, in those days before global air travel, bound for a summer training camp near Helsinki, and a racing tour of the fast, firm, cool cinder tracks of Finland. It was a four-week voyage.

In London, three Englishmen were counting the days. It had been a suspenseful winter. Alan Gordon, an Oxford University runner who at age 21 would finish fourth in the first sub-four mile, remembered that the months of watching and waiting were like the race to the moon. "It must have been agony for Bannister. Every day we expected to hear news from Australia that Landy had done the four-minute mile."

The agony of inaction ended for Bannister in April. Twelve days before May 6, he ran a solo three-lap time trial, and hit his exact target, 2:59.9. (As an admiring schoolboy, I watched from the rail and later begged his autograph.) "I felt a little sick afterwards and had the taste of nervousness in my mouth," he said (making me feel guilty now that I troubled him for his autograph). The nervousness would increase to fever-pitch, but he knew now that with pace-making help, he could do it. Santee had no major race in the weeks after his Berkeley treble. Landy was at sea.

****

Bannister and his two chosen pacemakers, Chris Brasher and Chris Chataway, decided to make their combined assault on the "Four-Minute Everest" on May 6, 1954, at the annual Oxford University versus Amateur Athletics Association match. It was a low-pressure, early-season evening event that enabled the AAA to give a competitive opportunity at near-national level to a mix of established and rising athletes, while the student team gained experience against strong competition. The overall team result didn't matter much, although that night the Oxford captain, Ian Boyd, chose to run the 880yd in hopes of gaining maximum team points. (Boyd later placed third in the 1954 Empire Games 880yd and eighth in the 1956 Olympic 1,500m, and became Chair of Athletics New Zealand, where he had moved after his competitive career was over.)

The main reason for Bannister's choice was, of course, that the meet was so early in the season. It was going to be a very long racing season, with the Empire and Commonwealth Games in Vancouver in July-

August, the European Championships in late August, and the first visit by a Soviet track and field team to Britain in October. With Santee blasting away at the barrier, and Landy in temporary exile on a passenger ship, the sooner the better. Bannister must have given the AAA a strong hint of the team he would like for the mile. For him and for Chataway it was a nostalgic return to the Iffley Road cinder track where their careers were established in their student years, while Brasher had been at Cambridge (whose Fenner's track at that date was still three-plus laps to the mile). For the media and public, turning out for the AAA without any special publicity would make it appear beforehand as if they merely wanted a warm-up race in a favorite venue to open the long season. If things worked out as they secretly hoped, they could be safe that it was a *bona fide* match race, with Britain's best time-keepers and officials present, and a good public and media attendance. They achieved all that without paying the price of sensationalism or stressful expectations beforehand. Someone who was in the know (probably the journalist McWhirter twins) made sure BBC television film cameras were present. We are all grateful for that.

Roger Bannister felt later that he was too much of a loner in his early running career. Already a shining star at university, he toured with small British teams, and placed third in the 1950 European Championships 800m, getting very close to a better medal. The three podium times were 1:50.5/1:50.7/1:50.7. He was invited to New Zealand and America, where he won the Benjamin Franklin Mile in Philadelphia in 1951. He shared in the world 4 x 1 mile relay world record by a British team, also including Chris Chataway, in 1952. But he had no coach, and raced rarely at home, leaving the public and press disappointed.

After he failed at the Helsinki Olympics in 1952, he increased and systematized his training, and through his friend Chris Brasher he met the coach Franz Stampfl. Bannister was at medical school in London now, and as was usual in those days, with the pressure of his medical work increasing, he didn't anticipate his running career lasting beyond the Empire Games and European Championships, at the end of that 1954 summer. But he was not so devoted to medicine that he was going to pass up the opportunity of the four-minute mile. Stampfl gave what control-freak Bannister conceded were "valuable hints" for his training, and he trained at Paddington with Brasher, and at weekends with Chataway. The group "rejuvenated my enthusiasm," he said, and made the severe interval training seem like fun. To freshen up as the day approached, Bannister made the decision to go hiking for five days in the Lake District, "so I was absolutely fresh and raring to go on the day itself" (Bannister, 1955).

He was also nervous and unsure, sharpening his spikes on a laboratory grindstone at St. Mary's Hospital, agonizing when he slipped on a polished hospital floor, feeling consumed with doubt, fretting about what he described as "the high wind." As he warmed up, he always said, he was anxiously watching the flag flapping on the square tower of the Iffley Road church. It was a cool evening, with a shower of rain early on, and more rain possible. The crowd and officials all wore overcoats, although the film of the race shows that they ran in sunlight, pale perhaps, but enough to show shadows of the runners on the track. At the beginning of the film, where they pull off their track tops, the flag on the church tower can be glimpsed flying out pretty vigorously.

Ian Boyd, whose career at Oxford University partly overlapped with Bannister's, found the great man too self-obsessed, and always told me that Bannister's accounts of that evening exaggerated the problem of the wind. Perhaps Bannister wanted to heighten the suspense narrative when he told the story in his book, or more likely at the time he genuinely needed a source of anxiety, as many of us do before taking on something momentous. Whatever the truth, Bannister's version is that in the minutes before the race, the flag drooped. "The wind was dropping slightly," are his words. He thought of Shaw's St. Joan waiting for the wind to change, he says in his book. He claims that he delayed making the final call until the race was about to start. "I made my decision. The attempt was on."

As Brasher led the first two laps, Bannister's simmering nervous energy nearly boiled over, and called out to Brasher, "Faster!" Brasher in fact took them through the first lap in a perfect 57 seconds. "I was shaken when Roger gave me the whip," Brasher recalled, and he feared they might wreck the whole thing by going too fast to halfway.

Bannister was moving "as if propelled by some unknown force" yet at the same time he was tense and impatient. During the second lap, a voice from crowd, in fact Stampfl, called "Relax!" which calmed his fretful temperament.

Brasher went through 880 in an immaculate 1:58, and led on until the beginning of the back straight. Many years later, in the Thames Hare and Hounds club pub, he sometimes confessed to the fantasy hope that he might be the one who would win and break the four-minute barrier. But his turn ended, Chataway moved past, and Brasher gratefully slumped back, finishing at the back of the field. Even more years later, as Chataway jogged round the same track (now with an all-weather surface) with other elderly friends in a long memorial relay put on soon after Brasher's death, he too suddenly joked as we came into the last bend, "This time I'll win." These were not men accustomed to playing a secondary role. Perhaps that's why they did it so well on that one all-important occasion.

It was Bannister who was destined for immortality, or had the inner conviction that it was his to seize. To understand the race precisely, you need to know that the start/finish line was in the middle of the straight, not immediately before the bend as has become customary since. So Chataway led from half way along the back straight, and they passed the bell in 3:00.1. Four minutes was possible but needed a sub-60 last lap. It would be close.

Fifty-five seconds from the finish, Bannister faced one of those fine-hair decisions by which history is made or lost: to pass the tiring Chataway by going wide on the first bend, or to wait and put everything on "unlocking my finishing burst." He waited till they hit the back straight, and unlocked. It was a long finishing burst, much longer than Bannister would deploy against Landy at Vancouver later that year, almost as long as Lovelock's at Berlin in 1936. The film shows Bannister still powerful and high-striding around the last curve, then holding on for the short final straight. No one watching would see that his last lap was in fact two seconds slower than his first, but Bannister knew: "My body had long since exhausted all its energy, but it went on running," he wrote. "With five yards to go the tape seemed almost to recede" (Bannister, 1955).

The image of his last lunging stride as Bannister broke the tape is one of the icons of the modern world. It was one of only three sports images chosen for *Life's* millennial "100 Photographs That Changed the World." (The others were Emily Davison's suffragette martyrdom under the hooves of the King's horse at Epsom races in 1913, and the attack on Kathrine Switzer in the Boston Marathon in 1967.) The photo is worth close attention. Bannister, in all white, at full stride, airborne, is at his heroic last gasp. One official clenches his pipe as he waits to press his stopwatch. One wears a clerical collar. Another, kneeling, is so overcome he can't watch the final strides. The infield is cluttered with athletes, coaches, and students in the scarf and sports jacket of that era, all intent or already jubilant. The flag on the church tower is no longer evident in the misty sky, its part in the drama done.

"I leapt at the tape like a man taking his last spring to save himself from the chasm that threatens to engulf him," Bannister wrote in his classic *First Four Minutes* (U.S. title *The Four-Minute Mile*). Running's most memorable moment was attained by someone who was also equal to the literary task of turning it into myth. Of his exhaustion afterwards he wrote, "I felt like an exploded flashlight with no will to live."

The time-keepers huddled to compare watches. No electronic timing in those days. There were complex rules about discrepant times being eliminated, and the valid ones averaged. The written record application would be sent for ratification later, but at this moment everyone on that ground breathed only for the result. The small crowd stirred and waited, then fell silently attentive, ready for history.

The public address announcer Norris McWhirter had a full sense of the importance of the moment, and made his contribution to it. As he read the results over the crackly PA system, he chose the sequence of

233

information with the skill of a great dramatist, arranging it in a rising crescendo of importance, with a perfect pause before the key word:

> *Ladies and gentlemen, here is the result of Event Number 9, the One Mile: First, number 41, R.G. Bannister, Amateur Athletic Association, and formerly of Exeter and Merton Colleges, Oxford, with a time which is a new meeting and track record, and which, subject to ratification, will be a new English native, British National, British All-Comers, European, British Empire, and World record. [Slight pause] The time was three...*

The rest of the announcement was impossible to hear.

The crowd shouted and cheered and cavorted, media, officials, and all. Bannister became as elated as an intense, anxious, reticent, and sometimes remote Englishman will allow himself to appear. He hugged Brasher and Chataway, he waved, he shook every hand, he was belabored with backslaps and dazzled by photographer's flashlights. In his book, he reflected on the united effort and the individual achievement, switching neatly from "we" to "I."

"We had done it – the three of us! We shared a place where no man had yet ventured – secure for all time, however fast men might run miles in future. We had done it where we wanted, when we wanted, how we wanted, in our first attempt of the year. In the wonderful joy my pain was forgotten...I thought at that moment I could never again reach such a climax of single-mindedness" (Bannister, 1955).

John Landy had disembarked in Europe on May 3. Santee's next meet was on May 29.

****

May 6, 1954, was not the end of the drama. Perhaps it will never end. Most of a century later, meet promoters in towns around the world still attract crowds by promising their area's first four-minute mile. In Whanganui, New Zealand, they keep an honors list of the sixty-six sub-fours run there (to February 2021), and award each successful runner a cap, numbered with their place in the sequence (Peter Snell got Number 1). In the English-speaking world, at least, to break four is still a special achievement, far more coveted than breaking 14:00 for 5,000m, say, or a 1:50 800m. It hasn't been cheapened by commercial vanity adventure tourism, like Mount Everest.

Yet for the first month it seemed that Bannister had moved into private territory, beyond mortal reach. Wes Santee hurled himself at the barrier again in Kansas City, and ran 4:01.3 (officially .4), equaling Haegg's old world record. Landy's first race in Finland was 4:01.6. On June 4, Santee broke the world 1,500m record (3:42.8) and gasped the extra 120 yards to break the mile tape in 4:00.6. A month earlier that would have been a world sensation. Now it was an obscure footnote, except as the American record. Landy and Santee each ran sub-4:02 again. But still only Oxford, England, knew the sound of the word "three." It seemed that Everest would be conquered only by Roger Bannister.

Until June 21, when Chris Chataway joined Landy in a mile race at Turku, Paavo Nurmi's town. Chataway always said that he went there to "make a race of it" and possibly help Landy through the barrier, not by pace-making but competing. It worked. Landy, as usual, did most of the leading, with Chataway in his footsteps. The threat from the resolute Chataway pushed Landy through three laps in 2:57.2, three seconds faster than Bannister six weeks before, shepherded so carefully by Brasher and Chataway. This time, Landy had no hot Melbourne wind or unreliable grass to cope with on his last lap, and no nails in his foot. It was a cool Finnish evening, he ran on firm Finnish cinders, and he had the threat of a very fit and determined Chataway just behind. Landy held 60-second pace, took the world 1,500m record in stride at 3:41.8, and reached the mile in 3:57.9. (Officially 3:58.0 for world record purposes.)

So in the end the persistent Australian did not scramble over the barrier – he leapt it. He leapt over Bannister, too, a yawning 1.7 seconds faster. His years of dedicated training at last had their reward. "I had improved my speed a bit," is as near as Landy would go to waxing eloquent about that night. Pushed, he added, "The Finnish crowds were excellent. They were track connoisseurs."

****

What if the church flag hadn't drooped on May 6th? Counterfactualities, or "What if?" is a branch of academic history that interprets what happened in the light of what might have happened. What if the rain had come? What if Bannister's five days' hiking had left him tired instead of fresh? What if the pacemakers erred, or if Bannister simply fell short as so many had done so often? Would the image of John Landy breaking the tape at Turku be part of the iconography of our age? Would that race head every list of sport's greatest achievements? Would the announcement of the word "three" have been as potent in Finnish? Or what if it had been spoken in Bendigo, Australia, the night of the football cleat? Or at that meet in Berkeley, California, what if Kansas University's coach had let Santee run only the mile? What if the British sport's governing body had enforced the full letter of their rules and disallowed the Bannister time as a record because it was assisted by pacing rather than a legitimate race?

The questions keep being asked, and should be asked. We need to keep re-examining something that has become so crucial to the history of our sport, and to the cultural narrative of the twentieth century. But competitive running has one special advantage. Any issue between two runners can be settled by a race.

****

The key moment in the "Miracle Mile," the Bannister/Landy head-to-head at the British Empire and Commonwealth Games in Vancouver in August 1954, is immortalized in a famous photograph, and a statue that stands outside the stadium. In an unforgettable split second as they come off the final bend, Landy, who had been leading the race by eight yards at half way, glances over his left shoulder, just as Bannister, so high off the track that he seems to be flying, surges past him on his right. The two greatest milers of all time had each run their best tactic. Landy set a remorseless pace from the front, Bannister hung on by what he called an "invisible rope," fermenting somewhere deep within him that extraordinary passionate upsurge of finishing speed. It had come down to that moment on the stretch, a microsecond of pure competition like the distilled essence of our sport. Both broke four minutes, 3:58.8 and 3:59.6. Landy lost the race but retained his world record. It was a dream come true for every track fan – except perhaps, Wes Santee.

****

Bannister's 1954 year of miracles ended with victory in the European championship 1,500m on August 29. Chataway and Brasher soon had their own moments of glory. On October 13, 1954, Chataway ran a world 5,000m record to defeat the USSR's Kuts in London (see my *When Running Made History*). Two years on, Brasher also rose to the big occasion, and won the Olympic gold medal in the 3,000m steeplechase in Melbourne in 1956. All retired from competition covered with glory, as did Landy, after taking the Olympic 1,500m bronze medal in Melbourne. In 1955 Santee ran an American record 4:00.5, meaning he had now run three of the seven fastest miles in history. He was promptly banned, by a federation that had never supported him, and was resentful of his fame and ability to fill a stadium. They banned him for "excess expenses," acting on a leak from a promoter who was also an AAU officer, and whose monetary offer to Santee to appear at his meet had been turned down. "The AAU officials knew exactly how much I was getting, they were the guys who were giving it to me. The whole case against me, and the lifetime ban that eventually followed, was a farce and a miscarriage of justice," Santee said later (Bryant, 2005).

It deprived him of the opportunity of the Melbourne Olympics in 1956. With Bannister retired, and Landy still lacking a sprint finish, Santee would have been at least a co-favorite for the 1,500m. He could have been the only American winner of the Olympic 1,500m between Mel Shepherd in 1908 and Matt Centrowitz in 2016.

They all made other major contributions, while also living out their lives under the strange light of sporting myth. Bannister had a distinguished career as a consultant neurologist, Master of an Oxford College, and Chairman of Britain's Sports Council. Knighted by the Queen, he was revered by the public and media. His legs and a stopwatch were on a commemorative British 50p coin in 2004. The Oxford University track, and an adjacent street, are named after him, and plaques decorate walls there and at St. Mary's Hospital in London, where he was studying at the time. His racing spikes sold at auction for GBP 266,500 in 2015.

Landy's successful career was in business and public service, and scholarly biology, including an important butterfly collection, until he was appointed Governor of the State of Victoria, a significant non-political position that he filled with his unfailing integrity and affable modesty, a universally respected Australian hero. Chataway was also knighted after service as a minister in the British government, time as a television news personality, and then a business career in aviation. He took up running again with remarkable success in his late fifties. The tirelessly enterprising Brasher became a leading sports journalist, founded a chain of sports goods stores, introduced orienteering to Britain, created and directed the London Marathon, owned race horses, and is famed in hiking circles as the inventor of a revolutionary boot.

Santee founded an insurance business and served in the Marine reserves, retiring as full colonel. He is commemorated in a silhouette statue at the Kansas University cross-country venue at Rim Rock Farm, Lawrence, but he has had little recognition nationally. He is not even in his nation's Track and Field Hall of Fame. Yet he was a key part of the story of the "Four-Minute Everest," and could well have won the 1956 Olympic gold medal.

Writing about his mythic moment, Bannister focused on the inward challenge, the personal striving for excellence:

"I had a moment of mixed joy and anguish, when my mind took over. It raced well ahead of my body and drew my body compellingly forward. I felt that the moment of a lifetime had come...that it was my chance to do one thing supremely well" (Bannister, 1955).

Achievement can be artistic, as it was for Jack Lovelock, yet is still never wholly individual. "Supremely well" means in comparison with others, at their most excellent. To say that the race for the four-minute mile was a competition is in no way to deflect from that individual drive to achievement. Competition is a strange and special thing, as the ancient Greeks knew – they believed that competition can put us mortals closest to being demi-gods. If you're a runner, you don't have to be ancient Greek to know that by pitting us against each other, competition can inspire achievement, and self-improvement.

When Bannister wrote, "we had done it – the three of us!" it was true in more ways than one. He may not have consciously thought about Landy and Santee as he forced himself around that last lap, but they were the ones who made him need to run under four minutes. Competition is contest, yet it can also foster the deepest kind of bonding, as it did between Long and Owens, or Sohn and Harper, in 1936.

I'm not being sentimental about the rivalry between the three. Each tried their utmost to be the first. They had never met. The Australian version, which took rather gauche form in David Williamson's script for the Australian TV movie, *The Four Minute Mile* (1988) is that Bannister was class-conscious and condescending to "colonials." In the real-life Vancouver "Miracle Mile," Kiwis Murray Halberg and Bill Baillie did their best to thwart Bannister and help Landy win. In fact, Bannister was no upper-class toff, but a suburban scholarship boy, whose family had moved south from cotton-mill Lancashire. His father was a public service clerk. Bannister's remoteness and reticence were a personal mannerism, a protection for shyness in the face of media attention, not class superiority. Landy never subscribed to that fiction of snobbery, and in later years they always met as old sporting rivals do, as good mates who respect each other for having shared the same struggle.

They were all three bonded by that struggle. The story of the four-minute mile belongs to all those who were part of its narrative, back to Nurmi, Lovelock, Bonthron, and Haegg. Every record broken, every close failure, made a contribution to the ultimate success. It really was like the first conquest of Everest, when two men took the crucial steps to the top, and gained the lasting name recognition, but only because of the commitment of the full team, and what was learned from the effort and sacrifices of those who had tried, and in some cases died, before them. That's not how the four-minute mile story is usually told, but from the perspective of the full mythic history, what was finally accomplished in 1954 was a shared achievement.

Chapter 12

The Most Sensational Last Lap in History: Billy Mills's Olympic Dream – Tokyo 1964

800 BC | 100 AD | 1719 | 1896 | 1908 | 1928 | 1936 | 1964 | 1984 | 2021

It was the greatest long track race in history before it even started. Standards had been rising meteorically as coaches and runners around the world experimented with the limits of quantity and quality in training. The successful training regimes of Jim Peters, Emil Zátopek, Vladimir Kuts, and coaches Percy Cerutty, Mihály Iglói, and Arthur Lydiard drove out old fears of "going stale" and "straining your heart." This was the era, these four years between the 1960 and 1964 Olympics, when training reached today's levels. For any runner from three miles/5,000m up who aspired to reach anywhere near national class, this was when it became commonplace to run two sessions a day, 100-plus miles (160-plus km) a week, and include high-volume sessions of interval training.

The world 10,000m record was broken three times in these four years, yet the most transformative improvement was in the depth of quality performances. At the Rome Olympics in 1960, the first eight in a global field ran under 29 minutes. In July 1964, eight from just one nation did the equivalent of that in the English six miles championships. All were training twice a day, and mixing high mileage with intense intervals. Hundreds if not thousands around the world were now doing that quantity and quality of training. Some were covert professionals. Most somehow fitted that commitment into their lives of work or study.

Two other radical changes combined with this increased training to raise standards. First, distance running was now truly global, with the USSR, Germany, Australia, and New Zealand becoming major powers for the first time, and Kenya, Ethiopia, and the USA emerging. Second, despite the still prevailing rules of amateurism, more people were staying on longer in serious competitive running. The 1960 Olympic champions at 5,000m and 10,000m, Murray Halberg and Pyotr Bolotnikov, both known for their ability to win under pressure, were back as strong contenders for the Tokyo 10,000m. Halberg had won a world-class Commonwealth 3 miles in 1962, and was ranked Number 1 at 5,000m every year from 1960 to 1963. Bolotnikov won the European 10,000m title in 1962, and broke the world record in 1960 and 1962. Barry Magee, bronze medalist in the Rome marathon, winner of the Fukuoka Marathon, and close to the world record at 10,000m, was another proven top-level contender in the Tokyo 10,000m field.

Threatening to overwhelm that strong returning generation was a flood tide of new talent, surging in from five continents. Ron Clarke (Australia, age 29) had matured to become, in December 1963, world record holder at 10,000m, after youthful brilliance that gave him a world under-20 one mile record, and the honor of lighting the Olympic torch at Melbourne in 1956. The Canadian teenage phenomenon, Bruce Kidd, had at age nineteen outclassed a superlative field to win the Commonwealth Games six miles in 1962. Even younger, Gerry Lindgren achieved at age eighteen one of the legendary feats of American sport only ten weeks before the Tokyo Games, when his 200-mile-a-week endurance training fused with his teenage fearlessness to outrun two world-ranked Soviet runners, Leonid Ivanov and Nikolay Dutov, in the politically-charged USA vs. USSR meet in Los Angeles. Lindgren, Ivanov, and Dutov were all there on the line again in Tokyo.

So were two future great runners who so far were best known for high placings in the International Cross-Country Championship, Ron Hill (Great Britain) and Mohammed Gammoudi (Tunisia). They were among many who were fast improving. That there were so many is testimony to the new normal in training. And there was something deeper. This was a generation who had come to maturity in a post-World War II world that seemed to call out for progress in every field, that needed achievement through dedicated work in some non-warlike activity. How else can you explain our willingness to undertake such huge loads of hard training, week after week, on top of full-time jobs or study, for absolutely no financial reward?

Another on the cusp of a major breakthrough was Jean Fayolle, a Frenchman who had forged his resilience in the smithy of the annual International Cross-Country Championship, and would have his culminating moment when he won that event, the world cross-country title, in March 1965, after a previous best place of twenty-first. Another was Kōkichi Tsuburaya, who had suddenly leapt from nowhere as a marathon runner in two races in 1964 to sneak a surprise third place in Japan's team at the Olympics. His finest hour would come a week after the 10,000m, when he astonished the world by finishing third in the Olympic marathon, losing second place on the finishing sprint. And there were two more future great names, Naftali Temu and Mamo Wolde, from two little-known running countries, Kenya and Ethiopia. Their big breakthrough moments also lay ahead. Temu's were in 1966, when he won the Commonwealth Games six miles, and then in 1968 the Olympic 10,000m. Wolde placed second to Temu in that Mexico City 10,000m, and reached the top by winning the Olympic marathon a few days later. Like Hill, Fayolle, and Tsuburaya, Temu and Wolde had not quite reached their zenith for the Tokyo 10,000m; but it was close.

It was quite a pantheon. Every one of the fourteen I've mentioned were worthy of the podium in Tokyo, on past or future form. There were another twenty-two in the field, hoping probably for a good day, and a place in the top six or ten. Among them, however, was one who was thinking, fervently and audaciously, only of winning – Billy Mills of the USA. The Tokyo 10,000m race now belongs so entirely to Mills, and he is so iconic as a legend of running, and so universally respected as a leader and spokesperson for Native American peoples, that it's hard now to realize how utterly unknown he was, how utterly unthinkable as a winner. Very few outside America, I can vouch for it, knew his name or his times or his origins. He was at most "the American Marine." Yet against all the evidence of the phenomenal strength of the field, Mills believed that he could beat the world, and wrote just that in his journal months before.

He tells the best story in his speeches. On the athletes' bus to the stadium, an Eastern European woman field event competitor asked him in a friendly way which event he was doing, and when he said the 10,000, "Ah! Bolotnikov, Ivanov, Lindgren, Clarke! Who will win?" she asked. "I will," said the unknown American. The conversation ended.

It was late on October 14, 1964, a gloomy fall day, with city smog clogging the air and some runners' lungs. "It was like a London fog," recalled New Zealand's Magee, who did his running with Halberg in cleaner air in the forested hills outside Auckland. The red cinder track was visibly damp. This was the last time Olympic track races were run on a surface other than all-weather. The smog and the soft track would be factors in the race, and so would the ill-advisedly large field of thirty-eight runners.

They lined up in two crowded straggly rows, and went out fast, towed first by the Soviet Dutov. The front group was full of compulsive front runners. Kidd, Jim Hogan (Ireland), and Clarke were all accustomed to leading, and needed that space and sense of control. Others too many to identify clustered around them. They were lapping at well under world record pace. Clarke, the tallest among them, looked dominant, serenely majestic with his high prancing stride whenever he surged into the lead. He pushed every second lap, seeking the clear space he loved, but on this day space was hard to find, or to keep. Wolde, Temu, Ivanov, and even the outsider Mills had turns in the front.

This pace, on this sluggish track, took its inevitable toll. Some in the long line began to be afflicted by the thousand natural shocks that flesh is heir to. Famous casualties were dropping back. Bolotnikov the defending champion was gone early, and so were Hill, Dutov, and Fayolle.

Lindgren, Magee, and Kidd all struggled with injuries. That sounds so commonplace, but the next Olympics were to be at high altitude in Mexico City, making this the last chance for most in the field except the altitude-bred Temu and Wolde. There are few things worse than knowing that you're ready for a major race, after maybe five years of dedicated work, and then having it all wasted by some trivial accident or injury. Lindgren had beaten Mills in the American trials, and thrashed the Russians, and was ardently ready, but two days before the race he rolled an ankle badly as he and Mills ran together, and was limping in pain. It can be so minor, yet so life-shaping. The frustration can last a lifetime. Magee, at age 86, wrote privately to me with a disappointment that clearly was still aching. A stress fracture crippled him, and he had to struggle along in "hopeless frustration" as the leaders lapped him twice, "a small pack of runners flying along past me."

The lead kept changing, but Clarke ensured that overall they flew along. His pace exacerbated any frailty. His best tactic was sustained high-pressure, creating a race of attrition, burning them off one by one. Halfway was 14:04, four seconds under world record schedule (Clarke's 28:15.6), and only one second outside the 5,000m personal best of Billy Mills, who was leading at that moment. The front pack was down to five, an odd assortment that no one could have predicted. Clarke, yes, but Wolde, Gammoudi, and Tsuburaya were almost unknown then, and came from unknown places in this context, Ethiopia, Tunisia, and Japan. Neither Africa nor Asia had ever won a medal in the 10,000m. And Mills! Who was Mills? Number two from a nation with no pedigree. America's only medal in the event was the 1912 silver by an earlier Native American (Hopi), Louis Tewanima. How could Mills still be there at this pace, when Murray Halberg was twelve seconds back, struggling to breathe in the smog, Ron Hill another eleven seconds behind him, and Bolotnikov the Olympic record holder almost half the track behind? The commentator who just before halfway dismissed Mills as "a man no one expects to win this particular event" understated the truth.

"I decided to lead a lap, so I would know at least I'd led the Olympics, even if I couldn't finish," is how Mills tells it. In fact, he led more than once, a presumptuous unknown undermining Clarke's confidence and need to control. Watching Kon Ichikawa's extraordinary film coverage of this race (in *Tokyo Olympiad*) over and over, it always looks as if Clarke lost because he lacked the sheer sprint of Mills and Gammoudi. In fact, I believe he lost because in the second half of the 25-lap race he allowed the relentless pace to relent. He now used surges rather than unremitting pressure. Clarke's own splits were 14:05 and 14:20. I know it's easy to sit in a cozy room half a century later and pontificate, but the point about the tactic of attrition, leading hard from the front, is that you have to sustain it until they all succumb. You can't do it only to halfway. You can't let them take breathers, as Clarke again fatally did in the Tokyo 5,000m a few days later. Mills and Gammoudi, already into new territory by almost a minute, would not have been with him at the bell if Clarke had continued at world record pace, as only he could. On that day, in that smoggy air, on that soggy track, could he? We'll never know.

This is what happened. Clarke kept surging, but he also kept easing. Mills, Gammoudi, Wolde, and Tsuburaya held with him. The big field straggled behind them, spread all over the track, and the front pack's progress became complicated by lapping. The air became gloomier. The floodlights were switched on. That seemed to heighten the intensity of the contest. Tsuburaya the unknown marathoner dropped from the front pack. Then, as Clarke cranked up the pressure with two laps to go, Wolde was gone. Three still there. Mills, with his sturdy shoulders and cropped Marine haircut, kept stubbornly challenging Clarke for the lead, pushing in very close to him, squeezing, and Gammoudi followed the two bigger men, looking small, springy, and cunning. Clarke, deprived of space and free running, seemed a little more perturbable than usual.

The bell. Mills was a fraction ahead, very close to Clarke on the pole line, almost leaning against him. Clarke kept him out as they went into the bend. Habitually courteous, Clarke tapped Mills to ask for space.

And then ensues the most sensational last lap in the history of long-distance track running.

It isn't simply three men racing. The cinder track is soft, the inside lanes are cut up, and the leaders have to weave through a confusion of lapped and double-lapped runners. There are ten of them to be negotiated on that final 62-second circuit, with six cluttered almost diabolically on the last bend. Only three move out to let the leaders through. These are elite athletes who don't know about getting lapped, and don't want to know.

Clarke in *The Unforgiving Minute* called the race "like a dash for the train in a peak-hour crowd." Coming off the first bend, Clarke found himself trapped in a bottleneck between Mills, "thumping along at my shoulder," and a slow lapped runner, Temu of Kenya, dead ahead on the inside lane. Clarke had a nightmare flashback to being hemmed in that way once before, in Melbourne, when it cost him the race.

Clarke tapped Mills "a couple of times," to indicate that he needed space to pass Temu, "anything so long as I wasn't forced into the back of the lapped runner." When Mills didn't respond, Clarke "crashed Billy with my right arm" (Clarke, 1966).

Mills later revealed (in an interview with Gary Cohen) that he knew of Clarke's earlier episode and hoped to repeat it.

"I wondered if that could duplicate itself. I felt Clarke bump me a little so I bumped him back. I accelerated and tried to cut in" (Cohen, 2014).

That's a less noble Billy Mills, more calculating and ruthless, less innocent and inspired, than the one who has been mythologized, but it rings true for young elite runners on a torrid last lap.

Moving on to the back straight, they are closing fast on Temu. Clarke and Mills are side by side, Gammoudi tucks in behind. Clarke, trapped, gives Mills a bump, then a well-deserved shove, and squeaks narrowly around Temu. Mills staggers out two lanes, reeling off balance, loses his stride a moment, recovers, and veers back in, shoulder to shoulder again with Clarke. Instantly comes the extraordinary moment when Gammoudi puts his two hands between the two leaders, forces his arms outwards, squirms his way between, and scoots into the lead.

"Poor Billy is out of the race, I must strike now," is how Gammoudi disingenuously told it years later (in 2012), when Mills visited him (Cohen, 2014). Mills stutters again, Clarke initially can't respond, and Gammoudi is away. As Gammoudi skims gleefully into the final bend, he has four meters on Clarke, and Mills is another four meters back, looking ponderous, defeated, out of it – surely.

Here they really hit the lapped traffic. Decent Bruce Kidd moves out to leave them ample space, and takes a long curious gaze at the unexpected trio. Others getting lapped also turn to look, but they don't move out. It's dangerously confused. Around the crowded bend, Clarke finds his full majestically prancing stride and closes on Gammoudi. They steer between more stragglers. Now they're coming off the bend, and it's Clarke's race as he levels with Gammoudi. No, Gammoudi finds another surge, head waggling, and it's his. Then, unbelievably, "Look at Mills! Look at Mills!" cries Dick Bank on ABC, wildly shouting over his race caller (and he got fired for it). As Gammoudi speeds away from Clarke in lane 3, the way to the tape clear at last, Mills charges into sight from among the lapped runners, and pounds down the stretch in lane 4, in a sprint that resembles a schoolboy imitation of a galloping horse, long high strides, knees lifting, head thrusting, arms pumping like pistons. He flings his arms up as he breaks the tape.

That momentary gesture is immortalized in a million internet images, and in a giant silhouette statue of Mills at Rim Rock Farm in Lawrence, Kansas, the Kansas University cross-country venue where he learned the craft of finishing fast on rough footing. Despite the heavy Tokyo track, he broke the Olympic record, with 28:24.4, well under Bolotnikov's 28:32.2 in 1960, only nine seconds outside Clarke's recent world record. Runners as great as Nurmi, Zátopek, and Kuts have won this Olympic title, but there has never been a race like this one.

It becomes more extraordinary the more closely you analyze it. Mills was eight meters behind as they went into the final bend, and still four meters behind as Clarke caught Gammoudi entering the straight. Starting his sprint at the top of the bend, Mills ran the last hundred meters two or even three seconds faster than they did. Think of that in terms of a 100m race. It's true that Mills found slightly firmer footing on an outer lane, and that like a good Marine he found a clear line of advance between the lapped runners. It's true that a less resolute competitor might never have recovered from that double shove at 300m to go. Not to blame Clarke, who needed and asked for space that Mills wouldn't give him. The second shove, by Gammoudi, the two-handed push to clear space, surely deserved disqualification. Later, Mills told Clarke, "our skirmish won the gold medal for me," because before the jostling he was about to launch his sprint, which would have been too early, and probably would have doomed him to get passed again.

I'm not convinced. Perhaps, as Mills now tells it, among his many interpretations, into his mind came the mantra of self-belief that saved his life in childhood, when his ailing father told him that "one day you will fly with the wings of an eagle." Or was it self-hypnosis, as Mills also now tells it? Or because his wife Patricia was in the stand above the end of the final bend? Perhaps it was Mills's luck or judgment in choosing the firmer outside lane, as Clarke came to believe (Clarke, 1966).

Most likely, to consider the whole race, not just its last half lap, it was the wet track, or inner self-doubt, that took the edge off Clarke's pace between lap 13 and lap 23. He was godlike when he ran alone.

Whatever the explanation, the plain simple reality is you can't argue with two seconds in a hundred meters. Especially at the end of a race that has gone close to the world record. The various explanations – self-hypnosis, the orphan's history, racial ill-treatment, the shove, the wet track, etc. – have really become prominent only because Mills has been too modest to state the essential truth, that out of the blue, way above anything he had done before, he suddenly ran one of the greatest long track races in history. Yes, Clarke after half way fell short of his best tactic, but Mills was there, always in the right place, running to win, racing clear of more than thirty of the world's best runners, in the strongest, deepest, most rigorously trained 10,000m field the world had ever seen, pushing the pace when he should have been struggling, surviving threats and surprises, surges and shoves, storming the finish, and ending with a time worth something under the world record if you take account of the conditions. Mills ran a race for the ages. Dick Bank said it best: "Look at Mills! Look at Mills!"

The Billy Mills Story

Sport is not about moral worthiness, but no winner has made worthier use of success than Billy Mills.

His story is well known, from his own public speeches, from a successful movie, and from many admiring writers and interviewers, but it deserves another brief retelling. His tribal name is Makata Taka Hela. (Spellings vary.) He was raised in poverty on the Pine Ridge Oglala Lakota (Sioux) Reservation, South Dakota, surrounded by alcoholism, depression, and disease. One sister died of tuberculosis when he was a boy. His parents separated, his mother remarried to his uncle, but died when Mills was eight. His father died four years later, leaving him orphaned as he entered his teens. Soon after the mother's death, his father, who sometimes read poetry to him, sat with the despondent boy, and told him he could rise from having broken wings, "and one day you will fly like an eagle." As Mills publicly tells that story now, once he discovered his running talent as a teenager, he always believed that "the Olympics would be my day to fly."

In later interviews, he has always been consistent about that belief, calling it "self-hypnosis," and saying, "I put in my journal that I must believe I can run with the best in the world and beat them in Tokyo." He cheerfully displays that journal to every camera. Lindgren, his roommate in Tokyo, tells the story differently. Mills didn't think he had a chance, Lindgren says, until the ankle injury put Lindgren out of contention. That, Lindgren said in a *Running Maniac* interview, made Mills think excitedly that he could win. "The only guy I know I couldn't beat is you." Whatever the truth is about Mills's pre-race self-belief, there's no question about the importance of his outdoor reservation childhood, with no family car, when he would regularly walk six miles to go fishing, and spent days on a one-speed bike. Like a young Kenyan, he gained "tremendous cardiovascular development just by lifestyle," he said later (Cohen, 2014).

He didn't know it when he started running, but he also had an age-old tradition behind him. Long-distance running is fundamental to Native American culture, for its practical importance in communications, and for its spiritual quality – see Chapter 3. In 2016, Mills was a powerful plenary speaker at a seminal Harvard University conference on Native American running. He was a good enough runner at the Haskell Institute (now Haskell Indian Nations University) to get a sports scholarship to Kansas University, where he was three times All-American in cross-country and a useful but not outstanding track runner.

His young adult years were not easy.

"I came so close to suicide my junior year in college. It had nothing to do with the University of Kansas. It was just the major changes America was going through. There were restaurants that I couldn't go into and the racism I was facing was extremely difficult. On one occasion, I was asked to get out of a photo of the top five athletes. I took it as racial, and I broke" (Cohen, 2014).

He was also proudly American, and after graduation he became proudly a Marine. Running seemed a way of affirming that part of his identity. As an aspiring young runner, he took inspiration from the teenage performances of Gerry Lindgren and Canadian Bruce Kidd.

After his triumph, Mills placed fourteenth in the Tokyo Olympic marathon (2:22:55.4), and in 1965 set a world record for six miles in a dead-heat with Lindgren (27:11.6). He retired with the rank of Captain from the Marine Corps, worked in business for a while, then became a speaker. He has given much of his life to being a passionate and cogent advocate for Native American needs and rights. The feature movie *Running Brave* (1983) revived public awareness of his unlikely transformation. Its Tokyo last lap recreated by running actors is pretty good, but nowhere near as sensational as the real thing.

Mills is a charismatic public speaker who knows how to tell a story. Deeper than that, if we're reflecting on his "fly with the wings of an eagle" mantra, and other stories, he comes from an oral storytelling culture, where stories are the expression of values (as in the parables of the New Testament). He brings that cultural force into his public speaking, telling a compelling rags-to-riches story, with emotion and wit. The incarnation of his own story, Mills can transfix an audience with his plea for support to help Native Americans rise out of the pit of poverty, addiction, and domestic violence, and have their rights recognized. He can be uncomfortably forthright about the ill-treatment that has been inflicted on them, and the injustice of their depressed position.

"From just my tribe, over $50 billion dollars' worth of gold was taken from us after the treaty was signed. Timber, uranium, gas, oil – all was taken. The raping of our lands was done and the government doesn't live up to the treaties. On the reservations we are billions of dollars behind in just funding according to the treaty rights...There is this whole confusion about not feeling that we belong. Most Native Americans take great pride in being citizens of the United States of America, as well as citizens of our tribal nation. We were the first Americans" (Cohen, 2014).

Not many great runners devote their later lives to such causes, or possess such eloquence, but with Mills, it is part of his story. In private, he talks with quiet sincerity about the follies as well as sufferings and rights of his people. You sense that he carries huge responsibilities as a leader and spokesperson, yet he has not allowed public rhetoric to be an end in itself. Don't even get him started on the name of Washington D.C.'s football franchise. And he goes beyond advocacy for his own people.

"Sport represents the future of the human race, unity in diversity," I jotted down, listening to Mills one day. I'm not sure now whether he said that, or it was my summary of what he was saying.

In 2012, President Obama awarded Billy Mills the Presidential Citizens Medal for his work for the movement Running Strong for American Indian Youth. He is the only track gold medalist to receive that honor for his later life work.

Chapter 13

Out of the Tunnel: Joan Benoit and the Women's Marathon – Los Angeles 1984

800 BC 100 AD 1719 1896 1908 1928 1936 1964 1984 2021

Prologue: 1896-1984

This is the story of a quest, and the championship that marked its triumphant outcome. It began with lonely unknown pioneers, and ended in the acclamation of a vast sunlit stadium. Like all quests, it features heroes, adventures, innovators, visionaries, entrepreneurs, exploiters, and antagonists. There are errors and enigmas in the story, some that will never be solved. But it's a good story, and it ends well.

In women's long distance running, most attention has been focused on the marathon, mainly because that is where women runners met most opposition and fought most vigorously against the constraints. Other areas have been overlooked, apart from episodes like the 1928 Olympic 800m (Chapter 9). In some other variants of running, though never wholly free from reactionary sexism, the women's story was less fraught. In cross-country, women's competition started in 1921, when a women's "harrier" (cross-country) club was formed in Dunedin, New Zealand. In England, the London Olympiades AC was also founded in 1921, after the successful women's games in Monte Carlo and Paris. Officially sanctioned national and international cross-country championships for women were held as early as 1923, over distances of two to three miles/ four to five km, less than men were running but enough to test endurance.

There seems to have been no opposition, perhaps because cross-country takes place mostly out of public view. The Dipsea trail race in California had to name its women's race a "hike" because of criticism, and eventually closed it down (Spitz, 1993). At the endurance extreme, women were prominent in ultra-distance professional "pedestrian" events in the late nineteenth century. They also made some early incursions into road races in Europe, the UK, and America.

Many of the pioneer women who first began to appear in the marathon, in the 1960s-70s, were already serious competitors, used to racing distances up to about five miles/8km in road and cross-country, or up to one mile/1,500m in track. With that reminder of a wider context, this prologue tells what is best called the pre-history of the women's marathon. It's somewhat beset by a lack of information and some wishful thinking.

The Mystery Woman of Athens

Did a Greek woman run, or try to run, the first Olympic marathon in 1896? Or is she a figment of retrospective fantasy?

It's a story that is a maze of conflicting versions. She was young, or she was thirty, or thirty-five, she was single, or had children, ranging in number from two to seven. She came from Piraeus, she came from Syros. She ran the day of the Olympic race, the day before, a month before, the day after. She tried to make an official entry, but was refused, say some versions, while others say she simply ran, unregistered. She ran on the Olympic course, or a different route. She ran 4hrs 30, or 5hrs 30.

Some accounts present themselves as definitive, like the Wikipedia entry "Stamata Revithi," but on close consideration are drawn almost wholly from secondary or unverified sources. Some get colorfully detailed. In one version, the mystery runner stops mid-run to admire the ships off Rafina, and chats with soldiers when she finishes her run in the middle of Athens, where she asks for a government job for her son. No mention is made of why she finished there instead of at the stadium, or whom she asked for the job. Another version, almost like an old fairytale, casts her as a poor woman looking for work, when by chance she meets a runner, who tells her the way to get rich is to win the Olympic marathon. Some supposedly historical retellings become fictionalized and exclamatory: "...she became obsessed and dreamed of participating...As she lunged forward she was swept up in her own momentum...Nothing could stop her! She was living her dream!" (Reese and Vallera-Rickerson, 2003).

Her name is most often given as Stamata Revithi, or Stamatia Rovithi (or similar), but for a century she, or a second putative woman runner, found fame as Melpomene (pronounced "Mel-pom-inny"). That seems to derive from a single newspaper reference to a Madame Melpomene running the course on March 8, 1896. Under that name, Melpomene, she was later honored by having an American women's health research institute named after her. Why an aspiring marathon runner in 1896 came to be known only by the ancient Greek name of the Muse of Tragedy no one has explained.

The problem is sources. The various stories as we currently have them derive mostly from work by Dr. Uriel Simri of Israel from 1980, the German Karl Lennartz, and the Greek Athanasios Tarasouleas, in the latter's book *Olimpiaka Dromena: Athens 1895-1896*, and articles in the *Journal of Olympic History* in 1994. These summarize a small number of reports stated to be from 1896 Greek- and French-language newspapers, with some masthead titles given. The only citations are very brief, just a few words quoted, with no context to inform us whether the episode was reported as witnessed fact or hearsay, and no precise page/column references. Those summaries were summarized again in *The Olympic Marathon*, by David Martin and Roger Gynn (2000), an excellent but not infallible book (its account of the Dorando Pietri marathon is wrong at several points – see Chapter 7). We are now three levels from a valid primary source.

The story is irresistible. Our culture gives affirmation to the innovative or rebellious actions of women seeking full acceptance. ("Well behaved women seldom make history" – Laurel Thatcher Ulrich.) We want the mystery woman runner of Athens to be true. We need an early women's marathon precursor. Some writers retelling her story get heated, protesting indignantly about gender bias, exclusion, and injustice to women. While that bias is obviously true of the early Olympic movement – de Coubertin said openly that his Games were only for men – the facts here are too flimsy and elusive to support much indignation. Journalists, we know only too well, are capable of concocting a good story from little evidence. Modern academic specialists in women's history also are not immune from imagining or exaggerating ill treatment. Some, for instance, inventively portray Kathrine Switzer as running her 1967 Boston Marathon disguised in male costume to a chorus of abuse from male runners and spectators, even (in one book) having food insultingly thrown at her. None of that is true. The 1896 story has been similarly appropriated.

It's a real whodunit. Or a did-she-do-it? And we so badly want her to have done it. We want a historical figure to stand revered at the head of the increasingly great tradition of the women's marathon, a myth of origin. I need one for this chapter. Think of the women's destination marathon in Greece if we could only verify the story and apotheosize Stamata Revithi.

But for a minimum level of belief, we depend on Greek scholars and sports historians, who have not provided the evidence we need. This was modern Greece, not ancient. Newspaper files must exist. A newspaper report doesn't necessarily mean the thing happened, but it's a necessary start to the research. I tried my best. I arranged a translator, and asked an eminent Athens sports scholar, an official historical advisor to the Greek Olympic Center, to help us locate that period's newspaper archives. He wrote down for me a detailed address on a street in the middle of the city. After two hours' searching, we had to conclude the address didn't exist.

If I can't consider the story as a historian, I'll consider it as a runner. How did she become capable of running 25 miles/40km? No one has ever said that she walked most of it. Accounts that give her a time specify 4hrs 30 or 5hrs 30. That range requires running all or almost all the way.

Twenty-five hilly miles in 4hrs 30 takes some real training, and sustained running; for sure not lingering to watch the shipping movements at Rafina. There was no sport of women's running of any kind in Greece at that time, and women of any social standing could certainly not be seen running on the streets. She must have been of lower socio-economic class to be that active. Many poorer women at that date would have routinely walked long distances, for sure, but (I'm considering likelihoods as open-mindedly as possible) a debut performance of non-stop running over that distance, in a time of 4:30-5:30, looks unlikely. One report attributes 5:30 to her as a 37-year-old mother of seven children. The necessary time out of the house for training for a woman with such family demands might be just possible in our era and economy, but it's hard to see it in the Greek poor in 1896.

The crux of the story as told now, and the source of all the indignation, is that the woman, whoever she was, tried to enter the Olympic race, and was refused. But that raises the problem of the Greeks' process of selection. There were two trial races preceding the Olympics (see Chapter 6), which were officially conducted, fully reported, and created considerable public interest. A total of at least fifty Greek men publicly tested themselves in one or other of the two trials. Only thirteen out of the fifty were selected for the Olympic race. The slowest time recorded in the trials by any runner who gained selection was 3:37:07. That's an hour faster than the fastest of the times estimated for the putative woman. No man was added to the team on the basis of a solo time trial, even though some were reported. The story that names her Melpomene has her running the course in four and a half hours two days before the first trial, without saying why she ran separately.

At the most generous and credulous estimate, she was 53 minutes away from being good enough for the selected team of thirteen. There was nothing sexist about not letting her run in the Olympics, if that decision ever happened. There wasn't a women's race, nor could such a thing be imagined in 1896. If we're talking about injustice, it's worth considering how unjust it would be to admit a last-minute walk-up, male or female, on the basis of an unauthenticated solo time of 4:30 or 5:30, giving her preference over thirty-seven eager aspirants who had been turned down after completing one of the required trials, 53 minutes faster than that.

The mystery woman of 1896 is a good story, but at present it is a long way from being history.

The Original Woman Marathoner

The loose meaning for many years of the word "marathon" (see Chapter 7) is responsible for two other doubtful candidates for the role of Original Woman Marathoner. A French newspaper reporting a marathon in Paris in 1918 gave a time of 5:40 for Marie-Louise Ledru, which has been called the first documented woman's performance. The time is credible, but in France at that date a "marathon" would have been 40km at most. The French resisted accepting the longer 1908 "London distance," until that was forced on them by the International Olympic Committee, for the 1924 Games in Paris. There is little likelihood that the 1918 Paris race would have been a "marathon" in our precise 26.2 miles/42.2km sense. Even Olympic marathons still varied. Stockholm 1912 was 40.2km, and Antwerp 1920 went longer again, to 42.75km. Boston, too, was a very approximate twenty-five miles until conforming with the Olympics in 1924. They were all legitimately called marathons; but they were not 26.2 miles/42.2km.

The name Violet Piercy enjoyed many years at the top of every list for the women's marathon world record, all taking her without query from this entry in David Martin and Roger Gynn's classic *The Marathon Footrace* (1979):

Violet Piercy   GBR   3:40.22.0   Chiswick   03 OCT 1926

The entry came from Roger Gynn, who later withdrew from running research; Dr. Martin was unable to give a source for the Piercy listing.

That mystery was solved in 2017. New research by Britain's Andy Milroy and Peter Lovesey, and the USA's John Brant, showed that a Violet Piercy did complete a well-publicized solo run starting at Windsor on that date, but her route was not to Chiswick, and was only about 22 miles (35.4km). It's the same problem, what does "marathon" mean? Despite the Olympic standardization, in those early years it still mostly meant "long road run," and could apply to anything from six miles up. Even today, every runner gets asked, "How far was your marathon this week?" Piercy's 3:40:22 for 22 miles was rare and admirable, a genuine pioneering performance, but it cannot qualify as a record in what we now call the marathon.

It's another intriguing story, thanks to Milroy and Lovesey for discovering it. There was a stage performer at the time called Violet Piercy, which fits with the well-managed publicity for her solo run. There was also a Violet Piercy who belonged to Mitcham Athletic Club, in the southern suburbs of London, which fits with the ability to cover twenty-two miles at that good pace. A likely identification is with a Violet Piercy who lived near Clapham Common, about 3 miles/5km from Mitcham. Perhaps, or even probably, the listed Violet Piercy was both the stage performer and the club athlete. More will be discovered, no doubt, as the story is too good to leave uncertain.

Whoever she was, she presumably enjoyed her first run from Windsor, because she did it again at least once, seven years later, in 1933, recorded this time as 4hrs 25. This seems to have been set up wholly as a media event, as she was followed by a car with reporters and a camera, and ended by running out on to a theater stage in front of a rapturous audience, at the Golders Green Hippodrome, again a different finish point. Again, there seems to have been no attempt to make it accurately the standard distance, although it must have been close to a modern marathon if she really did start at Windsor. But the point is that again, this seems to have been more a show than a race, and we have little idea how far she actually ran.

So Violet Piercy, considerable runner though she was, has to vacate the top spot she has occupied for forty years in the list of record progression for the women's marathon. Another candidate is Gazella Weinreich, age 16, who attempted to enter a marathon from Laurel to Baltimore, USA, but was excluded by the American Athletic Union. Later reports suggest she may have run in defiance, starting behind the men. (For the full research into Piercy and Weinreich, see www.nuts.org.uk/trackstats/Piercy.)

Things get more reliable later in the twentieth century. It's sure that in 1959, Arlene Pieper completed the Pikes Peak Marathon, in Manitou Springs, Colorado, a course with 7,000 ft. elevation change, in 9hrs 16min. In 1963, Merry Lepper and Lyn Carman, jumped into the Western Hemisphere Marathon, Culver City, California. After dodging officials, Lepper finished in 3:37:07, though the course is now believed to have been short. Carman persisted, three times finishing as the first woman in the Santa Barbara Marathon, 1966-68. The Lepper/Carman pioneering story is fully told by David Davis in *Marathon Crasher* and in Amby Burfoot's *First Ladies of Running*.

From 1964, at last we can talk of a world best performance, in authorized competitive conditions, on an accurate course; or as reliably accurate as any at that date. On May 23, Dale Greig, a Scot who was well established as a track, road, and cross-country champion, took herself to the well-established and notoriously hilly Isle of Wight Marathon. Race officials broke the rules to let her run, and were reprimanded for it. They were sensibly cautious, requiring her to start four minutes ahead of the men, and provided an ambulance to follow her. Her mother was also there in a car. Passed by many men, she re-passed a good number of them, "as they began to wane," she said, and finished in 3:27:25, warmly applauded by those same officials. Greig's is the first marathon "world best performance." She later ran the 55 mile/88.5km London to Brighton ultra race, and won the first international women's marathon championship, the world veterans/masters (35+) title in 1974.

Like Greig, Millie (Mildred) Sampson was a top competitor in track, road, and cross-country, all championship events in New Zealand by the

1960s. Her version of her marathon debut in Auckland is worth recording. "I'd been out late, dancing at a runner's party. My male Owairaka club-mates had to wake me, and practically pulled me out of bed. I'd promised to run because they thought I would get the race good publicity. I missed breakfast but managed to get hold of some ice-cream and chocolate during the run," Sampson recalled (in a private conversation) in her early eighties. She ran eight minutes faster than Greig, with 3:19:33 In 1966, she ran 3:13:58, so her 1964 world best looks authentic.

In 1966 America a new phenomenon appeared, young women with little running background who were inspired by the heroic romance of the marathon. That year, Roberta Gibb jumped into the Boston Marathon, claiming unofficially 3:21:40, and Debbie Hayes won Alaska's mountainous Equinox Marathon, in 5:24:30. The next year, 1967, Gibb was back at Boston, while twenty-year-old Kathrine Switzer did her best to do it officially by registering and getting the required medical certificate. Two miles into the race, she was attacked by race co-director Jock Semple, who tried to rip off her bib number in full view of the media vehicle, bringing iconic photographs and massive publicity to the cause of women's marathoning. She finished in 4:20.

Now the story began to move faster. In May 1967, thirteen-year-old Maureen Wilton ran 3:15:22.8 in York, Toronto, a world's best, with Switzer also invited to ensure a genuine women's race. Anni Pede-Erdkamp lowered that time in September 1967, with 3:07:26 in Waldniel, Germany. She was a protegée of Dr. Ernst van Aaken, who emerged as an important pioneering advocate for women's distance running.

Officialdom was not all Jock Semples. As early as 1970, the Road Runners Club of America put on the first championship marathon for women, won by Sara Mae Berman. In 1973, the first all-women's marathon was held in Waldniel, on the initiative of Dr. van Aaken. And in 1974, amazingly quickly looking back, the boring old AAU held the world's first official woman's national (USA) championship marathon, won by Judy Ikenberry in 2:55:18. The prologue ended.

The Goal in Sight

In the fourteen years from 1970 to 1984, women runners and their coaches, and a few enterprising race promoters, drove women's marathon training and performance forward by half a century. It was, I'm suggesting, like a heroic quest. Remarkably, male runners almost unanimously welcomed this incursion into their territory, but officialdom was often resistant, including women's own federations. Male journalists were mostly deprecatory to begin with, and non-running women were often hostile.

Women running marathons increased rapidly in number, but that increase could happen only because opportunities were created by a far smaller number of women and men who by persistence and hard work carved out the structures of the new global sport. Notable innovators were Dr. Ernst van Aaken in Germany; Alan Blatchford in England; Nina Kuscsik, Sara Mae Berman, and David Martin in the USA; and Kathrine Switzer also in the USA and globally. Kuscsik, Berman, and Switzer were active marathoners, and stand out among the pioneers of that era by adding all the labor of innovation, advocacy, and politics to their weekly mileage.

The passing of Title IX in America in 1972 gave federal endorsement to women's education and sports, and indirectly benefitted running, although the marathon was always post-collegiate. Existing races began to admit women (Boston in 1972), and most of the new generation of marathons welcomed them from the outset, notably New York City in 1970 and Vancouver in 1972. The equivalent of a league of their own for women began in 1978, when the Avon International Running Circuit created by Switzer brought corporate sponsorship to Dr. van Aaken's off-the-wall idea of marathons for women. Japan quickly came up with high-profile imitations, with the Tokyo Women's Marathon beginning in 1979, and Osaka in 1982.

Before that structure was ready, there were inevitably some problems. No one will ever resolve the enigma of Australian Adrienne Beames. A genuinely ground-breaking athlete, Beames's world-shaking sub-3 hours breakthrough with 2:46:30 in 1971 provoked big media coverage and was almost certainly real – yet almost certainly not valid. Like many pioneer women marathoners, she had to operate outside existing structures. We know from her male training partners that she was exceptionally well trained, running a hundred miles a week when American cross-country star Doris Brown Heritage was the only other woman in the world who was training at that level. But, Beames claimed later, the women's athletics federation of Victoria wouldn't give approval for her to run a marathon, which is probably true.

That created another complication that has not been recognized. She ran her world record in Werribee, Australia, in an event that was authorized by the sport of professional athletics. In Victoria, as also at that date in the Republic of Ireland, and some parts of Northern England and Scotland, there were two codes of athletics, strongly hostile to each other. Professional prize money was trivial, but the rivalry was fierce. Beames was athletically and personally enthralled to a fact-twisting Svengali of a coach, Fred Warwick, a former competitor in professional athletics, who recruited officials for her marathon debut, and supposedly some male runners, from the professional code. He then paced her. No other women were present. She claimed the course was "well-established for the professional sport," but no supporting evidence for that has been found. It's also impossible to establish whether Warwick paced her all the way, or only for parts of the course. He was, to say the least, possessive.

Most revealing for me was establishing that the only source for the news story was a phone call from the same coach/partner/pacer, Warwick, who contacted the *Melbourne Age* newspaper after the event. The paper then ran a "world record" story with off-the-cuff telephone reactions from great Australian male runners, all understandably impressed and supportive. Their quotes provided a false authenticity. It seems on close reading that no journalist or qualified observer was actually present. As with Stamata Revithi, a newspaper report does not necessarily mean that reporters were there as eye-witnesses.

It's doubtful that many people at all were there on the Werribee course that day, apart from the scattering of professional runners and officials. Nor so far as we know did anyone check the course or question the timing.

I interviewed Beames for a total of seven hours over two days in 2011, when she was living alone five years after Warwick's death, keeping a forlorn home in his dated and desolate chiropractic surgery. It was seven years before her own death, but she was faded and fretful, and limping badly from a car accident some years previously. As I patiently listened to her version of the truth, it was clear that she had been dedicated, perhaps obsessive, in training, including unprecedentedly high mileage and an extreme vegan diet that she still religiously maintained. It was equally clear that much of what she believed about her performances was delusional or mendacious. The daughter of one of Melbourne's greatest sports heroes, she was perhaps driven by a compulsion to please or emulate him. She was cast out by her family because of Warwick. When I visited, she seemed lonely, aimless, anxious, and plaintive. Hers may be one of running's greatest stories; it is for sure one of the saddest.

David Mark, an Australian journalist with the resources of the ABC, tackled the Beames story freshly in 2019, and reached the same conclusion about her enigmatic world record as I did – that it's impossible to reach a sure conclusion.

To be fair to her memory, I repeat, on very good authority from elite Melbourne runners who trained with her often, she was good enough to have run 2:46:30. The next ten years would prove that time to be no freak for a trained woman runner. Doubts must focus on the authentication of her race, not on her ability.

It's a relief that at Beames's date, 1971, this unofficial, marginalized women's marathon era of dubious courses and misty facts was near its end. The next steps in the process to full acceptance for the women's marathon came in full daylight, with reliable measurement and timing, and with extensive media coverage. The first Avon International Women's Marathon was in 1978, won by Martha Cooksey (USA); Norwegian Grete Waitz ran her world-record debut marathon in the bright light of New York City, also in 1978; there was a global field and global television audience for the Avon Women's Marathon in London in 1980; and the 1981 New York City Marathon, the first on American network television, had a record number of more than two thousand women runners, who all received huge support from the crowds, while the women's winner was the charismatic Allison Roe. (chapter 14). Another major step was effected in protest against the lack of women's distance events in the 1980 Moscow Olympics, when the Road Runners Club of America created its annual Women's Distance Festival.

The most momentous leap forward came when the International Olympic Committee in 1981 agreed to a proposal from the USOC that the women's marathon be added to the 1984 Olympic program. The motion came after persistent lobbying from Switzer, with the Avon Corporation's weight behind her. She put forward impressive evidence from their women's marathons, especially the massive success in London in 1980, supported by Dr. David Martin's myth-busting medical research (Switzer, 1980). Suddenly, the women's marathon was on the program for the next Olympics.

With no track race longer than 3,000m yet available, the Olympic marathon became the dream and the goal of almost every serious woman distance runner, whose numbers increased rapidly. For the first time in history, women could win international marathon championships. Rosa Mota (Portugal) won the first, the 1982 European in Athens, and Grete Waitz won the first IAAF World Athletics Championship women's marathon in Helsinki in 1983. The world record came tumbling down. In 1979, Waitz was the first to break 2:30. By 1983, Joan Benoit (USA) ran 2:22:43. Joyce Smith (Great Britain), Charlotte Teske (Germany), Patti Catalano (USA), Allison Roe (New Zealand), and Ingrid Kristiansen (Norway) also had world-record runs, depending how you interpret the disputed courses of Boston and New York.

More and more Olympic contenders emerged as the clock ticked to August 1984. Julie Brown (USA) was hugely impressive winning the June 1983 Avon Marathon on the Los Angeles Olympic course. Jacqueline Gareau (Canada) narrowly beat Anne Audain (New Zealand) in the

February 1984 Los Angeles Marathon, Lorraine Moller (New Zealand) won Boston in April 1984, and that same month track star Ingrid Kristiansen suddenly emerged as a marathoner with a 2:24:26 win in London. Almost miraculously, Joan Benoit recovered in seventeen days from knee surgery to win the U.S. Olympic trial in May 1984, beating Brown.

Even more important, there was new depth as well as new elite quality. Behind Benoit in the U.S. trial that day, thirty-one American women ran under 2:40:00. Only nine years earlier, that was the world record. It was in 1971 that the world record first went under three hours, and then 2:50. Yet in the one month of April 1984, 166 women beat 2:50, in the Boston, London, and American Trial Marathons. That progress was in thirteen years. That was the impact of making the women's marathon an Olympic event.

So came the day when these female knights fulfilled their quest and assembled for their greatest tournament. I choose my metaphor with purpose, because for centuries women had been culturally positioned as passive. The romance of the rose was their emblem, not the mighty gallop of hooves and the clash of lances. Their role was to admire men's adventures, inspire and support them, wait faithfully at home, letting men wear their scarves as they fought. Women were threatened by men, captured by men, and rescued by men. Men did the riding and fighting, as "champions" for the women. That's why this day was important, because women moved from the passive role to a totally active one. This was their ultimate and irreversible acceptance, no longer as spectators. They were the champions.

At 8 a.m. on August 5, 1984, forty-nine women stood on the start-line at Santa Monica City College, ready to race the first women's Olympic Marathon. The prologue is written, the quest completed. The story starts.

Out of the Tunnel

They came from twenty-eight nations and six continents, fully proving that this had become a global sport worthy of a place under the Olympic rings. The field of forty-nine was predominantly European (24) or English-speaking (16). The later powerhouse of Japan was represented (2), and there was one Kenyan, in 43rd place, but the top of the field looked very different from thirty years later, with East Africa not yet present. A political boycott excluded some strong but probably doped runners from Communist bloc countries.

The race for sure was going to be world class. Nine of the starters had won big international marathons and/or held the world record. Here's an announcer's introduction to the top rank, in reverse seeded order, with stats relevant up to that date:

12. Lisa Martin (Australia) is the 24-year-old ex-400m hurdler wildcard, who ran an exciting 2:32:22 debut marathon in 1983.

11. Priscilla Welch (Great Britain), a 39-year-old career army officer, became a kind of senior wildcard with her fast 2:30:06 second place in the April 1984 London Marathon.

10. Charlotte Teske (West Germany) has won marathons at Boston, Miami, and Frankfurt with sub-2:30 times, and if you count New York's course as short, she took the world record in 1983 with her 2:29:01 at Miami.

9. Joyce Smith (Great Britain) is one of the great pioneers. World-record breaker on the track in 1971, Olympian and European track medalist, and world champion in cross-country, she has twice won the London Marathon since turning forty, and at 46 is still among the world's best.

8. Jacqueline Gareau (Canada) was the 1980 Boston champion, the true winner after the exposure of the cheat Rosie Ruiz. Gareau was second at Boston in 1982 and 1983, and had an important and dramatic recent win at Los Angeles in February 1984.

7. Lorraine Moller (New Zealand) combines being a track medalist (third in 1500m and 3000m at the 1982 Commonwealth Games) with winning marathons (Grandma's 1979-81, Avon 1980, Boston 1984). Her 2:29:28 makes her one of only six sub-2:30 marathoners in this field.

6. Anne Audain (New Zealand) would have started as a favorite for the 5,000m and 10,000m if this Olympic program included them.

Winner of many road races in America, and with international honors in track and cross-country, Audain's proven ability to win ranks her high.

5. Julie Brown (USA) shot to the front rank on this actual course, when she won the 1983 Avon Women's Marathon in 2:26:26. In 1975, she won the World Cross-Country and set a world record for 10,000m on the track, and in 1978 won the Nike Oregon Marathon.

4. Rosa Mota (Portugal) won the first major international women's marathon title, the 1982 European Championship, in hot conditions in Athens. She also won the Rotterdam and Chicago marathons in 1983, and her continuing improvement and ability to win compensate for her lack of a super-fast time, her best being 2:31:12.

3. Ingrid Kristiansen (Norway) broke suddenly into the top rankings when she won this year's London Marathon in 2:24:26 (the world record if Boston is discounted). A world championship bronze medalist at 3,000m, she has also twice won the Houston Marathon, and improved to fourth in this year's world cross-country.

2. Joan Benoit (USA) holds the world's fastest time with her 2:22:43 at Boston in 1983, and has won five of the ten marathons she has raced. She came back dramatically from knee surgery to win the U.S. Trial in May.

1. Grete Waitz (Norway) won the first women's world championship marathon in 1983 by three minutes, soon after winning London in a world record 2:25:29. A five-time (so far) winner of the New York City Marathon, five-time world cross-country champion, and a superlative track and road racer, Waitz is coolly consistent in competition, and has all-round credentials to make her the pre-race favorite.

Conditions would be challenging, always humid, and becoming hot. The course started in Santa Monica, and stayed close to the Pacific coast until turning inland at 15 miles/25km. There, gray cloudy humidity (20° C/68° F) changed suddenly to radiant hot sun, with the runners exposed and unshaded on the Marina Freeway and Exposition Boulevard. Not all would cope.

They started on the Santa Monica City College track. Joan Benoit Samuelson recalls that they were lined up alphabetically by nation, and then each team according to height, making her think of her mother's favorite edict, "The last shall come first." After lapping the track, they turned on to the street, and soon went past the one kilometer marker, and then 1.5km. That point was not marked, as it's not significant in a marathon, except this one. Leaving that unmarked spot on the road behind them meant they had run farther than any woman in any race at any previous Olympics. The 800m track was restored in 1960, and the 1,500m was added in 1972. The heats for the inaugural women's track 3,000m were scheduled for August 8, three days after the marathon.

The first 4 miles/6km were somewhat uphill, climbing 190 feet, so the early pace was predictably watchful. A big pack cruised unperturbed behind some rash early leaders, gathering them in as they reached 5K in 18:15. That's 5:52 per mile, 3:39 per km, 2:34 marathon pace, appropriate on a slight uphill and a day that was going to become hot. The pack spread across the road, about twenty-five of them, with the three Americans visible in the front row, along with Mota and Waitz. Most took sponges at a station twelve minutes into the race, Benoit mopping her neck. There was no urgency. They all looked to be simply settling in to unroll the miles. It was going to be a race of moderate early pace and cautious tactics.

But then it wasn't. Eighteen minutes in, shortly before a water station, Joan Benoit simply moved a little ahead, and then skipped her drink. The way she always tells it, she makes it sound as homey as making jam.

"I actually wasn't bothered by the heat at all...I decided to break away because I felt hemmed in. If I had to be the pacesetter in order to run my own race, that was fine. Right after I broke free the first water station came up, and I was darned if I was going to get into a crowd again just for a drink, so I skipped it... I couldn't believe the other runners weren't coming after me" (Benoit, 1987).

And she was gone, just like that. Not with any great burst of speed, merely taking a five second gap at the water station, moving to a slightly higher rhythm, and edging further away. It was very early, and the pace seemed already fast enough. Waitz chose to let her go, coolly deciding

269

not to be lured into premature folly. The others watched Waitz, the supreme tactician, who had never lost a marathon, except two (New York 1981, Boston 1982) when she dropped out injured. Kristiansen, Mota, Audain, Brown, Moller, Sylvia Ruegger of Canada, Akemi Masuda of Japan, Laura Fogli of Italy, were spread across the road, watching Benoit recede. They wouldn't go after her if Waitz didn't. Kristiansen said later that if she had gone with Benoit, three or four others would have gone with her, "but I waited for Grete" (*Sports Illustrated*).

In fact, it's doubtful anyone but Waitz at her best could have lived with the pace Benoit was setting, although she seemed to do it so casually. Soon she was a runaway, out of sight. Between 5K and 10K (35:24) she in fact picked up the pace from 5:52 per mile to 5:31 per mile (3:26 per km), on the downhill slope heading to the ocean shore. On the flat shoreline she went even faster, 51:46 at 15K, 5:16 per mile (3:16 per km). Now she had a lead of 51 seconds, with nineteen hopefuls still in the following pack.

To the marathon connoisseur, this still was not a one-woman race, but an enthralling duel.

Waitz, as it seemed, was thinking that Benoit would slow down, "and we would catch her in the end." Most days that would have been a good call. We all know the danger of miscalculating your pace in the first half of a marathon by even one minute. That has been marathon truth since 1896. Waitz also had the advantage of sitting with the pack, relieved from the total responsibility for pace that Benoit was carrying. The reality was that despite the minute of space between them, those two were locked in a tactical combat, between the one who risked all and trusted to courage, and the one who stayed back, trusting to judgment.

Or perhaps (though it sounds less dramatic) it was only that Benoit's pace judgment was better than Waitz's. The splits show that Benoit in fact slowed between 15K and 20K, where she ran 5:24 per mile (3:21 per km). But instead of the pack closing, they allowed their pace to drop even more, and the gap increased from 51 seconds to 72 seconds.

Mota sensed the danger and surged, going through 20K twelve seconds ahead of the pack, but she couldn't sustain it alone. They all slowed in the next five kilometers. Benoit's pace dropped by two seconds a mile to 5:26 seconds (3:23 per km), while the pack slowed more, and lost another thirty-eight seconds on her, to be 110 seconds behind at 25K. They began to break up, as Brown and others dropped off. Waitz still waited.

You would never perceive those changes with the naked eye, but the analysis is (I think) fascinating. Those ten kilometers, 15K to 25K, are where Waitz lost the race. She needed to surge when Mota did, before halfway, and keep pushing till Benoit was within reach, or at least in sight.

Instead, she left it until 25K, where the chase finally began. Waitz, Kristiansen, and Mota emerged, followed by a half-minute by Moller and Welch. But Benoit's lead was undented, holding exactly steady at 110 seconds at 30K.

However you analyze it, Benoit proved indomitable. She admitted in her book that early on she had "one or two brief flashes of doubt and imagined the pack thundering by me," but by 16 miles/26km she "felt completely in control" (Benoit, 1987).

"I knew I wasn't going to be caught," she said. How many marathon runners can ever say that? She never lost her rhythm or the bounce in her seemingly short stride. From 30K to 35K, now on exposed roadway in blazing sun, and even higher humidity, she in fact slowed a little, to 5:34 per mile (3:28 per km), the slowest split of the race so far, and the chasing trio took nineteen seconds out of her lead, reducing it to 91 seconds. Now Waitz was really pushing, with Kristiansen, Mota, Welch, and Moller strung out behind her.

But it was too little too late, and Waitz could take only three more seconds out of Benoit's lead in the crucial five kilometers between 35K and 40K, where Benoit (by the unforgiving watch) slowed a little more to 5:39 per mile (3:31 per km).

Now the stadium was in sight, Benoit was running strong, her lead was still almost a minute and a half, and the race was as good as decided. The last moments were no anti-climax. The television camera showed Benoit swerve confidently into the tunnel, and her stocky figure fade from sight in the gloom. Then came the moment that still most potently expresses what that day in history would mean. A hundred thousand people within the stadium gazed at the tunnel exit, and as Benoit emerged, they rose with an acclamation for the ages.

That was the essential symbolic moment, as the first woman Olympic marathon champion ran springy and strongly out of the tunnel, out of dark invisibility into bright sunlight and acclaim. For everyone who was there, or watching on television, or who has seen it in the many years since, she represented all women, proving beyond dispute that they were emerging from centuries of obscurity to claim their proper role on earth, as active, visible, and capable of being heroic.

Benoit understood the significance. "Once you leave this tunnel, your life will be changed forever," she was thinking. But with her downbeat humor, she also reports that, "My mother said later that I looked like a little gray mouse skittering out of a hole" (Benoit, 1987).

Benoit ran 2:24:52, the third fastest in history, behind only her own 2:22:43 at Boston in 1983, and Kristiansen's 2:24:43 at London in April 1984. It was a phenomenal run in hot and humid conditions, almost wholly solo. It's easy to praise Benoit's opportunism for grabbing that early break, so early that no one took her seriously. It was a far more rare achievement to run alone, and achieve such near-perfect pacing, out in front, and in rising temperatures. Her half-marathon splits were 1:12:17 and 1:12:35. Waitz (2:26:18) ran true to her tactic, with negative splits of 1:13:45 and 1:12:33. That acceleration ought to have been enough to catch Benoit, but the bold little American wasn't there for catching. She was nowhere to be seen.

Resolute Mota passed Kristiansen for third (2:26:57), and then came Moller (5), Welch (6), Martin (7) and Ruegger (8). Of the other pre-race picks, Joyce Smith at age 46 ran 2:32:48 for eleventh, which on age-graded calculations would take the gold medal. Teske was sixteenth. Brown (thirty-sixth), Gareau (DNF) and Audain (DNF) all succumbed to the humid heat. But something that has not been noticed is that despite the heat, the race was a spectacular success in terms of quality in depth. There were only six drop-outs, nine broke 2:30, twenty-five broke 2:40, and the last finisher, Eleonora de Mendonça of Brazil, ran 2:52:19. At risk of repetition, only thirteen years earlier that would have broken the world record.

There was one last momentous episode in this momentous race. On a fully respectable 2:45 pace, Gabriela Andersen-Schiess, an American-domiciled Swiss, shuffled dazedly out of the tunnel. Emergence from the cool tunnel into the ferocious microclimate heat inside the stadium was for her no symbolic moment of triumph, but one when biological reality asserted itself. Dehydrated and heat exhausted, Andersen-Schiess's body could scarcely respond to her still lucid mind.

She had accidentally missed the last drinks station, and had to slow down. Serious dehydration struck as she entered the stadium. Even when her body effectively ceased to respond, she forced herself to keep moving. In the years since, she has always insisted that her mind was still lucid and capable of making decisions, and she was driven by the knowledge that if she stopped or sat down or received assistance, that would end it. "I'm in the Olympics, I'm thirty-nine, this is my one and only chance."

Agonizingly slowly, with the world urging every uncertain stride, Andersen-Schiess completed her one lap around the track. A medical official followed close by and watched, checking that she was still mentally capable, and still perspiring. Staggering, reeling, weaving side-to-side across four or five lanes, touching her face with twitching fingers that seemed outside her mental control, yet she never stepped over the curb, and never quite fell. The crowd at first thought they were watching an act of horror. After almost six minutes, they knew they had watched an act of heroism.

The reaction to Andersen-Schiess was as significant as her arduous achievement. In the television commentators' booth, Kathrine Switzer at first dreaded that she was witnessing the undoing of years of work, the overturning of the race as evidence of women's capability. "My God, don't tell me we have to fight it all over again, with them all saying women are too frail for distance running," she thought. The world at that time still believed that the 1928 Olympic women's 800 meters had been an embarrassing display of women's weakness.

This time, Andersen-Schiess herself was eventually the only one who felt embarrassed.

"I wished I could have placed twelfth or fifteenth, not to end this way. But what surprised me was all the compassion, the reaction of all the athletes, they were so supportive. People kind of identify with you, because they see the struggle. In life, you have to get over some bad experiences."

No lasting harm was done. Little more than two months later, Andersen-Schiess encountered even more oppressive marathon conditions (95% humidity), in the notorious "hot fog" New York City Marathon, when more than two thousand succumbed and failed to finish. Andersen-Schiess ran without serious problem to record 2:42:24, in eleventh place overall.

Strangely, unexpectedly, Andersen-Schiess's last lap became the best thing that could have happened to end the story of that day. Her struggle and her survival made it evident that the women were indeed pushing themselves to the very extreme, were going beyond boundaries, despite Benoit looking so indestructible and in control, despite Waitz's composure. No one openly suggested that Andersen-Schiess's sufferings were improper or unfeminine. Instead, as she stumbled forward at the very edge of consciousness, spectators and television viewers acclaimed her resolve, and praised the officials for not intervening in her fascinating struggle.

Looking back, this first women's Olympic marathon was a story that went beyond the highest hopes of those who envisioned and created it. It proved that women can run marathons competitively and supremely well. It proved that the world will eagerly watch and admire them doing so. It proved that women can overcome difficulty, adversity, extreme physical and mental stress, and respond not with tears or swoons, but resilience and attainment. Perhaps more than any other single running story in modern history, this race positioned women as active, not passive, as fully entitled participants in sport and in life. And finally, and most unexpectedly, it also showed that women have at last gained the right to suffer exhaustion in public.

Chapter 14

The New Atalanta: Allison Roe

800 BC   100 AD   1719   1896   1908   1928   1936   1964   1984   2021

Allison Roe had an easier childhood than Atalanta, but with many things in common. She wasn't abandoned or raised by bears, but she did live in quite close contact with the natural world, and she was born with supreme natural talents in all kinds of sports. Her father Allan Deed was an admired family doctor at Milford on the North Shore of Auckland, New Zealand, small-town and rural in those days, with the Hauraki Gulf and beyond that the Pacific Ocean always a potent presence. She has never lived at any distance from a beach.

Her mother Pamela was loving, supportive, and inspirational in her commitment to altruism. Both parents had family histories of bad health, heart problems in Allan's family, diabetes in Pamela's, and they reacted by adopting a lifestyle of healthy diet, holistic medicine, and regular exercise, convinced that those are the key to an enriched and longer life. (Allan in 2021 is 95 and still in his own home.) They were also early environmentalists, valuing the earth and active in conserving it. That was the regimen that Allison and her sister grew up with as normal, not too different from Atalanta's nurturing by the goddess of wild nature, Artemis. She also absorbed from both parents, through a childhood in the idealistic 1960s, the driving belief that we all have responsibility to help others less fortunate. The focus of life in that family was to identify and fulfill our special talents, and then use our successes to a greater good.

With those origins, it's no surprise that Allison in her teenage years became outstanding at several sports, and in her sixties could commit her energies to community service in the health sector. Along the way, she created a series of races to fund a women's health charity, she leads the development of a recreation trail, and she often confirms her commitment: "The health stats are alarming. I want to make a difference in the community, doing something positive." (Quotes in this chapter without other citation are from private conversations or emails, and much biographical information has been sourced in the same way, including the next paragraph.)

As a child, she met Sir Ed Hillary, and learned from that encounter that a straightforward and unpretentious Kiwi could be the first to climb the world's highest mountain, one of the most historic accomplishments of the modern age. She also took note of his matter-of-fact attitude to success, and that he always scrupulously shared the credit with Sherpa Tenzing Norgay. Enterprising accomplishment and genuine egalitarianism are two facets of the New Zealand psyche.

As a girl, always near a beach, Allison was good at swimming and water-skiing. Beaches for her have always been for moving on energetically, not for lying inert. She also excelled at netball (a women's variant of basketball that is big in the British Commonwealth), and at tennis and high jumping, winning high school championships in both. She was increasingly drawn to track and cross-country running, but without seeming to be driven by the competitive intensity that attracts many to those sports at elite level. Her temperament is sunny and positive. "My philosophy in life is to see the bright side." Her laughter is ready and engaging. (On the family diabetes problem, she predicts, "When I go, it will be with a bang or a sugar rush.")

Ironically for a woman who would go on to be an icon of a new kind of beauty, and see herself rated in print as more attractive than Bo Derek (the "Perfect 10" movie star of the 1970s) her self-image as a child was self-effacing and negative.

"I find it confronting now to be thought of as 'beautiful' because as a child I thought I was the ugly duckling and needed to 'do something' to get noticed. My father always thought my pretty sexy little sister would have all the children and I'd be the career woman," she recalled in 2020.

Her sporting talents gave her one way to "do something." She began to focus on running when the former British Olympic medalist and world record-breaker Gordon Pirie, then resident in Auckland, offered to coach her. That proved to be a challenge as well as an opportunity. Pirie had charisma, but he was intense, competitive, domineering, unpredictable, and sometimes tortured and paranoid, obsessed with what he considered to be lack of recognition. In the congenial and welcoming Auckland running scene, he remained an outsider, mainly because of his compulsion to dominate any conversation. He was a passionate advocate of his personal training principles, which he completely changed about every three months. He also lived for a while in a ménage à trois relationship that was not the norm in 1960s/70s New Zealand. Later, inappropriately, his personal life and his coaching of young women overlapped. If there was a menacing centaur in Allison's young life, it was Pirie, but like Atalanta, she was unfazed. Of equable temperament, she found him "motivating but eccentric," and she moved on.

On the track, the teenage Roe had "lots of seconds and thirds" at the national level, and represented New Zealand on the track in early 1975. But at that time, women's long-distance track meant 800m and 1,500m/mile, too short for Roe. The 3,000m was beginning to be available, introduced as a New Zealand championship in 1976. A more significant opportunity came in cross-country, then usually at 2.5 miles/4km for women. In 1974, at age eighteen, on a hilly national championship course, Roe defeated Lorraine Moller, who would precede her into the world marathon rankings, and would follow her as a winner of the Boston Marathon. Roe is the youngest woman ever to lift the New Zealand cross-country title. That earned her a place in the New Zealand team at the 1975 World Cross-Country in Rabat, Morocco.

That experience was memorable in many ways, and her mother's voice was strong within her.

"For the first time in my life I saw real poverty, young children, blinded and maimed, begging for a living, on the sidewalk as Mercedes Benzes rolled by. I began to think that if I could get recognized as a reasonable sport, then it might help me to find a way to do something that really mattered."

In Morocco she also suffered from an adverse vaccine reaction. She ran below form to finish twenty-ninth, fourth scorer in the New Zealand team. They won the silver medals, behind USA, going frustratingly close to emulating the New Zealand men, who won a historic team victory on the same day.

At this time, Roe was offered an attractive sports scholarship at the University of California, Los Angeles, but she opted to stay in New Zealand, despite the restrictive amateurism that prevailed there. By the mid-1970s, there were semi-licit ways for an elite runner to make money in America and elsewhere, but not in New Zealand's tiny and watchful community. Soon Roe would play a part in ending that muddled and obsolete code.

Her track career was hindered by frequent injuries, but she got on the championship podium most years on muddy cross-country courses and flat fast road courses. She was selected again for the World Cross-Country in 1977, but plantar fasciitis kept her outside the scoring four in Düsseldorf.

Full disclosure: I was on the New Zealand men's team for the three-week trip required for those championships, and, at age 37, I found Allison at age 20 always good company in training groups or at team social events – natural, relaxed, and friendly, free from competitive brittleness and totally free from any inclination toward negative gossip. She did, however, keep me entertained throughout one training run all the way around a north German lake with an account of Gordon Pirie's bizarre personal life that slowed my pace because I was laughing so much. Yet she was still kind and not judgmental.

Between injuries, she ran some decent track races, on one occasion in 1979 finishing an Auckland 3,000m behind visiting Norwegian star Grete Waitz. They would meet again. Roe was running well on different surfaces, but had not yet found her real event. The crucial moment came in February 1980. Finding that her track season was not going well, she made an apparently impulsive decision to enter the Choysa Marathon on the Auckland waterfront. Some of her women runner friends had "raved" about marathons, so she thought she would try it.

"It was quite by accident that I ever ran that marathon. I didn't train. My longest ever run had been eighteen miles [29km]. I thought that after twelve or fifteen miles that would be it, and that I'd give it away. And I actually tried to at one stage, when I walked a bit, but the crowd was too persuasive. When I found a stretch without any one to see, I'd look about and stop, and walk for a while, I was so tired."

As an account of a life-shaping debut marathon, that's, in Roe's engaging way, slightly out to lunch. The seeming casualness of the decision to run is typical of her lack of calculated ambition or planning, which somehow co-existed in her peak years with a capacity for absolute focus once she got going in a race that mattered.

This time, she ran 2:51:45, overshadowed by American Joan Benoit's extremely focused second-fastest-in-history 2:31:23. More importantly, despite all the secret walk breaks, Roe was the first New Zealand woman, and that brought an expenses-paid trip to the Nike Oregon Track Club Marathon seven months later.

"Without that trip as the prize, I'm not sure that I would ever have run another marathon," she says.

Now, as she turned 24, her life changed in important ways. She married chiropractor Richard Roe, she built up her training to about 68 miles/110km a week, doubling her previous level, and she included long Sunday runs, with men, that increased from 18 miles/30km upward, on Arthur Lydiard's famous and demanding circuit in the Waitakere (Why-tack-erry) hills outside Auckland. There was plenty of banter and laughter.

"The guys used to say, 'Alli, you've got to learn to run like a man, and stop pussyfooting around.' Soon I'd say to them, 'Time you learned to run like a woman, guys, perhaps you'd be faster then'" (Gifford, 1981). Runners always accept other runners, and respect is given as soon as it is earned.

At this time, Roe went to one of those Sunday training partners as her coach. From the outside, it was a surprising choice. Perhaps Pirie had made her suspicious of celebrity runners. Gary Elliott was a good club runner, best known for his ability to run above form in the fiercely-contested inter-club road relays of that era. His 1981 record still stands for one famed downhill relay lap. He had no international marathon experience, but like most New Zealand runners he adhered mainly to Arthur Lydiard's training principles, and he brought special skills that Roe believes were crucial to her progress to the top of the marathon.

"Gary and I really worked on the mental side of training. It wasn't until I learned self-hypnosis that I was able to overcome my string of seconds and thirds. A record is only a barrier in your mind and a fear of the unknown." Before major races, she became a strong advocate of the psychological trick of listing possible things that can go wrong in order to be prepared to confront them. She valued Elliott's contribution so highly that she later named her and Richard's son and second child Elliott Roe in his honor. When she was inducted into the New Zealand Sports Hall of Fame, her first acknowledgement was to him. "Gary was the one that helped me believe in my dreams and achieve whatever I wanted to achieve."

Under Elliott's guidance, Roe sharpened for the Oregon marathon with winter cross-country, placing third in the national title. In assessing such championship placings, it's well to remember that during those years New Zealand was one of the world's strongest in women's running, twice on the team's podium at World Cross-Country, an event they could afford to attend only every second year. Roe's speed and strength were built on the traditional New Zealand formula of hard miles on scenic (i.e. extremely hilly) terrain, topped off with structured quality work. While the weekly long run on Lydiard's road course built her distance base, Roe mostly ran on beaches and golf courses ("natural surfaces are important for prevention of injuries") and later added sessions of 20 x 200m. That balance again was worthy of Atalanta.

The Nike Oregon Marathon at Eugene in September 1980 gave American and New Zealand runners some consolation for the disappointment of the American-led boycott of the Moscow Olympic Games the previous month. Dick Quax had been a potential Olympic marathon champion but was deprived of that chance. He won the Oregon men's race sixteen seconds faster than Waldemar Cierpinski's drug-boosted Olympic winning time. Lorraine Moller made Oregon a Kiwi double by taking the women's race, and in a strong field Roe had the race of her life so far to place third. Her 2:34:29 made her the eighth fastest woman in history.

Now Roe was riding the surging wave of the road running boom, and she was instantly invited to an all-women's marathon in Tokyo in November 1980. It taught her that marathons could still go wrong.

"I was on 2:26 pace until new shoes caused blisters that visibly bled on to the road. I had to walk and then muster courage to run into the stadium in fourth, when I'd kind of known I could win. Great lesson. The only time I cried at a race." She ran 2:42:24, twelve minutes behind the winner. In an earlier take on that experience, she admitted she "hit the wall" in the time-honored manner, and was not yet trained to "switch to my fat reserves."

She may have simply been over-raced. In the ten weeks between those two overseas marathons in Oregon and Tokyo, Roe had also won the Auckland Road Champs and placed second in the National Road Champs, behind Mary O'Connor, who became another world-class marathoner. If she had overdone it, her own love of the process was at fault.

"Some people say you can't do everything, but I really do enjoy it," she told Tim Chamberlain for *New Zealand Runner* (October 1980).

The Tokyo experience taught her to become more focused, at least by skipping the January-February 1981 track season. Not selected for the World Cross-Country, she won a low-key City of Auckland Marathon in February, now able to treat 2:36 as a less than full-effort run. Then she popped over to Japan to break the world best for 20K in Miyazaki, with 68:22. She was now sponsored by the Japanese shoe company Asics/Onitsuka Tiger, their first female runner. She also won three late-summer 10K road races in Auckland, each in 33-34 minutes. As the New Zealand summer ended, she decided to go to the Boston Marathon, a decision she described (again!) as "last minute."

"I decided to run only two weeks before, after a good Sunday 20-miler in the Waitakeres, when I felt so strong and everybody started talking me into going," she wrote, in her own account of her now legendary Boston run, for *New Zealand Runner* (Roe, 1981).

The local favorite was Patti Catalano, who (as Lyons) had twice been second, and was desperate to win. But the field also included two formidable previous winners, Joan Benoit, who had finished twenty minutes ahead of Roe in Auckland fourteen months earlier, and Jacqueline Gareau, the Québequoise 1980 Boston champion.

"I was a little nervous, but I felt in good shape and quite confident. I liked the look of the course, too. I remember thinking on the start line, 'I'd like to win this'" (Roe 1981). She aimed for sub-2:30, but in those days, splits at Boston were called only at arcane local landmarks. Roe "forgot all about time, and decided instead to stick with the top guns." She tracked Catalano and Benoit, and the lesser-known Julie Shea. Near halfway, Catalano, accompanied for most of the distance by her runner husband, got away by about twenty seconds. Roe relaxed her concentration a little. The feared Newton hills were to come.

That's where the only other New Zealander to have won Boston until then, Dave McKenzie (in 1967), had broken away. Roe closed to ten seconds behind Catalano on Heartbreak, the last and most notoriously killing of the hills, which she had the effrontery to describe as "actually over-estimated." Perhaps so, to someone hardened to hills in training and racing in New Zealand, and still running within herself.

Roe affirmed her New Zealand identity by wearing all-black, with a prominent silver fern above her bib number, and white gloves that became her trademark that year. She felt confident enough to lurk ten seconds back from Catalano and choose her moment.

"I wanted to let her feel the pressure of me behind her. That way I thought I was relaxing and having a holiday." She made "one decisive move at 23 miles [37km]. Patti was wobbling and she didn't respond at all" (Roe, 1981).

Boston runner/writer (now coach/writer) Tom Derderian was in the race and running alongside Catalano as the expected winner, so was able to provide a genuinely close-up eye-witness account of the key moment (so close-up, he could apparently note eye color). Smitten on the spot by Roe's heroic glamor, Derderian was inspired to write this richly embellished narrative, in his classic history, *Boston Marathon*:

> *As Catalano began the descent past [Bill] Rodgers's store and into Cleveland Circle, I heard a second roar of the crowd behind us and coming closer. Just as I expected – here comes Joan [Benoit], or maybe Julie [Shea]. But I turned to see a tall, blond woman runner, wearing black, approaching us, a woman a head taller than Joan. It was not Julie. Where was Joan?*
> *The blond was Allison Roe, a woman I hadn't met, but whom I had heard of...She stood 5' 8" at 129 pounds. Roe's interests and talents were eclectic... She had a plan. Everything she did she did well. She was intelligent, astute, and beautiful...*
> *Catalano knew someone was coming. For the first time she showed fatigue. I could sense the hesitation in her stride...At the 23rd mile Roe pulled even... Neither spoke to the other. I watched both carefully. Catalano...looked gaunt, hollow. She seemed to be digging as deep as she could go. Like the crew of a steamship out of coal she threw her own decking into the furnace. She wanted to win this race.*
> *Roe's face, by contrast, looked peaceful, in control. She looked like an actress coming onstage to take the leading role. Other than sharing beautiful*

*running form, the two could not have looked more
different – blue-black hair versus blond, brown
eyes versus blue, a dark face with chiseled features
versus a pale baby face...I looked at Catalano
and saw her face frozen like a department store
mannequin... She could not respond to Roe's
challenge. Roe took a downward, backward glance
at Catalano, then looked forward and smiled. No
one but me could see that Mona Lisa smile sneak
across her face as contact broke (Derderian, 1994).*

Roe smiled again as she crossed the finish line. As she approached, she saw 2:26 on the clock, and thought "Impossible! Must have been a power cut." But it was true, Roe had won the Boston Marathon against top competition in 2:26:46. It was the world's second fastest time, and broke the Boston record by 7 min 42 sec, a margin that is unlikely ever to be repeated. Poor Catalano, second again, 1 min 5 sec behind, had the consolation of breaking the American record. Derderian had deserted her, and in photographs is to be seen, memorably hirsute, finishing a stride ahead of Roe.

****

The "Year of Miracles" for the modern running movement was 1981. Numbers boomed, professionalism arrived, the women's marathon was voted into the Olympics, Ethiopia and Kenya made their team debut at the world cross-country, the inaugural London Marathon made charities central to the sport's mission, and the New York City Marathon was on network and global television for the first time. Running as we know it – as we knew it until the 2020 pandemic – was shaped by the miracles of 1981.

At the time, nothing seemed more miraculous than the sudden emergence of this wondrous talent of Allison Roe. She didn't simply win Boston and break the record by seven minutes, she gave the world a new image of the elite woman marathon runner. One judicious journalist, Phil Gifford, calling her "a superb figurehead for the boom in women's running," praised her friendliness and intelligence, and her lack of any trace of rivalrous malice. For the women's viewpoint, he quoted a successful professional woman, also a jogger, who enthused: "She's a heroine to me. She looks like a heroine with that blonde hair flowing, and her good looks. And this heroic figure can run marathons. She's perfect" (Gifford, 1981).

America was where most of the action was in that era's exploding running boom. Roe's next major race landed her in more action than she wanted. The Cascade Run Off 15K in Portland, Oregon, in June 1981, was backed by the rising shoe company Nike, which for the first time openly provided $60,000 as prize money, in defiance of the amateur code still prevailing. The atmosphere in Portland among the leading athletes was passionate for rebellion, but it took a lot of courage, first to run in a race that was not "sanctioned," and then actually to take the cash, infringing two rules that each brought loss of amateur status. Some declined to race or did not accept the money. In the women's race, Roe was second to Anne Audain, with Lorraine Moller third, a New Zealand sweep. Their prize money was $10,000, $5000, and $2000. The story of what ensued is complex and contested, and this is not the place for a full account, but I will provide some overlooked information that impacts on Roe's situation.

One complication that has received no attention is that an official move to end amateurism had already begun, with New Zealand a leader in advocating the change. Three months earlier, in March 1981, the New Zealand AAA (now Athletics New Zealand), passed a motion "to inform the IAAF that we are in favour of liberalising the amateur rules" (NZAAA, 1981). The IAAF initiated an international consultation process. The different priorities, to express it simply, were that the shoe companies and the elite runners wanted prize money for elite runners, while the international stakeholders wanted a fully professional sport, including provision for developmental and support structures. The debate can be interpreted as the federations fighting to preserve their control against the new challenge from the commercial sector. Or you can see it as organizations that depended almost entirely on volunteer officials, coaches, and administrators, wanting a share of the big new cake to help run the sport; some contribution, for instance, toward the costs of travel to team championships that had been important in the early development of all three New Zealand women. The Cascade rebellion made no provision for anyone but the prize-winning elites, and thus the emergent profession of agents and managers.

Roe, like most elite athletes at the time, was largely unaware of these wider issues. Before the race, she joined the majority of elites in agreeing to run for the prize money. Moller's account renders her as speaking about "crusades," with "infectious enthusiasm," and calls her "gung-ho" (Moller, 2007). (Moller's book, merging autobiography with comic-satiric caricature, is often not a reliable source.) After the race, Moller and Roe placed their prize money in a trust account with the race director in Portland.

During July, letters and faxes flew across the globe. Roe upset her fellow rebels by taking a less-confrontational stance. August 4, the inexperienced new chairman of NZAAA, obedient to draconian messages from America's TAC, issued bans on all three athletes. The media went into a frenzy; the IAAF distanced itself from TAC's "hard line;" and Roe moved into competitive mode. She instructed a vigorous lawyer, who castigated NZAAA for not following its own rules about banning athletes, and threatened High Court action. Under a wiser acting chairman, the bans were rescinded on August 18. (For full details and documentation, see Robinson 2021).

In September 1981, NZAAA issued an uncompromising public statement of policy: "What we would like to see is for the payments to be made direct to the athletes" (*New Zealand Runner,* Sept-Oct 1981). There are of course different versions of who were the villains, and who banned whom and for how long, but to stay with the record, "the eligibility of [the three athletes] to compete in events under IAAF rules has been satisfactorily resolved after numerous discussions between the three athletes, officers of [the NZAAA], the IAAF, and The Athletic Congress of USA" (NZAAA, 1982). The American TAC had been prompt to declare the event unsanctioned. Despite her accommodation with her national federation, Roe was not cleared to run the New York City Marathon until October 8, the day before she flew to America, only seventeen days before the race. With all the public outcry, media attention, conflicting pressures, and disapproval from her peers, the controversy was a stressful time for Roe, who is not an antagonistic personality. In a rare moment of impatience, she once declined to answer questions on the issue, saying "I'm sick and tired of talking about it."

Her more collaborative posture with officialdom may in fact have helped move things forward. And she was not inactive during these difficult months. After Cascade, she turned the tables on Audain by winning the prestigious Peachtree 10K in a course record 32:38.5, an outstanding time for a hot, humid, and hilly race. She also won the Sydney City to Surf, at that time the Southern Hemisphere's premier road race. Back in New Zealand, she had to steer through two potentially serious injuries as well as anxiety over the professionalism controversy, but with chiropractic support from her husband Richard, acupuncture, and Gary Elliott's guidance she continued to improve. In a *New Zealand Runner* feature (January/February 1982), Elliott noted that she had logged her best long runs, best 10 miles (51:36), best interval sessions (5 x 1mile in 4:40), a tempo win in the Auckland road champs, and a 33-minute 10K at Warkworth. Her equable temperament and ability to stay positive served her well at this contentious time.

She and Elliott flew out early for New York, stopping first in Boston, where she ran the Bonne Bell 10K in a personal best 32:22, second to Jan Merrill's American record. She stayed on in Boston for two weeks, lodging with Ellison Goodall, the American women's half-marathon champion, in a house full of athletes. Kevin Ryan, a top New Zealand marathoner who was working with New Balance in Boston, arranged it, to give Roe a better training base than a downtown hotel. She enjoyed the experience, trained hard, and made many friends. As record-breaker at Boston and Peachtree, Roe was a huge star among knowledgeable runners, bigger than any woman in the world other than Grete Waitz, yet she won affection from the Bostonian running community.

"She hung out with the Boston runners, training with us, just one of the crowd, never showing any vanity," recalled TV commentator Toni Reavis many years later. He is one of several now distinguished members of the running community who were young and in Boston in 1981, and who still fondly remember the bliss and very heaven of that dawn, especially running with Roe. That is despite (or perhaps because of) the fact that, as she brightly remarked, "I had no trouble keeping up with the male athletes on training runs." Her gift for winning friends is a consistent sub-theme beneath the story of her winning races.

At a more mundane level, an ankle injury was becoming so troublesome that she had to do her intensive work in the pool. Then she encountered New York for the first time.

"It was a big thrill for a Kiwi girl. We were picked up by this enormous stretch limo. But I was scared about running there. TV showed New York as a dangerous city, with people murdered every day, and I had these terrible dreams about having to run fast to dodge all the bullets" (Robinson, 2011).

Roe's Boston record made her famous and a factor, but Boston is a point-to-point course with net elevation drop. When the wind is fair, it can be fast. The undoubted New York race favorite was still Grete Waitz. The cool Norwegian seemed never to lose, she had supreme track and cross-country credentials, and at that point a New York City Marathon career of three victories and three world records. She was beloved of the First Avenue crowds. Some days before the race, Roe and Waitz met by chance when they both went in for physiotherapy. Deeply admiring of Waitz and all she had accomplished, Roe also took some hope from seeing that "the queen of New York...had a problem." The problem was in fact severe shit splints that would put Waitz out of the race at 17 miles/27km.

On race day, Roe was so nervous that she forgot her bib number. Race officials had to track down a spare F2000-something number and trim it to equip her with a somewhat tatty "F2."

"Julie Brown took off fast and went miles up the road, but I hung around with Grete, and quite a bunch, including Ingrid Kristiansen and Julie Shea. It was my first tour of New York, and I found it a great trip, trundling along with Grete and taking in the neighborhoods"(Robinson, 2011). Yes, she did say "trundling."

Once Waitz dropped out, it was all Roe, majestic in her sky-blue outfit with the silver fern of New Zealand, and shining white gloves. This was the first city marathon to be broadcast live on network television, so it was not only the First Avenue crowds that were excited by her power and grace, but a global audience. Unaware of this instant celebrity, she was simply racing, and enjoying the tour.

"Harlem was great. They shouted 'Hey, sister, go!' Really neat."

Overtaking male runners by the handful, Roe turned the jets full on through Central Park's hills. Pace judgment had been a problem, and often in the past in her enthusiasm she went out too fast. But she had worked on it.

"I'd done a lot of reading about how to apportion speed. My last three miles were the fastest – 5:12, 5:14, 5:12," she said, revealing a thoughtful student of the sport within that warrior goddess exterior. She was going so fast she missed seeing the finish marshals.

"I ran under the wrong banner, with the men. Fred Lebow was running around like a chook [New Zealand for chicken] with its head cut off. It took a while for it to sink in that I'd broken the world record" (Robinson, 2011).

Her time was 2:25:29. As a world record it was later qualified when the course was found to be 150 meters short, and Roe's time is often omitted from record progression lists, or included with an asterisk. But the previous three world records had been set by Waitz on exactly the same course, and Roe's time was four and a half minutes faster than the best on any other course to that date. She thus unquestionably ran the greatest and fastest marathon any woman had ever run. It seems less than sensible, or fair, to pretend that she didn't.

****

Now the world was crazy for Allison Roe. She was not only the best woman marathon runner of 1981, but one of the most admired of all world sportswomen. She was besieged by media, sought after by American TV shows, and she got endorsement contracts, advertising decaffeinated coffee along with David Bowie and Dustin Hoffman – that's how big she became. Life changed.

"Up until then I'd bought all my own shoes. After New York I never paid for an air ticket, a pair of shoes or a hotel room again." Her many honors included the award of Year's Best Amateur Sportswoman by the American Press Association.

She kept winning. That 1981-82 New Zealand summer, new, big, sponsored road races were booming, prize money was permitted (via the "trust fund" administered by NZAAA) and in March Roe won the Christchurch final of the national "Big M 10K" series. She then flew to the Seoul Marathon, where stifling humidity and pollution slowed her victory to 2:43:12. The brave new world of women's road running seemed hers to command.

But that new world was bigger and tougher than it used to be. A new generation was responding to the news that there would be a women's marathon in the Los Angeles Olympics. Roe struggled with injuries that kept her out of the big marathons in 1982. She went back to Boston in 1983 with better than ever Auckland training times in the bank, but there she encountered a fired-up Joan Benoit.

Determined not to have Roe sit behind and play cat and Catalano-mouse with her in a repeat of 1981, Benoit used a preemptive strike, taking off at world record pace. She held it as only she could, and shattered Roe's course record and the world record with a historic 2:22:43.

Roe ran with former winner Jack Fultz for a while, still holding 2:25 pace, which would have given a personal best, but seemed to lose concentration with Benoit out of sight. Jacqueline Gareau (the 1980 winner) passed her for second, and Roe slowed, and then at 17 miles, she gave it away. By Derderian's account, Fultz also stopped, and they dropped in on a marathon party at the house of some of his friends (Derderian, 1994).

Perhaps the cause was that old lack of intense competitiveness. The perfect magic can be elusive when you try to recapture it. Perhaps it was something national, the confidence quirk that besets many New Zealand sports people, who typically perform better as outsiders than as favorites. Perhaps it was the pressures of being a superstar, for someone essentially modest. Being an inspiration for others and a figurehead for women's running is another form of pressure. That April 1983, among many other demands, Roe and her coach Elliott were also finishing a book, "experiences to direct your thinking along positive lines in training and racing." When you write a book, Winston Churchill truly said, it begins as an amusement and ends by being a tyrant. Or perhaps it was simply that Roe's happy personality thrives best when she is enjoying the experience – "relaxing and having a holiday," as she said about her Boston win. That's not unique or necessarily bad. Deena Kastor's advice in *Let Your Mind Run* is to be positive, and smile in races. But it's hard to smile when Joanie has just scuttled off out of sight on a pace three minutes faster than you've ever run.

Roe tried to get herself recharged and refreshed by venturing into the triathlon, an emergent sport at that date. Although that was strange move for someone seen as a favorite for the Olympic marathon, it seemed to work at first, and in December 1983, she cruised to a comfortable 1:16:04 course record in an Auckland half-marathon. But as 1983 turned into Olympic marathon year of 1984, a 1:16 half doesn't predict the hot weather 2:24/2:25 she was going to need to be competitive in Los Angeles. Roe's last chance for selection, Boston 1984, started well despite lingering injury problems, but became a disaster. The pressure of needing a fast time to make the team sent her out at 2:25 pace, faster than either of her great 1981 marathons. She walked off the course two miles from the finish.

Then it all ended. Roe didn't get turned into a lioness like the first Atalanta but it was nearly as bad. It ended with a home accident that could strike any of us, yet ought not strike an epic hero and beloved figurehead. During house renovations, she stumbled and fell down the stairs. She chipped a bone, inflicted a major hematoma, and catastrophically tore her upper hamstring.

Fortunately, her positive personality is resilient, and her commitment to physical fitness and health goes deep. She has varied talents. She enjoyed the Los Angeles Olympics after all as a corporate host for the American magazine *Sports Illustrated*. She did some television commentaries in America and New Zealand, and established her own television production and sports promotion company in Auckland. She became a proficient race director, mostly of women's road races. She succeeded as a competitive triathlete, and became a cyclist, winning New Zealand titles. Through her forties, fifties, and sixties, she has continued to kayak, swim, bike, and run, she goes to the gym, and she gets injured kickboxing. She won her age group in mountain biking in the World Masters Games in Auckland in 2017.

"I live each day with purpose and passion," she said at age 56.

Her personal life hit a bad patch when she and Richard Roe divorced after eighteen years of marriage, with two teenage children. "The separation was the worst time of my life," she says. In time, she married again, to realtor Alan Barwick, whose previous marriage was to another distinguished and even more dedicated runner, ultra-marathoner Sandy Barwick. Roe became step-mother to Barwick's two children, and her role as grandmother and step-grandmother is now centrally important.

Looking to make a contribution in areas that concern her most, she established the Allison Roe Trust, in support of women's health. She produced and promoted health products, including an Allison Roe jogger's baby stroller. She instigated a series of fun runs to raise funds for women's health projects. Then she tried politics, still in the health area, elected to a regional health board as an advocate for preventative health policies, and also serving in local government. She retained her seat in later elections, but her benign temperament is not suited to that contentious culture, and she describes herself as "out of politics."

That experience taught her a lot about governance, the strengths and problems of bureaucracy, and how to make things happen. She decided to focus on "something that is simple and truthful, that I know is for the greater good." She threw her energy, her optimism, and the power of her celebrity into developing a coastal recreation trail. That enables her to contribute to health, outdoor exercise, and the natural environment, things that she grew up with, things she learned early were her responsibility as well as a source of pleasure. Her late mother never let her daughters forget their duty of philanthropy. "The Matakana Coast Trail Trust ticks all the boxes, it's a legacy project," Roe says. The trail is in easy reach of the beach.

****

Throughout this book, I have told running's greatest stories and then reflected on them, trying to establish the truth, but also considering their significance, the way they have passed into our culture, what they might mean to today's runners, and why the stories are worth retelling. Allison Roe is still vital and busy, and she has a husband, family, and many friends, and several kinds of activity that sustain her contribution to society. Her story isn't finished, and it would be premature to say too much about what it means. Nevertheless, it's worth pausing one more time, especially to think about why she became such an iconic figure, on the basis really of only two races, and about what her similarities with Atalanta might signify in our very different world.

Like all true epic heroes, Roe was representative as well as extraordinary. Her impact on a public far beyond regular athletics fans came from five things. Two were personal – the superlative quality of her performances, and her striking combination of power and grace in appearance. More of that shortly. The other three were matters of history. Her peak coincided with the miraculous year of 1981. The global boom in the exciting new sport of road running created a mass readership for running magazines and women's magazines eager for celebrity material, and put hundreds of thousands out on the sidewalks of New York eager for recognizable stars. Secondly, women's running was booming even ahead of the main curve, and entries by women in the marathon were accelerating meteorically. In 1970, one sole woman entered the inaugural New York City Marathon. In 1971, there were four. In 1981, Roe was the first of 2,029 women. "The crowd's cheering goes berserk at the sight of every woman competitor," wrote one journalist who ran it mid-pack. The world wanted a heroine runner.

The third historic innovation was the arrival of live television coverage, and probably that was the most critical in making Roe into a superstar. When the 1981 New York City Marathon was the first big city road race to be on network television start to finish, and ABC distributed it live worldwide, Roe literally became a global star in two hours and twenty-five minutes. It's no exaggeration to say that those screen images of her in such commanding motion, visually memorable in her sky-blue singlet and shorts, with blond hair and white gloves, gave her a lasting place in the global culture of running, and in the minds of millions of viewers. When I ran Boston in 1984, Roe was the main attraction. As I ran somewhere ahead of the first woman at about ten miles, a man leaned out from the crowd to peer behind me. "Where's Allison?" he demanded impatiently. Elderly runners, mostly but not only male, still remember the impact of those images with affection.

A similar tribute came in the American running novel, *The Purple Runner* (1983), by Paul Christman. The main female character is a long-legged blond New Zealand runner, "blessed with very supple limbs" and "incredible athletic ability," named Solian D. Lede, an anagram for Allison Deed. At the end of the novel she wins the London Marathon in a world record.

Male spectators were smitten in their thousands by the real-life Roe, and responsible writers worked hard to describe her impact and allure without resorting to sexist clichés.

"The sight of Allison Roe at full power commands respect. Her long, purposeful stride makes her racing look effortless," carefully wrote

Tim Chamberlain, editor of *New Zealand Runner* (Oct 1980). "Roe performed like a beautifully oiled machine," wrote Richard Benyo and Joe Henderson in *Running Encyclopedia*, adding that she was "movie-star attractive."

The traditional glamor of movie stars tends to be posed and static, whereas Roe's appeal was entirely natural and dynamic. Her physically powerful beauty was greatest when she was in full motion, when her high stride made her seem much taller than her actual 5ft 8in/1.7m. It is not fanciful to say that Roe was thus at the forefront of a new definition of femininity. Every culture in every era grapples with the issues of defining gender. The ideal of dynamic female beauty, a combination of power and grace in motion, has simmered in the cultural consciousness of the human race since Atalanta. In the four decades since Roe ran Boston and New York, in the age of Warrior Queens and Wonderwomen discussed in chapter 1, it has become a popular stereotype.

When Roe ran, it seemed new. She displaced old stereotypes of female appeal as weak, passive, and static. Roe never looked as if she needed to be rescued. Yet she was entirely feminine. After she won New York, a picture of her in full mid-race action featured on page 3 of the Auckland *Sunday News*, displacing the page's customary topless sunbathing image. The female editor later described it as "a blow for feminism." Women's organizations conspired to buy multiple copies in support.

Despite her career being cut so short, she shows no inclination to present her story as one of disappointment.

"I know I had better marathons in me and, yes, naturally, I would love to have an Olympic medal. But that's not the measure of a life well lived. I was lucky to accomplish more as a runner than I ever thought I could. I had wonderful experiences, I made lifelong friends, and I learned things that I still value." She will be remembered as the superstar runner, but she does not allow that to define her.

She seems to be moving contentedly and creatively through the later years of her story. In her mid-sixties, she is regretful but good-humored about aging.

"Looking back on old photos we can see how youthful we were, and checking the mirror, how old we look now. I think if you put a smile on your dial it helps enormously, so that's my ploy....oh and don't look at yourself in the mirror with reading glasses on. Now that's scary...no wonder God gave us failing sight as we start to lose our looks...but [she says, moving from laughter to the underlying health mission] it's all relative, and the important thing is that we keep moving, keep evolving."

A few years ago, Allison dropped a casual remark that I thought summed up the kind of runner she was – one whose competitive pride was strong, but deep, co-existing with a ready humor and a positive delight in the simple process of running, and being able to do it well. It also showed that she has her life in perspective, and can link the triumphal past with the less public present. It's a good quiet note to end this book of great running stories. She was talking about her run that morning, at age 56, on the beach:

"Passing joggers like I passed all those guys in the last miles at New York. It still feels so good to run."

BIBLIOGRAPHY

Abrahams, Harold, *XVII Olympiad Rome 1960*, 1960

Anninos, C., *The Olympic Games 776 BC- 1896 AD*, 1896, trans. C. Beck, 1996

Audain, Anne, and John L. Parker Jr, *Uncommon Heart*, 2000

Baker, W. J., *Jesse Owens: An American Life*, 1986

Baldwin, Barry, "Re-running Marathon." *History Today*, May 1998, 44-49

Bannister, Roger, *First Four Minutes*, 1955

Batten, Jack, *The Man Who Ran Faster Than Everyone: The Story of Tom Longboat*, 2002

Beck, Jason, *The Miracle Mile. Stories of the 1954 British Empire and Commonwealth Games*, 2016

Benoit, Joan, with Sally Baker, *Running Tide*, 1987

Benyo, Richard and Joe Henderson, *Running Encyclopedia*, 2002

Berlin, Irving, *Dorando*, 1909

Bible, The Holy, Jeremiah, Samuel 1.

Booth, Martin, *The Doctor, the Detective and Arthur Conan Doyle*, 1997

Browning, Elizabeth Barrett, *The Battle of Marathon*, 1820

Browning, Robert, "Pheidippides," in *Dramatic Idyls*, 1879

Bryant, John, *3.59.4: The Quest to Break the 4 Minute Mile*, 2005

___, *Chris Brasher. The Man Who Made the London Marathon*, 2012

___, *London Marathon, The* 2005

___, *Marathon Makers, The*, 2008

Bulger, Dr. Michael, "Medical Officer's Report" in Cook, T. A., below

Bull, Andy, "The Forgotten Story of Sohn Kee-chung, Korea's Olympic Hero," *The Guardian*, August 27, 2011

Burfoot, Amby, *First Ladies of Running*, 2016

Butler, Samuel, *Butleriana*, 1932. Ed. A.T. Bartholomew

___, *Correspondence of Samuel Butler with his sister May*. Ed. Daniel F. Howard, 1962

___, *Family Letters of Samuel Butler, The, 1841-1886*. Ed. Arnold Silver, 1962

___, *Life and Letters of Dr. Samuel Butler, The, Headmaster of Shrewsbury School*, 1896

___, *Way of All Flesh, The*, 1903. Ed. Roger Robinson, 1976

Byron, Lord George Gordon, *Childe Harold's Pilgrimage*, 1812

Carnegie, David, Paul Millar, David Norton, and Harry Ricketts (eds.), *Running Writing Robinson*, 2011

Carli, E., *Dorando Pietri*, 1973

Cather, Willa, *Death Comes to the Archbishop*, 1926

Clarke, Geoffrey, *The Post Office of India and its Story,* 1921

Clarke, Ron, *The Unforgiving Minute*, 1966

Cohen, Gary, Billy Mills interview. Garycohenrunning.com/interviews, 2014

Colquhoun, David (ed.), *As If Running on Air. The Journals of Jack Lovelock*, 2008

Cook, T.A. (Comp.), *The Fourth Olympiad, being the Official Report of the Olympic Games of 1908,* 1909

Cooper, J. Fenimore, The Last of the Mohicans, 1826

Davis, David, *Marathon Crasher. The Life and Times of Merry Lepper*, 2012

___, *Showdown at Shepherd's Bush*, 2012

Dee, Harry, "Bouquet to Kathy Miller (America's Atalanta)," 1972, cited in Switzer, *Marathon Woman*, p. 174

Depping, Guillaume, *Wonders of Bodily Strength and Skill*, 1871

Derderian, Tom, *Boston Marathon: The History of the World's Premier Running Event*, 1994, 2014

Dobers, Ernst, *Die Judenfrage. Stoff und Behandlung in der Schule,* 1936

Doyle, Arthur Conan, *Memories and Adventures*, 1924

___, "The Adventure of Wisteria Lodge" (1908), in *Sherlock Holmes: The Complete Short Stories,* 1928

Dyreson, Mark, "Icons of Liberty or Objects of Desire? American Women Olympians and the Politics of Consumption," *Journal of Contemporary History*, 2003

English, Colleen, "'Not a very edifying spectacle.' The Controversial Women's 800-Meter Race in the 1928 Olympics." *Sport in American History* (ussporthistory.com), October 8, 2015

Eusden, Laurence, *Ovid's Metamorphoses*, 1717, cited in Robinson, *Running in Literature*, p. 40

Fontes, Justine and Ron, *Atalanta: The Race against Destiny*, illustrated by Thomas Yeates, 2008

Giller, Norman, *Marathon Kings,* Pelham, 1983

Glickman, Marty, *The Fastest Kid on the Block: The Marty Glickman Story*, 1999

Gotaas, Thor, *Running: A Global History*, 2012

Graves, Robert, *The Greek Myths*. 2 vols., 1955

Green, D., *Blenheim Palace*, 1951

Green, P., *The Greco-Persian Wars*. University of California Press, 1997

Hadgraft, Rob, *The Little Wonder. The Untold Story of Alf Shrubb,* 2004

Hall, Harry, *The Pedestriennes: America's Forgotten Superstars*, 2014

Hanson Victor Davis, *The Western Way of War. Infantry Battle in Ancient Greece,* 2009

Harris, H.A., *Greek Athletes and Athletics*, 1964

Harris, Norman, *The Legend of Lovelock*, 1964

___, *The Lonely Breed*, 1967

Hart-Davis, Duff, *Hitler's Games. The 1936 Olympics*, 1986

Heidenstrom, Peter, *Athletes of the Century. 100 Years of New Zealand Track and Field*, 1992

Herodotos, *Histories*, Book 6, 430 B.C. This version by Roger Robinson, 2021

Hillenbrand, Laura, *Unbroken. A World War II Story of Survival,*

Resilience, and Redemption, 2010

Hughes, Thomas, *Tom Brown's Schooldays*, 1857

James, C.P.R., *Beyond a Boundary*, 1963

Jobling, Ian, "'Teddy' Flack was the 'Lion of Athens.'"*Journal of Olympic History*, 26.1, 2018

Johnson, Len, *The Landy Era. From Nowhere to the Top of the World*, 2009

Karnazes, Dean, *The Road to Sparta*, 2016

Kastor, Deena, *Let Your Mind Run*, 2019

Kidd, Bruce, *Tom Longboat*, 1992

King, Marian, *The Story of Athletics*, 1931

Kipling, Rudyard, "The Overland Mail," in *Departmental Ditties and Other Verses*, Second Edition, 1886

Krentz, Peter, *The Battle of Marathon*, 2010

Large, D.C., *Nazi Games*, 2007

Lovelock, J.E., "Youth and Modern Sport," in A. C. Johnson (ed.), *Growing Opinions: A Symposium of British Youth Outlook*, 1935

Lovesey, Peter, *Kings of Distance, The*, 1968

Official Centenary History of the Amateur Athletic Association, 1979

___, "The Most Famous Marathon Runner of All," *Athletics Weekly*, April 6, 1966

___, "Spyridon Louis: Champion or Cheat?"

Lucian of Samosata, *Works*, 1905

MacAloon, John J., *This Great Symbol: Pierre de Coubertin and the Origins of the Modern Olympic Games*, 1981

McConnell, Lynn, *Conquerors of Time*, 2009

McGrath, Roger, "Running Rings Around the Empire: the 1908 Olympics," *Irish America*, August/September, 2012

Mansfield, Katherine, "The Daughters of the Late Colonel," 1920, in *The Stories of Katherine Mansfield*, ed. Antony Alpers, 1984

Martin, David, and Roger Gynn, *The Marathon Footrace*, 1979

___, *The Olympic Marathon*, 2000

Middleton, P(eter) J., *The Royal Shrewsbury School Hunt. A History:*

1831-2011, 2011

Mills, Billy, *Lessons of a Lakota*, 2005

Milroy, Andy, "The Great Running Traditions of the Basques," www. ultrarunninghistory.com

___, "24hr Run History,"www.ultrarunninghistory.com

___, and Lovesey, Peter and Brant, John, www.nuts.org.uk/ trackstats/Piercy

Moller, Lorraine, *On the Wings of Mercury. The Lorraine Moller Story*, 2007

Montillo, Roseanne, *Fire on the Track. Betty Robinson and Triumph of the Early Olympic Women*, 2017

Morites, K., *Spiridon Louis – A Legend in the Olympic Games 1896-1996*, 1997

Murray, J. "Alfred Shrubb, Champion of the World," in Shrubb, *Running* (1908), q.v.

Nabokov, Peter, *Indian Running: Native American History and Tradition*, 1981

New York Times, files 1908-1912, accessed via New York Public Library

New Zealand Amateur Athletic Association, *94th Annual Report, 1980-81*, 1981

___, *95th Annual Report, 1981-82*, 1982

Original Weekly Journal, The (later *Applebee's Original Weekly Journal*), 1718-22

Ovid, *Metamorphoses*, various English translations

___,Hoffman, Michael and Lusden, James (eds.), *After Ovid: New Metamorphoses*, 1994

Paling, Bruce, *India: Literary Companion*, 1992

Pepys, Samuel, *The Diary of Samuel Pepys*, Wikisource

Pliny the Elder, *Natural History*, 74 A.D.

Plutarch, *Moral Essays*, 110 A.D.

___, *Life of Aristides*, ca. 100 A.D.

Pringle, Patrick, *The Thief Takers*, 1958

Pritchett, W. K. *Marathon*. University of California Press, 1960

Raby, Peter. *Samuel Butler. A Biography*, 1997

Reese, Anne C., and Irini Vallera-Rickerson, *Athletries. The Untold Story of Ancient Greek Women Athletes*, nd (2003)

Robinson, Roger, *Heroes and Sparrows: A Celebration of Running*, 1986, 2011

___, *Running in Literature*, 2003

___, *Spirit of the Marathon*, 2014

___, *When Running Made History*, 2018, 2019

___, "From Canterbury Settlement to *Erewhon*: Butler and Antipodean Counterpoint." James G. Paradis, ed., *Samuel Butler. Victorian Against the Grain*, 2007

___, "Life and Opinions of Dr. Jack Lovelock, The" *Turnbull Library Record*, 35, 2002

____, "What you know about how running became a pro sport is only half the truth," *Podium Runner*, September 2, 2021

Roe, Allison, "I'd Like to Win This," *New Zealand Runner*, 16, September 1980 www.runningpast.com

Ryan, James, and Fraser, Ian H. (eds.), *The Annals of Thames Hare & Hounds*, 1968

Ryan, Mark, *Running With Fire. The True Story of 'Chariots of Fire' Hero Harold Abrahams*, 2011

Sandford, Mike, in "Road course measurement board, 26.2 centenary," 2008

Scott, Walter, *The Bride of Lammermoor*, 1819

Sears, Edward S. *Running Through the Ages*, 2001, 2015

Shakespeare, William, *Antony and Cleopatra*, 1606, *As You Like It*, 1599, *Hamlet*, 1601, *Henry VI Part 3*, 1589, *Romeo and Juliet*, 1595

Shearman, Montague, *Athletics and Football, Badminton Library*, with cross-country by Walter Rye, 1887

Shirley, James, *Hyde Park*, 1632

Shrubb, Alfred, *Running and Cross-Country Running*, 1908

Sillitoe, Alan, "The Loneliness of the Long-Distance Runner," 1959

Sobanja, Dreydon, *The Kiwi Runners' Family Tree*, *1800s-1999*, 2020

Spenser, Edmund, *Amoretti* (1595), Sonnet 76

Spitz, Barry, *Dipsea: The Greatest Race*, 1993

"Stamata Revithi," Wikipedia.org, ed. 2021

Stevens, John, *Marathon Monks of Mount Hiei*, 2013

Strutt, Joseph, *Sports and Pastimes of the People of England*, 1801

Swift, Jonathan, "Directions to Servants," 1731

Swinburne, Algernon, *Atalanta in Calydon*, 1865

Switzer, Kathrine, *Marathon Woman*, 2007, 2017

___ and Roger Robinson, *26.2 Marathon Stories*, 2006, 2007

___ and Valerie Andrews, *The Avon Report on the Status of Women's Distance Running*, 1980

Tamini, Noel, *La Saga des Pédestrians,* 2 vols, 1997, 2009

Tarasouleas, Athanasios, *Olimpiaka Dromena: Athens 1895-1896*

Thackeray, William, *The Four Georges*, 1860

Thomas, William J., "Running Footmen," *Notes & Queries*, series 2:1, 1985

Tobin, Christopher, *Lovelock: New Zealand's Olympic Gold Miler*, 1984

___, *Runners in Black. The Early Years*, 2020

Tripp, Ellen, *My Early Days*, 1915

Tulloh, Bruce, *Four Million Footsteps*, 50th Anniversary Edition, 2019

van Aaken, Ernst, and Lennartz, Karl, *Das Laufbuch der Frau*, 1985

Vance, Louis Joseph, *The Fortune Hunter*, 1910

Watman, Mel, *Encyclopedia of Track and Field Athletics*, 1964, 1967, 1981

Wells, H.G., *The History of Mr. Polly*, 1910

West, J. M., *Shrewsbury*, 1937

Young, Derrick, *The Ten Greatest Races*, 1972

ABOUT THE AUTHOR

Roger Robinson is a widely admired writer who is also a literary scholar, historian, sports journalist, and long-time world-ranked runner. All those skills are used in the research and writing of *Running Throughout Time*.

Roger is known for *When Running Made History* (Syracuse University Press 2018; Canterbury University Press, 2019), his sixth book on running, which was called "the best book ever about running" (Amby Burfoot, USA), "one of the very best athletics books I have reviewed in sixty years" (Mel Watman, UK), "ranks with C.P.R. James and Ernest Hemingway as sports writing" (Richard Meyer, South Africa), and "a work of literature, an ode to running, and an eye-witness account of some of the sport's most poignant and significant moments" (Eugene Bingham, New Zealand).

His previous running books, *Heroes and Sparrows: A Celebration of Running* (1986, 2011), *Running in Literature* (2003), and *26.2 Marathon Stories* (with Kathrine Switzer, 2006, 2007) are all regarded as classics in running literature. His other work includes the *Oxford Companion to New Zealand Literature* (1998), *Robert Louis Stevenson: His Best Pacific Writings* (2003, 2004), and literary classics editions for Penguin, Pan, and Louisiana State University Press.

Born in England in 1939, Roger Robinson was a scholar at King's College School, Wimbledon, and Queens' College, Cambridge, and obtained his PhD from Cambridge for work on the English eighteenth-century novel. After lecturing at Cambridge and Leeds, he moved to New Zealand, first as lecturer/senior lecturer at the University of Canterbury, then at age 35 he moved to a full chair at Victoria University of Wellington. He reached the position of Pro Vice-Chancellor (Academic), led the revision of the New Zealand schools' English curriculum, and has been recognized in awards for outstanding teaching. He is now Emeritus

Professor. The Festschrift *Running Writing Robinson* was published in his honor by Victoria University Press.

As a writer on running, Roger has been published in all major magazines and online outlets in the USA (*Runner's World, Running Times, Marathon & Beyond, New England Runner, New York Runner, Podium Runner*, with columns in the first three), the UK (*Athletics Weekly*), Canada (*Canadian Runner*), Australia (*Runner's World*), New Zealand (*New Zealand Runner, VO2Max*), and several European publications (especially the French *VO2Run*). He is a frequent contributor to *Runner's World* (USA) and *Podium Runner*, reaching wide international readerships.

As an athlete, Roger represented England in the 1960s, New Zealand in the 1970s, and won world championships in the over-40 and over-50 categories. He set masters records at the Boston, New York, Vancouver, and Canberra marathons, and returned to elite age-group competition after knee replacements in his seventies. He was a stadium announcer for fifty years, from the national level to the Commonwealth Games, and a commentator for TV (including the Olympics) and radio. He has been involved as writer, consultant, and/or expert contributor in several documentary feature films on running and its history. He is a frequent invited speaker/celebrity guest at major running events in the USA and Canada, and literary festivals in New Zealand.

Roger has been married for 34 years to women's running pioneer Kathrine Switzer. They live in New Paltz, NY (in non-Covid times), and Wellington, New Zealand.

Credits
Cover and interior design: Anja Elsen
Layout: DiTech Publishing Services, www.ditechpubs.com
Cover photo: © AdobeStock
Copyeditor: Stephanie Kramer
Managing editor: Elizabeth Evans

MORE GREAT NARRATIVES

Paperback, 5.5 x 8.5"
320 p., b/w
ISBN: 9781782551973
$16.95 US

Holly Zimmermann

RUNNING EVEREST

ADVENTURES AT THE TOP OF THE WORLD

Running Everest tells the story of a group of adventurers from around the globe who embark on a remarkable journey through the Khumbu Valley of Nepal, battling high-altitude sickness, deplorable sanitary conditions, freezing temperatures, and enjoying every minute of it!

Paperback, 5.5 x 8.5"
312 p., in color
ISBN: 9781782552406
$18.95 US

Hilary JM Topper

THE BUMPY ROAD FROM COUCH POTATO TO ENDURANCE ATHLETE

A PORTRAIT OF A NON-ATHLETIC TRIATHLETE

Readers will be inspired as they follow the author on her decade-long journey as she turns her life around by training for different endurance events. They will walk away feeling that no matter what, they can cross the finish line, too.

MEYER & MEYER SPORT

MEYER & MEYER Sport	Phone	+49 02 41 - 9 58 10 - 13
Von-Coels-Str. 390	Fax	+49 02 41 - 9 58 10 - 10
52080 Aachen	E-Mail	sales@m-m-sports.com
Germany	Website	www.m-m-sports.com

FROM MEYER & MEYER SPORT

Mara Yamauchi

MARATHON WISDOM

AN ELITE ATHLETE'S INSIGHTS
ON RUNNING AND LIFE

From planning training, optimizing nutrition, and preparing effectively for racing to coping with disappointments and struggles with mental illness, Mara shares everything she has learned as one of the world's top marathoners.

Paperback, 6.5 x 9.5"
304 p., in color
ISBN: 9781782552451
$22.95 US

Paul C. Clerici

BORN TO COACH

THE STORY OF BILL SQUIRES,
THE LEGENDARY COACH OF
THE GREATEST GENERATION OF
AMERICAN DISTANCE RUNNERS

Bill Squires was the key figure in the creation of the greatest generation of American distance runners. This book shows his journey to a record-setting runner and ultimately the leading running coach in the US.

Hardcover, 6 x 9"
312 p., b/w
ISBN: 9781782551966
$28.95 US

MEYER & MEYER Sport
Von-Coels-Str. 390
52080 Aachen
Germany

Phone   +49 02 41 - 9 58 10 - 13
Fax   +49 02 41 - 9 58 10 - 10
E-Mail   sales@m-m-sports.com
Website www.m-m-sports.com

MEYER
& MEYER
SPORT

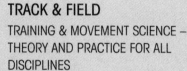